"This is a timely and interesting volume that will appeal to those interested in using technology in their instructional and assessment practices. It is a much-welcomed addition to the literature on technology-mediated language assessment. It also offers important guidelines for navigating assessment in different instructional settings in times of crisis. I strongly recommend this book!"

Atta Gebril, *The American University in Cairo, Egypt*

"This important book is both timely in its message and massively encouraging in the way in which the individual chapters reflect the creativity of language testers from across the world in dealing with the disruption caused by COVID. In challenging our perceptions of how to establish evidence of test quality in terms of development and delivery the authors call into question much current thinking on validation. Two strong messages ring out from these pages. The first relates to the need to broaden our validation evidence base to embrace qualitative as well as quantitative evidence. The second is the way in which context is rightfully recognised as a critical factor in any validation argument. This book should be seen as core reading for any language testing program."

Professor Barry O'Sullivan, *British Council*

"Technology-assisted language assessment has been with us for something like 40 years. One would think we know everything there is to know about it, but this is far from the case. As the authors of the various chapters document, technology-assisted language assessment is a complex undertaking with issues of the security of the test content itself and of the test-takers' environment, fairness in terms of access to computers and the internet, validation concerns when test-takers may be unfamiliar with certain aspects of technology-assisted tasks, and reliability may be a challenge owing to diversity of test-taking situations and interaction between human and computer-based scoring. The chapters in this book address these concerns in a scholarly but approachable manner and readers will find much of value as they develop their own technology-assisted language assessments for their own contexts."

Dan Douglas, *Professor Emeritus, Iowa State University, USA*

"This timely edited collection of chapters addresses a critical matter of language assessment due to the COVID pandemic. It takes as its starting point the use of technology: online assessment, video technology, and remote learning. In addition, chapters provide overviews and opinions on validation and fairness during the pandemic. As editor, Sadeghi offers an overview as well as concluding thoughts of lessons learned and not learned. As repercussions of the COVID era are still unfolding, this collection will serve as a leading collection of ideas on technology and language assessment."

Professor Antony Kunnan, *Nanyang Technological University, Singapore*

TECHNOLOGY-ASSISTED LANGUAGE ASSESSMENT IN DIVERSE CONTEXTS

This timely collection explores the role of digital technology in language education and assessment during the COVID-19 pandemic. It recognises the unique pressures which the COVID-19 pandemic placed on assessment in language education, and examines the forced shift in assessment strategies to go online, the existing shortfalls, as well as unique affordances of technology-assisted L2 assessment.

By showcasing international examples of successful digital and computer-assisted proficiency and skills testing, the volume addresses theoretical and practical concerns relating to test validity, reliability, ethics, and student experience in a range of testing contexts. Particular attention is given to identifying lessons and implications for future research and practice, and the challenges of implementing unplanned computer-assisted language assessment during a crisis.

Insightfully unpacking the 'lessons learned' from COVID and its impact on the acceleration of the shift towards online course and assessment delivery, it offers important guidelines for navigating assessment in different instructional settings in times of crisis. It will appeal to scholars, researchers, educators, and faculty with interests in educational measurement, digital education and technology, and language assessment and testing.

Karim Sadeghi is a Professor of TESOL at Urmia University, Iran. He is the founding editor-in-chief of the Iranian Journal of Language Teaching Research.

Routledge Research in Language Education

The *Routledge Research in Language Education* series provides a platform for established and emerging scholars to present their latest research and discuss key issues in Language Education. This series welcomes books on all areas of language teaching and learning, including but not limited to language education policy and politics, multilingualism, literacy, L1, L2 or foreign language acquisition, curriculum, classroom practice, pedagogy, teaching materials, and language teacher education and development. Books in the series are not limited to the discussion of the teaching and learning of English only.

Books in the series include:

Pluricentric Languages and Language Education
Pedagogical Implications and Innovative Approaches to Language Teaching
Edited by Marcus Callies and Stefanie Hehner

The Acquisition of English Grammar and Phonology by Cantonese ESL Learners
Challenges, Causes and Pedagogical Insights
Alice Yin Wa Chan

Using Digital Portfolios to Develop Students' Writing
A Practical Guide for Language Teachers
Ricky Lam and Benjamin Luke Moorhouse

Enhancing Beginner-Level Foreign Language Education for Adult Learners
Language Instruction, Intercultural Competence, Technology, and Assessment
Edited by Ekaterina Nemtchinova

Technology-Assisted Language Assessment in Diverse Contexts
Lessons from the Transition to Online Testing during COVID-19
Edited by Karim Sadeghi

For more information about the series, please visit www.routledge.com/Routledge-Research-in-Language-Education/book-series/RRLE

TECHNOLOGY-ASSISTED LANGUAGE ASSESSMENT IN DIVERSE CONTEXTS

Lessons from the Transition to Online Testing during COVID-19

Edited by Karim Sadeghi
URMIA UNIVERSITY, IRAN

NEW YORK AND LONDON

First published 2023
by Routledge
605 Third Avenue, New York, NY 10158

and by Routledge
4 Park Square, Milton Park, Abingdon, Oxon, OX14 4RN

Routledge is an imprint of the Taylor & Francis Group, an informa business

© 2023 selection and editorial matter, Karim Sadeghi; individual chapters, the contributors

The right of Karim Sadeghi to be identified as the author of the editorial material, and of the authors for their individual chapters, has been asserted in accordance with sections 77 and 78 of the Copyright, Designs and Patents Act 1988.

All rights reserved. No part of this book may be reprinted or reproduced or utilised in any form or by any electronic, mechanical, or other means, now known or hereafter invented, including photocopying and recording, or in any information storage or retrieval system, without permission in writing from the publishers.

Trademark notice: Product or corporate names may be trademarks or registered trademarks, and are used only for identification and explanation without intent to infringe.

Library of Congress Cataloging-in-Publication Data
Names: Sadeghi, Karim, editor.
Title: Technology-assisted language assessment in diverse contexts : lessons from the transition to online testing during COVID-19 / edited by Karim Sadeghi.
Description: Abingdon, Oxon ; New York, NY : Routledge, 2023. | Series: Routledge research in language education | Includes bibliographical references and index. |
Identifiers: LCCN 2022036643 (print) | LCCN 2022036644 (ebook) | ISBN 9781032117683 (hardback) | ISBN 9781032117690 (paperback) | ISBN 9781003221463 (ebook)
Subjects: LCSH: Language and languages--Ability testing--Technological innovations. | Language and languages--Study and teaching--Technological innovations. | COVID-19 Pandemic, 2020---Influence. | LCGFT: Essays.
Classification: LCC P53.4 .T44 2023 (print) | LCC P53.4 (ebook) | DDC 418.0078/5--dc23/eng/20221116
LC record available at https://lccn.loc.gov/2022036643
LC ebook record available at https://lccn.loc.gov/2022036644

ISBN: 978-1-032-11768-3 (hbk)
ISBN: 978-1-032-11769-0 (pbk)
ISBN: 978-1-003-22146-3 (ebk)

DOI: 10.4324/9781003221463

Typeset in Bembo
by KnowledgeWorks Global Ltd.

This book is dedicated to language assessors across the globe, past and present, who have shaped the field of language assessment and those from the frontline who continue to push the frontiers of technology-mediated language assessment. I also humbly dedicate this volume to the souls of two pioneers in language assessment who passed away in 2022: Liz Hamp-Lyons and Bernard Spolsky.

CONTENTS

Acknowledgements xii
Foreword by Paula Winke xiii
List of Contributors xvii

SECTION I
Theoretical and Methodological Concerns in Online L2 Assessment   **1**

1 Technology in Language Assessment: An Overview   3
 Karim Sadeghi

2 Seeking Empirical Evidence to Support Online Test Validation: Building on the IELTS Indicator Assessment Model   16
 Tony Clark, Martine Holland, and Richard Spiby

3 Emergency Remote Assessment (ERA) Narratives from the UK English for Academic Purposes (EAP) Sector: Examining Validity and Longevity of Technology-Driven Solutions   34
 Emma Bruce and Heléna Stakounis

4 Language Testing and Assessment in COVID-19 Pandemic Crisis   54
 Hossein Farhady

5 Argument-Based Validation in the Time of the COVID-19 Pandemic 69
   Erik Voss

6 Assessment without Borders: Modernising Placement Tests for Diverse Contexts 84
   Mahmoud Amer and María J. Cabrera-Puche

SECTION II
Reactions to L2 E-Assessment during the COVID-19 Pandemic   101

7 Responding to the Pandemic in New Zealand: Opportunities and Challenges for Language Assessment in One Tertiary Institution 103
   Martin East, Deborah Walker-Morrison, and Viviane Lelièvre-Lopes

8 Online Remote (at-Home) Assessment of Language Modules during COVID-19: Changes, Challenges, and Students' Perceptions 117
   Isabel Balteiro

9 Assessing University Students' Writing Development and Performance during Remote Instruction 131
   Bahiyyih Hardacre

10 Fairness in Remote English Placement Testing at Iowa State University during the COVID-19 Pandemic 148
    Reza Neiriz, Shireen Baghestani, Ananda Astrini Muhammad, and Jim Ranalli

11 Integration of Data-Driven Learning and Assessment through a Multimodal Corpus of Learning Objects at the Time of the COVID-19 Pandemic 163
    María Luisa Carrió-Pastor

SECTION III
Managing L2 Assessment at the Time of the Crisis: The Way Forward   179

12 Test Usefulness of e-Portfolios: An Alternative Approach during and Beyond the Pandemic   181
    Ricky Lam

13 Can Interactions Happen across the Screens?: The Use of Videoconferencing Technology in Assessing Second Language Pragmatic Competence   196
    Shishi Zhang and Talia Isaacs

14 The Use of Technology for Redesigning L2 Language Assessments: Tasks, Rubrics, and Feedback in Emergency Remote Teaching Contexts   212
    Ana Maria Ducasse

15 Rethinking the Online Placement Test for a College-Level Japanese Language Program during the COVID-19 Pandemic   228
    Akiko Imamura, Catherine Ryu, and Mariko Kawaguchi

16 Conclusion: Lessons Learned and Lessons Not Learned   243
    Karim Sadeghi

Index   *249*

ACKNOWLEDGEMENTS

This book is the outcome of collaborative effort among some of the experts in technology-mediated language assessment. I am deeply indebted to researchers in computer-assisted language assessment who answered my call and accepted my invitation to contribute to a volume that reflects attempts in diverse contexts to respond to language assessment challenges at the wake of the COVID-19 pandemic. My next note of gratitude is due to Emilie Coin, Elsbeth Wright, AnnaMary Goodall, and their colleagues at Routledge who welcomed the proposal and worked with me to bring it to fruition. My thanks also go to Alice Salt, Shivranjani Singh, Deepanshu Manral, and their production team who made sure that the manuscript production was completed professionally and on time. I am also grateful to anonymous reviewers as well as chapter contributors who also acted as peer reviewers, all playing a direct role in the quality of the current work. Dan Douglas kindly offered constructive feedback on the first chapter; thank you so much Dan! All remaining faults are mine; and I welcome suggestions to improve the volume in future editions.

Karim Sadeghi
Urmia, Iran

FOREWORD

When Karim Sadeghi put out an open call for abstracts for chapters for this important edited volume on technology-assisted language assessment in diverse educational contexts in early 2021, he was, in essence, putting out a call to language test developers and researchers to pause and reflect on their current work during the COVID-19 pandemic. Karim's timely call rang out strong and clear. Let's take a break and write. Let's reflect on what we have done and are doing. Let's document this tumultuous time, so we will not forget, and so that we can learn from what we have done to keep language assessments afloat as best possible (to meet the needs for the tests' outcomes and score interpretations) during this chaotic time of COVID-19.

At that time, when Karim's call went out back in early 2021, the COVID-19 vaccine was predominately unavailable. Disparate vaccination roll-out plans were beginning to unfold in unequal and disordered manners, causing social unrest and calls for equity and fairness world-wide in health care initiatives and international vaccine sharing. We were still at home, online, and many of us in lockdown. But I believe Karim was seeing something very clearly: fresh off of finishing his 2021 (Springer) book 'Assessing Second Language Reading: Insights from Cloze Tests', he was observing that technology applications in language testing were taking a giant leap forward.

I know I was not clearly seeing the forest for the trees because I, like many people, was simply too busy: I was editing the journal *Language Testing*, teaching in and directing Michigan State University's Second Language Studies Ph.D. Program, and managing the at-home-learning of two children. Luke Harding, my co-editor at *Language Testing*, and I had just overseen the print publication of Daniel R. Isbell and Benjamin Kremmel's (2020) review in *Language Testing* of at-home language proficiency tests for making high-stakes decisions. We thought that Isbell and Kremmel's work would be popular and was needed, and we were right about that; but we were not prepared for the extremely large volume of traffic the work would receive: It was the most cited and downloaded paper in *Language Testing* in 2020. In early 2021, when Karim's call came, I had just read the online-first articles that had just come out in *Language Assessment Quarterly's* (2021) special issue (edited by Gary Ockey) with commentaries from language test program leaders who explained how they were revising their assessments due to the ever-unfolding global pandemic. Over the stretch of a few months, I thought I saw the language testing field somewhat pivot from the question of 'What tests can I give, given that we are now online?' to 'What tests can I make and give locally to meet our testing needs given the new learning context and my local resources?' The 'local language testing' movement, it indeed seemed, was born, and this movement was well documented by Dimova et al. (2020) and Yan et al. (2023) in their Routledge and Springer, respectively, books on the topic. These practitioner-efforts in expanded local language testing demanded a higher-than-ever level of language assessment literacy among the test-development community, and ushered in a treasure trove of locally spurred, online-assessment innovation.

The 15 chapters in this book describe how language assessment work was, in 2021 and 2022, replete with pandemic-mandated scaffolding and rebuilds, untested and rapidly implemented administrations and rating programs, unstable internet connections that hijacked even the best of plans, and worries and speculations about whether the recently transitioned tests would need to remain in their new formats for the long haul. Language testers' work was all at once newly and wondrously innovative and yet dangerously (perhaps thrillingly so) experimental in early 2021. Language assessment was fuelled by working groups with rather significant amounts of pandemic-related urgency. Those groups were at the same time thinning in person-power, as universities and industries were faced with the hard reality that the pandemic was a longer-than-expected reality, negatively affecting the budgets of economic institutions world-wide, especially those of universities, colleges, and units that normally provided in-person testing. Staff shortages and hiring embargoes followed, and yet, language testing needed to go on, just not quite in the same form. And as chapters in this book attest, the results were amazing: tests were created that are more modern, more learner-oriented, more efficient, easier to access, and more aligned with the curriculum and curricular goals (see in particular Amer & Cabrera-Puche, Chapter 6; East, Walker-Morrison, & Lelièvre-Lopes, Chapter 7; Zhang & Isaacs, Chapter 13; Imamura, Ryu, & Kawaguchi, Chapter 15). Language testing programs as a result became more nimble, relaxed, and expecting of the unexpected.

Foreword **xv**

As Karim and authors in this edited volume noted, language test validation arguments are *always* context bound. As such, a test's validation argument can be thrown to the wind in times of crisis. Voss (Chapter 5) in particular wrote about how language-test-program claims regarding the beneficial consequences of a program's test in some cases dissolved during the pandemic simply because students could not take the test in person: Remote and reimagined testing re-opened the possible claims for beneficial consequences, especially when remote testing tasks matched or better mirrored those given and prioritised in the online or hybrid language classroom environment (see Neiriz, Baghestani, Muhammad, & Ranalli, Chapter 10; Carrió-Pastor, Chapter 11). And this is what we saw with the pandemic. When the context of life drastically changed, test scores, all of a sudden, were not valid for their prior specific uses. The tests' prior stakes were neutralised. We saw this sudden shift in assessment contexts world-wide during the height of the pandemic, and we see this now in Ukrainian testing contexts due to the war in Ukraine. A question we now face is whether we want to return testing to its former contexts *and* consequences, or keep moving forward as collectively described by Karim and the other chapter authors in this book. We have the power as a society and as a professional guild to not go back. We have learned first hand that test-security needs rise and fall in consort with test stakes. So if we keep test stakes low, we can keep costs and test-taker anxiety down, because costs and anxiety also go up with stakes and security needs. We have learned that online testing reduces our carbon footprint and can allow tests to be better aligned with test-takers' more natural circadian rhythms and needs for accommodations. We have also learned that language testing research has much to benefit from qualitative inquiry. In this book, for example, several chapter authors used qualitative measures, such as open-ended surveys (Balteiro, Chapter 8; Ducasse, Chapter 14), focus groups (Clark, Holland, & Spiby, Chapter 2), test-taker reflections (Farhady, Chapter 4), interviews (Bruce & Stakounis, Chapter 3), and case studies (Hardacre, Chapter 9; Lam, Chapter 12) to investigate the psychological, perceptual, and cognitive-development-level appropriateness of COVID-19 language assessment measures.

In sum, this book is important because, as Clark, Holland, and Spiby (Chapter 2) eloquently alluded, it provides a timely forum for reflection and discussion on the emergency, rapid-fire advances in online assessment that happened out of necessity during the pandemic. East, Walker-Morrison, and Lelièvre-Lopes (Chapter 7) rightly emphasised that the COVID-19 pandemic was 'the most disruptive event to have occurred on a global scale in many decades', and it upended language testing programs around the world, as the chapters in this book demonstrate. Language testing program directors and managers swiftly converted tests to online formats, enacting 'Emergency Remote Assessment (ERA)' conditions, as described by Bruce and Stakounis

(Chapter 3). Language teaching and language testing moved online in a hurry, with variable support (East et al.), very little employer-provided training (Hardacre, Chapter 9), or – in worse-case scenarios – with no support at all (as in a case described by Lam, Chapter 12). Most researchers and test developers, without a doubt, had little time to reflect on these changes, let alone document them. The process of test revision was, quoting Imamura, Ryu, and Kawaguchi (Chapter 15), 'rushed'. As the pandemic wanes, or at least as society comes to live with COVID-19 and its less-intensive risks thanks to vaccine proliferation and raised immunity levels, some of the highest-stakes and riskiest (or, one could say, most ground-breaking) emergency language-assessment measures are either staying on for the long haul, or are being dismantled or softened, necessitating, in all cases, the documentation of their development, lest their reasons for being and their lessons for future researchers be forgotten over time. Thus, I thank Karim and his team of authors for taking the time to pause, reflect, write, and share with us. These words are here so we will remember, know, and learn.

Professor Paula Winke
Editor, Language Testing
Fulbright Scholar, Herder-Institut, Leipzig University, Germany
Director of the Second Language Studies Ph.D. Program,
Michigan State University

References

Dimova, S., Yan, X., & Ginther, A. (2020). *Local language testing: Design, implementation, and development.* Routledge.

Isbell, D. R., & Kremmel, B. (2020). Test Review: Current options in at-home language proficiency tests for making high-stakes decisions. *Language Testing*, 37(4), 600–619. https://doi.org/10.1177/0265532220943483

Ockey, G. (Ed.). (2021). The quest to maintain language assessment quality during a pandemic: Stories from higher education. [Special Issue]. *Language Assessment Quarterly*, 18(1), 1–79.

Sadeghi, K. (2021). *Assessing second language reading: Insights from Cloze tests.* Springer.

Yan, X., Dimova, S., & Ginther, A. (Eds.). (2023). *Local language testing: Practice across contexts.* Springer.

CONTRIBUTORS

Dr. Mahmoud Amer is a Professor of Arabic and Applied Linguistics and Chairperson of the Department of Languages and Cultures at the West Chester University of Pennsylvania. He is an Executive Board Member of the American Association of Teachers of Arabic, an Adobe® Certified Expert®, and a CompTIA® Certified Technical Trainer.

Shireen Baghestani is a PhD student in the Applied Linguistics and Technology program at Iowa State University. Her research interests include L1 and L2 writing assessment and argument-based test validation.

Isabel Balteiro is a Senior Lecturer at the Department of English at the University of Alicante. She has published extensively on Word-Formation, Lexicology, ESP, Language Contact and Language Teaching. Dr. Balteiro received the Extraordinary Award for her PhD thesis and the national AEDEAN Linguistics Award in 2007 and 2008.

Dr Emma Bruce is a Researcher with the Assessment Research Group at the British Council. She specialises in research and validation of IELTS and also works on a range of projects for assessment systems designed and developed by the British Council. Emma has over 25 years of experience working in the tertiary sector, both in the UK and overseas, initially as a teacher, and later as a testing and assessment specialist. Emma's main research interests are in EAP assessment and integrated assessment tasks.

Contributors

Dr. María J. Cabrera-Puche is a Professor of Spanish, Language Pedagogy, and Linguistics at the Department of Languages and Cultures, WCU. Co-author of *Tu mundo* (1st, 2nd & 3rd editions), co-editor of *Romance Linguistics 2006*, Department Assessment Coordinator, University Assessment Director of General Education and trained tester/rater of ACTFL exams.

María Luisa Carrió-Pastor is a Professor of English language at Universitat Politècnica de València, Spain. Currently, she is the head of the Department of Applied Linguistics. Her research areas are contrastive linguistics, pragmatics, and the study of academic and professional discourse both for second language acquisition and discourse analysis.

Tony Clark is a Principal Research Manager at Cambridge University Press and Assessment, managing research on IELTS, test preparation, pedagogy, diagnostic assessment, and lexical studies. Addressing the challenges of conducting high-stakes assessments for university entrance has been a particular area of research interest since the Pandemic began.

Dr Ana Maria Ducasse lectures in Spanish language and culture, while researching and supervising Applied Linguistics at RMIT's Social and Global Studies Centre. IELTS and TOEFL iBT awarded her grants to research speaking but recently L2 feedback on writing tasks has been her main research focus including the Inter_Ecodal team.

Martin East is a Professor of Language Education in the School of Cultures, Languages and Linguistics, Waipapa Taumata Rau/the University of Auckland. He is an experienced teacher and teacher educator in the language field, and his research interests include innovative practices in language teaching, learning, and assessment. He publishes widely in these areas.

Hossein Farhady received his PhD in Applied Linguistics from UCLA in 1980. He has taught graduate courses in many universities, presented papers at professional conferences, conducted workshops, and published at national and international levels. His major areas of interest are research methodology, language assessment, and ESP. He is presently a Professor of applied linguistics at Yeditepe University, Istanbul, Turkey.

Bahiyyih Hardacre is an Associate Professor of TESOL at California State University Los Angeles. She has a PhD in applied linguistics, and her research interests include second language assessment and second language learning and teaching. She has over 25 years of teaching experience, both in Brazil and in the United States.

Martine Holland works for IELTS UK as an Assessment and Research Advisor; her research interests include applications of traditional pedagogical and assessment theory in digital implementations; integrated reading-into-writing assessment, academic language skills, and learning-oriented assessment. She has a strong interest in language assessment literacy, including enhancing stakeholder understanding of the IELTS test construct.

Akiko Imamura is an Assistant Professor and the Japanese language program coordinator at Michigan State University. Her research centres on language use and social interaction in first and second languages. Her most recent paper on Japanese compliments has been accepted for publication in *Discourse Studies*. Her broader research interest includes language pedagogy and language program direction.

Talia Isaacs is an Associate Professor of Applied Linguistics and TESOL and Programme Leader for the MA TESOL In-Service at IOE, UCL's Faculty of Education and Society, University College London. Her research interests include assessing speaking, English for academic purposes, classroom-based assessment, health communication, and assessment interfaces with second language acquisition.

Mariko Kawaguchi is an instructor of Japanese at Michigan State University. Her teaching and research interests include Japanese pedagogy, multicultural education, teaching Japanese to heritage learners, and computer-assisted language learning. In collaboration with an English instructor in Japan, she conducted multiple projects, e.g., a team-blog project for Japanese and virtual language exchanges.

Ricky Lam is an Associate Head and Programme Director of the Master of Education in the Department of Education Studies at Hong Kong Baptist University. His research interests include L2 writing assessment, digital portfolios, and language assessment literacy. His publications have appeared in numerous top-tier journals. Ricky is the author of *Portfolio Assessment for the Teaching and Learning of Writing* (2018, Springer) and *Using Portfolios in Language Teaching* (2019, New Portfolio Series 4, SEAMEO Regional Language Centre).

Viviane Lelièvre-Lopes is a Professional Teaching Fellow of French language and linguistics in the School of Cultures, Languages and Linguistics, Waipapa Taumata Rau/the University of Auckland. She is an experienced teacher and teacher educator over multiple secondary and tertiary teaching environments. She specialises in innovative practices in course design, language teaching, learning, and assessment.

Ananda Astrini Muhammad is a PhD student in the Applied Linguistics and Technology program at Iowa State University. Her research interests include second language pragmatics in language teaching/learning and assessment, as well as teacher professional development.

Reza Neiriz is a PhD student in the Applied Linguistics and Technology program at Iowa State University. His research interests are computer-mediated second language assessment, oral communication assessment, interactional competence, and automated scoring of oral communication.

Jim Ranalli, PhD, is an Assistant Professor in the TESL/Applied Linguistics program at Iowa State University. His research addresses the intersection of L2 writing, technology, and self-regulated learning. He is particularly interested in innovative uses of computers for scaffolding and assessing the development of English for academic purposes and writing skills.

Catherine Ryu is an Associate Professor of Japanese literature & culture and director of the Japanese Studies Program at Michigan State University. Her teaching and research interests include Classical Japanese, Heian women's narratives, Japanese culture and literature, Korean literature, Zainichi literature, game studies, translation studies, children's literature, digital humanities, and global studies. She also holds a U.S. patent for a language learning platform and is the PI of ToPES (tone perception efficacy Study), M-ToPP (Mandarin tone perception and production), Picky Birds, and Tone Perfect.

Richard Spiby works with the British Council Assessment Research Group. He works on the development and validation of British Council tests, including research into receptive skills components, oversight of operational analysis, and various development and training projects worldwide. His interests include language assessment literacy, test-taker strategies, test analysis and inclusivity in language assessment.

Heléna Stakounis is a Teaching Fellow in Applied Linguistics and TESOL at the University of Durham. Previously EAP Co-ordinator at the University of Lancaster and Associate Lecturer at the University of Salford, Heléna has worked in the UK HE sector for over ten years. She founded her own British Council-accredited private language school and has experience working in assessment for Cambridge International Examinations, British Council, Pearson, and NCUK. She is currently a final-year PhD student investigating student integration on the multilingual, multicultural, internationalised campus.

Erik Voss is an Assistant Professor in the Applied Linguistics and TESOL program at Teachers College, Columbia University. His research interests include language assessment and technology and validation research. He has served on the board of the Midwest Association of Language Testers (MwALT) and the International Language Testing Association (ILTA).

Deborah Walker-Morrison is an Associate Professor of French in the School of Cultures, Languages and Linguistics, Waipapa Taumata Rau/the University of Auckland. Her wide-ranging teaching and research interests include a long-standing focus on the creation of communicative, student-focused, multi-media materials for blended language learning and the use of technology for assessment.

Shishi Zhang is a PhD student at IOE, UCL's Faculty of Education and Society, University College London. Her research interests include second language pragmatics, assessing pragmatics, and intercultural communication. She worked as a project manager at Foreign Language Teaching and Research Press (FLTRP) in Beijing, China before commencing her PhD.

SECTION I

Theoretical and Methodological Concerns in Online L2 Assessment

1
TECHNOLOGY IN LANGUAGE ASSESSMENT

An Overview

Karim Sadeghi
URMIA UNIVERSITY, URMIA, IRAN

1.1 Introduction

While until fairly recently the use of computer technology in language assessment was generally very limited and primarily confined to large-scale testing, the global outbreak of the COVID-19 pandemic in early 2020 turned the page. This health crisis left no sphere of life untouched and turned educational and assessment systems and practices upside down. Despite its grave health and economic consequences (which were still on the rise, with more than 510,000,000 confirmed cases and more than 6,225,000 death worldwide by the end of April 2022), the pandemic was a blessing in disguise in some respects, especially in reviving a reimagination of education (Liontas, 2013). Although computers and digital technology have been part of educational enterprises since the 1970s and have similarly been employed in language education in certain contexts, their application remained restricted for various reasons including lack of widespread access to relevant infrastructure, the availability and speed of the Internet, the cost of the hardware and software for educational institutions, teachers and students, and the like. As such, technology was looked upon as a luxurious commodity, only affordable to a niche group of society and an asset to be benefited by people lucky enough to live in certain (primarily western) countries.

Despite extensive research about the affordances of technology in facilitating language teaching and learning (as documented by numerous studies published in journals like *Language Learning & Technology, Computer Assisted Language Learning, System, ReCALL, CALICO Journal*, and so on), not many learners were able to practically benefit from this educational innovation. When it comes to language assessment, the situation becomes worse due to

DOI: 10.4324/9781003221463-2

the complexities involved in delivering tests from a distance such as issues with test security, fairness, validity, and reliability. Despite these complexities and even before the pandemic, attempts were made by major testing bodies such as Educational Testing Service (ETS) in the United States to administer tests online, an initiation which continued at a faster pace after 2020 with an aim to make large-scale high-stakes tests available to a larger population of test takers worldwide at a time when restrictions were in place in taking tests on site. Apart from this, delivering tests from a distance (whether synchronously or asynchronously) had not until very recently found its way to small-scale testing. The Emergency Remote Education (ERE) (Sosa Díaz, 2021) period emerging from the COVID-19 pandemic at the start of 2020 forced all educational (including assessment) practices to go online. While some educational organisations and testing bodies were more or less prepared for such a change as they had been experimenting with at least partial online practices for decades, most of the world was introduced to a shocking and puzzling scenario which needed immediate attention. It is in this sense the pandemic has worked as a blessing in disguise to evaluate, rethink, and renovate the language assessment territory, and as Ockey (2021) recognises, it led to innovations in language assessment: 'It forced language assessment developers to be creative and bold in their approaches to ensuring a safe testing environment without compromising the validity of the decisions based on their assessments' (p. 5). Indeed at the start of the pandemic and during the first few months, most educational attempts concentrated on making teaching and learning happen virtually, with assessment neglected for some time. Some institutions, for example, disregarded any formal assessment for one or two semesters and relied on teacher's formative assessments while teaching, while others with the needed infrastructure in place administered whatever already existing online tests and some others opted for accommodating some aspects of existing tests to make them suitable for delivery through the medium of computer. While delivery through the medium of computer was nothing new for some organisations, its unsupervised delivery was what remained a challenge to be dealt with. This chapter (and the whole volume) is accordingly meant to review (and document) the affordances computer technology offers the field of second language (L2) assessment as well as the challenges involved in using this technology extensively and innovatively in large- and small-scale testing at the time when most testers were neither ready nor had the relevant knowledge, expertise, and training nor had access to the needed technological infrastructures to make this transition from traditional to remote assessment happen smoothly when there was an urgent need for that. Although there are book publications, book chapters as well as special journal issues (like *System* and *Language Assessment Quarterly*) attending to the use of technology in language assessment (as briefly outside below), this volume is the only one we are aware of that discusses and reports affordances and challenges of using digital technology in assessing L2 when such applications happen on an emergency basis where constant on-the-spot decisions are to be made at different stages of constructing, adapting, and administering the relevant tests as well as in interpreting the yielded scores.

One of the first and the most authoritative treatments of the topic of technology in L2 assessment or computer-assisted language assessment (CALA) is by Chapelle and Douglas (2006). The book treats theoretical, methodological, and practical issues in CALA, overviews the work in the field of CALA, evaluates examples of assessment through computer technology, and provides language teachers and researchers with practical guidelines for implementation. There is, however, no information or advice on how computer technology can be used at a global scale and a time when there is an abrupt shift to online education and an urgent need for online assessment, especially at the classroom level, a gap which the current volume is hoped to bridge. Apart from Chapelle and Douglas's (2006) authoritative treatment of CALA, there are very few books available on the market on the role of technology in language assessment (like Kunnan, 2015, which is a collection of papers already published elsewhere). There are devoted handbooks on language assessment by Winke and Brunfaut (2021) and Fulcher and Davidson (2012), with no space allocated for the use of technology in L2 assessment. There are also chapters within books or encyclopaedias related to the role of technology in language assessment like Brown (1997), Chapelle and Voss (2016), Milliner and Barr (2020), Winke and Fei (2008), and Winke and Isbell (2017). However, all of these volumes focus on the planned use of technology for language assessment in technologically rich contexts where users (both test takers and givers) can both afford the technology and have been trained in using it. As such, this book, as one of the first to tackle online testing at the time of the COVID-19 pandemic, is all about theoretical issues, practical concerns as well as the earliest experiments in this regard. Before closely looking at the content of the chapters that constitute this volume, we attend briefly to the history and then to some affordances and pitfalls that the application of digital technology has been reported to afford the field of language assessment.

1.2 Technology and Language Assessment: History, Affordances, and Challenges

1.2.1 A Brief Historical Overview

There is no shortage of terms like computer-assisted language testing, computerised language testing, technology-assisted language testing/assessment, technology-mediated language testing/assessment, computer-based testing, computer adaptive testing, web-based testing, online assessment, mobile-assisted language testing/assessment, and the like. Terms starting with the word 'computer' were coined in late 1970s and early 1980s when computers started to have personal applications (Godwin-Jones, 2001). According to Chalhoub-Deville (2001), although computer-based testing was already in practice since the early 1970s, computerised and computer adaptive language tests emerged in the mid-1980s with the 1985 Language Testing Research Colloquium (LTRC) conference proceedings published by Stansfield (1986) with the title *Technology and Language Testing*. Fulcher (2000) traces the history of computer-based testing even backwards to 1935, when an automated technology was used for scoring papers (see below). In those early days (1970s and 1980s), the computer was primarily a medium through which paper and pencil tests were delivered; indeed the test was the same except for the delivery mode and items and instructions were delivered on a computer screen rather than on paper. As the computer technology advanced, computer adaptive testing found vogue, where in addition to delivering the test with the medium of computer, changes were also introduced to the way the test was delivered to candidates of different ability levels such that different test takers who sat the same test received different number and type (in terms of difficulty) of items. This made the test more individualised and efficient. Comparing a computer adaptive version of the Word Part Levels Test with its traditional paper-based version, Mizumoto et al. (2019, p. 101), for example, found that the computerised version can provide diagnostic information on candidates' knowledge of word affixes 'with the same or greater precision' than its paper-based predecessors.

With the invention of the World Wide Web and the Internet in 1989, more unprecedented advances followed. While in both computer-based and computer adaptive testing, the test was still administered at a test centre and was supervised, the Internet- or web-based testing offered additional affordances such that testees could sit a test at a more convenient place and time and with limited supervision conditions. Internet-based testing, accordingly, marked a drastically different stage in language testing and has since been adopted by large-scale tests such as Test of English as a Foreign Language (TOEFL) and International English Language Testing System (IELTS) for assessing the receptive skills of reading and listening, with limited application to productive skills of writing and speaking. Internet-based TOEFL (TOEFL iBT) with a focus on integrated speaking and writing tasks, was, for example, introduced in 2005 by ETS to be delivered online at secure test centres in most parts of the world. Since the 2000s, the computer technology has seen further advances and with the increasing use of laptops, tablets, and smartphones for the administration of language tests, terms beginning with 'technology' have now taken over, with the word 'assessment' also gently replacing testing as more commonly technology has found its way to small-scale classroom testing contexts as well.

Despite all these advances in language testing, most technology-assisted language assessments so far have required human supervising in one way or another, primarily for security reasons. Although some large-scale tests (see Clark et al., this volume, for example) have had some measures in place to prevent cheating in distance administrations of the tests, such unsupervised testing was generally limited to a few large-scale tests. Despite the fact that test security is still a serious issue (see Sadeghi & Douglas, 2023, for example), the COVID-19 pandemic forced migration of almost all language assessment to a virtual world, with large-scale assessments like TOEFL iBT introducing a Home Edition since November 2020 (Papageorgiou & Manna, 2021). Although attempts are ongoing as the contributors to this volume have documented, the language assessment field is now experiencing a real taste of what can truly be called a 'new generation of technology-mediated language assessment', which spans from online delivery of traditional tests to those assessing productive skills of writing and speaking in real-time and in interaction with a 'virtually live' human being to automated scoring and feedback. Despite all these advances, there is a need for further research on whether technology-mediated language assessment taps the underlying constructs appropriately, accurately, and authentically enough (or whether the addition of technology had contributed to a better assessment of underlying traits) and what other theoretical and methodological concerns there may be.

1.2.2 Affordances and Challenges of Technology-Mediated Language Assessment

No doubt one of the major advantages of computer-delivered language tests, whether synchronous or asynchronous, whether supervised or unsupervised, whether delivered at a test centre or remotely, is, as Chapelle and Douglas (2006) identify, their higher practicality in terms of administration:

> Computer-assisted tests offer the possibility of diminishing the administrative burden of invigilating, or proctoring, by making the test available wherever and whenever the test taker can log onto the Internet or can insert a disk into a CD-ROM drive. Similarly, computer-assisted tests can reduce administrative burdens by transmitting test materials electronically, and requiring fewer personnel to hand out test papers, collect answer sheets, operate equipment, and so on.
>
> (p. 25)

Despite an existing challenge with test security which is discussed in some of the chapters in this volume (with measures suggested by Davidson & Coombe, 2023, for example, that can reduce the severity of any cheating), technology-assisted language assessment has also offered greater access chances to those who, especially at the time of the COVID-19 pandemic, would otherwise be unable to take tests, given the availability of computing hardware and software and a stable Internet connection. This may be regarded as a big logistical advantage of web-based tests, making them flexible in time and space. Referring specifically to DIALANG and the affordances technology has offered this test in terms of its administration only, Chapelle and Douglas (2006, p. 26) itemise the many practical benefits which similar web-based tests can also boast of:

> … [in addition to keeping variations in administration such as the rubric and instructions to a minimum] the test is entirely self-managed … it may be possible for administrators [and researchers] to collect data on item performance; the amount of time users take for each item, sub-tests, and the entire test; self-assessment; test–retest; and self-reported demographics on the users. Routine collection of these data would make constant revision a possibility.

Another major affordance technology has offered language assessment is in the domain of scoring in general and scoring writing and speaking in particular. With its 26 chapters, the *Handbook of Automated Scoring: Theory into Practice* (Yan et al., 2020) offers a comprehensive account of the background history and theory underlying automated scoring as well as operational methodologies and applications of computer technology, artificial intelligence, and natural language processing in assessing productive components of language. The practice of machine or automated scoring of objective or multiple-choice test items dates back to 1935 when IBM introduced its Model 805 test scoring machine based on the premise that such machines score more accurately and faster than human beings (Fulcher, 2000). In writing assessment, Cotos (2011), for example, observes that there has been an increasing interest in automated writing evaluation (AWE) since 2020. Although the concern in AWE is on providing feedback on learners' writing, the benefit of saving time, energy, and human resources (its cost-effectiveness) is likewise evident when computer technology is deployed to facilitate the scoring of writing papers as well as oral performance. In a recent study, Chan et al. (2022) compared the performance of an automated essay scoring system called Intelligent Essay Assessor (IEA) with holistic assessment by 19 experienced assessors. A total of 3,453 essays were assessed and both single and multi-facet Rasch models were used to analyse the data and make comparisons, with the results indicating that automated scoring ratings were equal to (and more consistent than) those of human beings. Latifi and Gierl (2021) also found that Coh-Metrix (an automated essay scoring software) scored the writing quality as reliably as the 'gold standard' of two human ratings (p. 62).

Similar affordances have been reported for computerised scoring of speaking using SpeechRater, an automated scoring engine developed at ETS (Wang et al., 2018; Zechner & Evanini, 2020). In comparison to its use with reading, listening, and writing skills, automated scoring of speaking has been more challenging, however (Kang & Johnson, 2018). Their own experiment with automated soring of a corpus of 120 Cambridge English Language Assessment (CELA) audio speech files (English monologues) indicated that there was 0.718 correlation coefficient between the proficiency levels (from B1 to C2) assigned by the computer and those by official CELA raters, a relationship indicating around 50 percent variation overlap, which may seem satisfactory given the gain in practicality. While faster scoring is guaranteed by machine scoring of writing and speaking and there is no doubt that technology offers enormous practicality especially when large-scale testing is involved, the quality of assessment as well as the accuracy of feedback may however not be comparable to that performed by human beings (as can be deciphered from Kang & Johnson's 2018 study). Indeed, for valid interpretations to be made of the resulting scores, human supervision and judgment will always be needed until further advances in the thinking mind of technology, i.e., artificial intelligence, even at which time a human role cannot be expected to be fully disregarded since artificial intelligence, however advanced it may become in the future, gains its intelligence from human intelligence. It is based on such considerations that designers of TOEFL Essentials (Davis et al., 2023) propose only human rating for the interview task, since 'automated scoring systems do not yet provide robust measurement of propositional content and discourse-level language phenomena (Zechner, 2020)' (cited in Davis et al.). This does not however understate limitations in human scoring of writing and speaking such as inconsistency, halo effect, rater drift, fatigue, subjectivity, leniency/severity, cost, and so on.

Numerous other affordances of technology have been documented in previous research on language assessment, to some of which we make a brief reference in this section. Darhower (2014), for instance, used a synchronous computer-mediated environment to understand how two university Anglophone learners of Spanish developed in terms of producing past narratives over six sessions and found that such computer-mediated environments offer an ideal medium for dynamic assessment of learning. In a similar dynamic assessment experiment, Yang and Qian (2019) compared the development of two groups of Chinese English as a Foreign Language (EFL) learners in reading comprehension after four sessions of treatment. While the experimental group was exposed to computerised dynamic assessment, the control group received conventional treatment, and the results indicated the superiority of the experimental group in reading comprehension at the end of the study, which implies that (dynamic) assessment delivered through the medium of computer leads to better learning outcomes. Oskoz (2005) too used dynamic assessment within a synchronous computer-mediated environment for assessing learners' language development, highlighting the affordances such technology offers in assessing instructional processes (as opposed to products) as well as allowing for collaborative assessment (compared to individualistic performance targeted by traditional tests).

In an attempt to understand whether reducing the tempo of speaking speed will lead L2 test-takers to perform better in listening tests delivered at normal speed, East and King (2012) find technology beneficial in this regard, and acknowledge that although it may be unlikely for testing bodies to use such technology to deliver listening tests, the technology can prove effective in scaffolding learners as they prepare for such tests. Park et al. (2022) report experimenting with listening tests accompanied by unscripted audio-visual stimuli from the target language use domain which render a more authentic listening assessment without compromising validity and reliability of test scores. In the context of second language speaking assessment, and as a measure to overcome the challenges of bringing together test-takers and a tester in one physical place, Ockey et al. (2017) introduced a web-based virtual environment which allows real-time voice communication among test-takers and test-administrators, and discussed their potential for delivering oral tests, as well as the theoretical and methodological issues concerned. Current technology is however much more advanced where video-conferencing facilities offered by platforms like Skype, FaceTime, Zoom, and Microsoft Teams have made online communications more real-life and authentic, improving over the limited authenticity of avatars (computer-animated human characterisations) in virtual environments that were used in Ockey et al. (2017) and offered only voice communication and limited non-verbal interactions.

Compared to advantages of using technology to deliver language tests, very few disadvantages have been reported, apart from issues such as security and fairness in remote, at-home, online assessments. Table 1.1, adapted from Chapelle and Douglas (2006), nicely summarises some of the main affordances and challenges of the use of technology in language assessment as reported by some of the scholars referred to above and others. The affordances and challenges are listed in terms of Test Method Characteristics proposed by Bachman (1990).

Evidently, the above affordances and challenges have been offered with planned language assessment in mind. The emergency language assessment contexts definitely pose new opportunities for the use of technology as well as fresh challenges, some of which are documented for the first time by the contributors to this volume. A recent special issue in *Language Assessment Quarterly* attends to the challenges and opportunities associated with migration from face-to-face testing to computerised at home remote assessment in the context of university placement and admission testing. With an editorial by Ockey (2021) and six commentaries, this collection is one of the first coverages of early experimentations with technology-mediated language assessment at the time of the COVID-19 pandemic, where the contributors discuss the

TABLE 1.1 Advantages and Limitations of Computer-Assisted Language Tests (CALT)

Test method characteristics	CALT advantages	CALT limitations
Physical and temporal circumstances	Computer-Assisted Language Tests (CALTs) can be taken at many convenient locations, times, and largely without human intervention.	Security is an issue in high-stakes tests; equipment not standardised nor universally available; IT expertise required for establishment, maintenance.
Rubrics/instructions	Test task and instructions are presented in a consistent, uniform, and automatic manner; making for enhanced fairness.	Different levels of instructions, voluntary help screens, different languages of instructions can detract from uniformity.
Input and expected response	Multimedia capabilities allow for a variety of input and response types, enhancing contextualisation and authenticity.	Input and response types are limited by available technology.
Interaction between input and response	Computers can adapt input in response to test-takers; responses and actions, allowing for computer adaptive tests (CATs) and rapid feedback.	Interactiveness is more controlled than certain other formats; computer's ability to sample fairly may be limited; CATs are expensive to develop.
Construct definition criteria for correctness scoring procedures	Natural language processing (NLP) technology allows for automated scoring of complex responses, affecting the construct definition, scoring criteria, and procedures.	NLP technology is new, expensive, and limited, creating potential problems for construct definition and validity.

Source: Adapted from Chapelle and Douglas (2006, p. 23).

challenges they faced in moving online (or making adaptations to traditional tests) as well as the lessons they learned for the future. Talking specifically about IELTS Indicator, Clark et al. (2021), for example, highlight challenges as follows: 'the change process was stressful … there were no organisational structures in place for the Indicator project … Important support systems … had to be set up from scratch and could not be made immediately available' (p. 22). Similarly, reporting on adaptations made to a placement test to screen international teaching assistants at Temple University, Wagner and Krylova (2021, p. 14) list challenges like 'identifying and integrating the various software and communication platforms' and 'ensuring the test-takers' technology would be compatible' among others that they needed to tackle in making their traditional test delivered through technology.

Although obstacles like test security, fairness, and social equity are still there and require ongoing attention and further research for proper tackling, the greatest benefit of technology in language assessment at the time of the recent global health crisis has been preventing assessment from dying: were it not for the role of whatever available technological resources in different contexts, language assessment could have simply been stalled or at best limited to contexts where chances existed for limited onsite or off-site supervised testing practices. Although lessons are still being learned on how to make accommodations to our traditional testing practices in light of technological innovations, this book provides us with significant theoretical positions and first hand data, some by frontliners, on successful emergency application of technology to both large-scale and small-scale assessment practices across the world. The hope is that we learn from these early attempts and possible failures to make language testing a more sustainable and secure enterprise in the wake of another future catastrophe. Despite the multitude of new opportunities afforded by technology, language testing experts may not be very willing to go too far too fast in availing themselves of the full range of technology-mediated language assessment options since there are still theoretical and methodological issues surrounding CALA which remain unresolved. A parallel Routledge volume by Sadeghi and Douglas (2023) investigates some of these less touched perennial issues including how the integration of technology into language assessment mediates with test-taker performance and the interpretation of test results as well as whether this integration has a bearing on the underlying constructs measured and whether and how the traditional key concepts of validity, reliability, authenticity, interactiveness, washback, and practicality require revisiting.

1.3 Structure of the Book

In addition to a Foreword by Paula Winke (Michigan State University, Co-editor of *Language Testing*) and two introductory and concluding chapters by the editor, this volume is made of 14 other full-length chapters (contributed by some of the best-known scholars in the field of L2 assessment, a few of whom being frontliners in large-scale assessments). The book is structured around three major themes in three sections: Section I: Theoretical and Methodological Concerns in Online L2 Assessment; Section II: Reactions to L2 E-Assessment During the COVID-19 Pandemic; and Section III: Managing L2 Assessment at the Time of the Crisis: The Way Forward. The first section comprises six chapters on the topics of online test validation of IELTS Indicator (by Tony Clark and his colleagues), validity and longevity of UK English for Academic Purposes assessments (by Emma Bruce and Heléna Stakounis), language assessment in the COVID-19 pandemic crisis in a Turkish context (by Hossein Farhady), argument-based validation in language testing at the time of the COVID-19 pandemic (by Erik Voss), and modernising a placement test for diverse contexts (by Mahmoud Amer and María J. Cabrera-Puche).

With its five chapters, papers in Section II focus on reactions in such diverse contexts as New Zealand, Spain, and the USA to emergency assessment of L2. Martin East and his colleagues share opportunities and challenges they identify for language assessment in one tertiary institution in New Zealand; Isabel Balteiro reports on COVID-19 related challenges and attitudes in at-home online language modules assessment at a Spanish University; Bahiyyih Hardacre experiments with assessing students' writing development and performance at a US context; Reza Neiriz and his co-researchers share their experience of adapting an Iowa State University placement test, highlighting fairness issues; and María Luisa Carrió-Pastor examines formative assessment in synchronous language teaching in a Spanish higher education institute.

The final section concentrates on successful stories of applications of technology to L2 assessment and offers recommendations for future research in this area. In Chapter 12, Ricky Lam examines validity, practicality, and washback of E-Portfolio as alternative assessment during the pandemic; Shishi Zhang and Talia Isaacs in the next chapter report an investigation into the use of videoconferencing technology in assessing L2 pragmatic competence; Ana Maria Ducasse introduces some tasks and rubrics for virtual and distance classroom assessment; and before the Conclusion, the chapter by Akiko Imamura and her colleagues evaluates a Japanese college level online placement test. The Conclusion by the editor summarises the lessons learned for emergency L2 assessment during the pandemic, and outlines areas of further research in technology-mediated language assessment and the lessons that we are yet to learn.

References

Bachman, L. F. (1990). *Fundamental considerations in language testing*. Oxford University Press.

Brown, J. D. (1997). Computers in language testing: Present research and some future directions. *Language Learning & Technology, 1*(1), 44–59.

Chalhoub-Deville, M. (2001). Language testing and technology: Past and future. *Language Learning & Technology, 5*(2), 95–98.

Chan, K. K. Y., Bond, T., & Yan, Z. (2022). Application of an automated essay scoring engine to English writing assessment using many-facet Rasch measurement. *Language Testing*, 1–25. https://doi.org/10.1177/02655322221076025

Chapelle, C. A., & Douglas, D. (2006). *Assessing language through computer technology*. Cambridge University Press.

Chapelle, C. A., & Voss, E. (2016) Utilizing technology in language assessment. In E. Shohamy, I. Or, & S. May (Eds.), *Language testing and assessment. Encyclopedia of language and education* (3rd ed.). Springer. https://doi.org/10.1007/978-3-319-02326-7_10-1

Clark, T., Spiby, R., & Tasviri, R. (2021). Crisis, collaboration, recovery: IELTS and COVID-19. *Language Assessment Quarterly, 18*(1), 17–25. https://doi.org/10.1080/15434303.2020.1866575

Cotos, E. (2011). Potential of automated writing evaluation feedback. *CALICO Journal, 28*(2), 420–459.

Darhower, M. A. (2014). Synchronous computer-mediated dynamic assessment: A case study of L2 Spanish past narration. *CALICO Journal, 31*(2), 221–243.

Davidson, P., & Coombe, C. (2023). Keeping them honest: Assessing learning in online and digital contexts. In K. Sadeghi, M. Thomas, & F. Ghaderi (Eds.), *Technology-enhanced language teaching and learning: Post-pandemic lessons*. Bloomsbury.

Davis, L., Norris, J., Papageorgiou, S., & Sasayama, S. (2023). Balancing construct coverage and efficiency: Test design and validation considerations for a remote-proctored online language test. In K. Sadeghi, & D. Douglas (Eds.), *Fundamental considerations in technology mediated language assessment*. Routledge.

East, M., & King, C. (2012). L2 learners' engagement with high stakes listening tests: Does technology have a beneficial role to play? *CALICO Journal, 29*(2), 208–223.

Fulcher, G. (2000). Computers in language testing. In P. Brett, & G. Motteram (Eds.), *A special interest in computers* (pp. 93–107). IATEFL Publications.

Fulcher, G., & Davidson, F. (2012). *The Routledge handbook of language testing*. Routledge.

Godwin-Jones, R. (2001). Language testing tools and technologies. *Language Learning & Technology, 5*(2), 8–12.

Kang, O., & Johnson, D. (2018). The roles of suprasegmental features in predicting English oral proficiency with an automated system. *Language Assessment Quarterly, 15*(2), 150–168. https://doi.org/10.1080/15434303.2018.1451531

Kunnan, A. (2015). *Language testing and assessment*. Routledge.

Latifi, S., & Gierl, M. (2021). Automated scoring of junior and senior high essays using Coh-Metrix features: Implications for large-scale language testing. *Language Testing, 38*(1), 62–85. https://doi.org/10.1177/0265532220929918

Liontas, J. (2013). Reimagining education is dead. Long live reimagining education! New technological innovations in second language teacher education and professional development. In K. Sadeghi, & M. Thomas (Eds.), *Second language teacher professional development: Technological innovations for post-emergency teacher education*. Palgrave Macmillan.

Milliner, B., & Barr, B. (2020) Computer-assisted language testing and learner behavior. In M. Freiermuth & N. Zarrinabadi (Eds.), *Technology and the psychology of second language learners and users. New language learning and teaching environments* (pp. 115–143). Palgrave Macmillan. https://doi.org/10.1007/978-3-030-34212-8_5

Mizumoto, A., Sasao, Y., & Webb, S. A. (2019). Developing and evaluating a computerised adaptive testing version of the Word Part Levels Test. *Language Testing, 36*(1), 101–123. https://doi.org/10.1177/0265532217725776

Ockey, G. J. (2021). An overview of COVID-19's impact on English language university admissions and placement tests. *Language Assessment Quarterly, 18*(1), 1–5. https://doi.org/10.1080/15434303.2020.1866576

Ockey, G. J., Gu, L., & Keehner, M. (2017). Web-based virtual environments for facilitating assessment of L2 oral communication ability. *Language Assessment Quarterly, 14*(4), 346–359. https://doi.org/10.1080/15434303.2017.1400036

Oskoz, A. (2005). Students' dynamic assessment via online chat. *CALICO Journal, 22*(3), 513–536.

Papageorgiou, S., & Manna, V. F. (2021). Maintaining access to a large-scale test of academic language proficiency during the pandemic: The launch of TOEFL iBT Home Edition. *Language Assessment Quarterly, 18*(1), 36–41. https://doi.org/10.1080/15434303.2020.1864376

Park, Y., Lee, S., & Shin, S.-Y. (2022). Developing a local academic English listening test using authentic unscripted audio-visual texts. *Language Testing,* 1–24. https://doi.org/10.1177/02655322221076024

Sadeghi, K., & Douglas, D. (Eds.) (2023). *Fundamental considerations in technology mediated language assessment.* Routledge.

Sosa Díaz, M. J. (2021). Emergency remote education, family support and the digital divide in the context of the COVID-19 lockdown. *International Journal of Environmental Research and Public Health, 18*(15), 7956. https://doi.org/10.3390/ijerph18157956

Stansfield, C. W. (1986). *Technology and language testing.* TESOL.

Wagner, E., & Krylova, A. (2021). Temple University's ITA placement test in times of COVID-19. *Language Assessment Quarterly, 18*(1), 12–16. https://doi.org/10.1080/15434303.2020.1862849

Wang, Z., Zechner, K., & Sun, Y. (2018). Monitoring the performance of human and automated scores for spoken responses. *Language Testing, 35*(1), 101–120. https://doi.org/10.1177/0265532216679451

Winke, P., & Fei, F. (2008) Computer-assisted language assessment. In N. H. Hornberger (Ed.), *Encyclopedia of language and education.* Springer. https://doi.org/10.1007/978-0-387-30424-3_110

Winke, P. M., & Isbell, D. R. (2017) Computer-assisted language assessment. In S. Thorne. & S. May (Eds.), *Language, education and technology. Encyclopedia of language and education* (3rd ed.) (pp. 1–13). Springer. https://doi.org/10.1007/978-3-319-02328-1_25-2

Winke, P., & Brunfaut, T. (2021). *The Routledge handbook of second language acquisition and language testing.* Routledge.

Yan, D., Rupp, A. A., & Foltz, P. W. (2020). *Handbook of automated scoring: Theory into practice.* Routledge.

Yang, Y., & Qian, D. D. (2019). Promoting L2 English learners' reading proficiency through computerized dynamic assessment. *Computer Assisted Language Learning,* 1–25. https://doi.org/10.1080/09588221.2019.1585882

Zechner, K., & Evanini, K. (Eds.) (2020). *Automated speaking assessment: Using language technologies to score spontaneous speech.* Routledge.

2

SEEKING EMPIRICAL EVIDENCE TO SUPPORT ONLINE TEST VALIDATION

Building on the IELTS Indicator Assessment Model

Tony Clark

CAMBRIDGE UNIVERSITY PRESS & ASSESSMENT, CAMBRIDGE, UNITED KINGDOM

Martine Holland

IELTS UK, LONDON, UNITED KINGDOM

Richard Spiby

BRITISH COUNCIL, LONDON, UNITED KINGDOM

2.1 Introduction

The socio-cognitive framework (Weir, 2005) is a model used to guide test development, research, and validation – including considerations of test use and consequences. Its central role underpinning International English Language Testing System (IELTS) test development and validation is well-documented, with the framework applied to 'scrutinise, in a rigorous and systematic way, all aspects of test validity' (Taylor & Chan, 2015, p. 28). Refining this application of the framework based on operational testing experience is required; it is important to collect evidence to support validation activities as part of an ongoing process (Chalhoub-Deville & O'Sullivan, 2020; Geranpayeh & Taylor, 2013). Within this remit, Taylor and Chan (2015) note the responsibility of major test providers to respond appropriately to changes in an evolving assessment landscape, including documentation of the reasoning and logic behind decisions that affect large numbers of test-takers and test score users. The COVID-19 global pandemic – and the catapulting of technology to the

DOI: 10.4324/9781003221463-3

forefront of delivering high-stakes language assessment – continues to raise a series of pertinent questions for test providers. Related areas include fairness, test-taker rights, and access issues (Muhammad & Ockey, 2021), all of which require further consideration for the emerging new world of language testing.

In their review of at-home assessment options, Isbell and Kremmel (2020) call for test providers to adopt a proactive stance on such topics, maintain solid record keeping about the impact of post-pandemic assessment models, and prepare for potential future disruption. The purpose of this chapter is to support the implementation of online assessment capabilities, take stock of relevant existing research findings, and identify some of the remaining questions. While earlier work (Clark et al., 2021) described the practical and logistical rollout of IELTS Indicator,[1] a more detailed consideration of the subsequent implications for candidates is now required. The present inquiry goes beyond the featured test (also IELTS Indicator) and is intended to inform high-stakes online assessment more broadly. We are cognisant of the limitations; constructing a definitive validation argument for an online assessment model would be a significant longer-term undertaking. However, starting to contribute to this – by documenting our findings and reasoning – is a more realistic aim. The unifying and coherent validation approach offered by the socio-cognitive framework (Chalhoub-Deville & O'Sullivan, 2020; Weir & O'Sullivan, 2011) in defining and collating a range of complementary validity evidence (He & Jiang, 2020) underlines its continued importance, guiding key questions in a post-pandemic setting. Aspects of particular relevance to online assessment include test-taker characteristics (e.g., test anxiety), context validity (test administration), scoring validity, consequential validity (test impact, fairness), and criterion-related validity (comparability and interchangeability of different forms of the same test).

Although IELTS Indicator was retired from use in 2022, reflecting on what has been learned from the experience is important to inform future decision-making. We believe that a strong theoretical basis to support future validity arguments (see Spiby & Clark, forthcoming) around online testing will be central to language assessment – and, in this chapter, we aim to demonstrate where theory begins to meet empirical evidence.

2.2 IELTS, IELTS Indicator, and the Impact of the Global Pandemic

IELTS is a large-scale multilevel test of language proficiency, used for university entrance (IELTS Academic module), vocational or migration settings (IELTS General Training module, and IELTS Academic in some cases). It assesses four skills (Speaking, Writing, Listening, and Reading) on a nine-band rating scale. IELTS[2] is owned by three partner organisations (British Council, IDP Education, and Cambridge University Press & Assessment), and is ordinarily available at 1,600 test centres in over 140 countries worldwide. In addition to widespread availability, two of IELTS' strengths are test security and the opportunity for candidates to interact with an examiner, both of which were compromised by the closure of test centres due to COVID-19. This dialogue between the candidate and examiner requires the use of interactional skills – comparable to a shared and co-constructed exchange between interlocutors (Galaczi & Taylor, 2018) – and prepares candidates for spoken discourse after the test by allowing them the chance to use their language to speak to a human contact, supporting the cognitive validity of the chosen approach (Weir, 2005).

IELTS Indicator provided a temporary online testing capability (April–September 2020 was the main period of deployment, but it remained in use at some test centres until 2022). Indicator provided candidates an advisory score only, owing largely to limitations on the ability to fully implement test security measures in the online environment. Beyond this, test content, format, timing, and structure replicated the IELTS Academic test. Although security practices improved over the course of 2020 in particular (using identity checks and some degree of remote proctoring), measures for IELTS Indicator were not considered sufficiently robust for high-stakes testing purposes.

2.3 Validity Issues in Remote Testing

As with much educational instruction, the pandemic prompted a rethink of approaches to language assessment and a switch to online testing as the main mode of delivery (Chapelle, 2020). This meant a pivot to remote, at-home solutions (Isbell & Kremmel, 2020) and was particularly acute in the case of tests informing high-stakes decisions. Test providers reacted by suspending testing activity, creating remote-proctored delivery of existing or adapted tests, or using pre-existing online tests (Wagner, 2020), whose uses have been extended in response to the temporary non-availability of other tests.

The Standards for Educational and Psychological Testing contain several standards applicable to the issue of validity in an online context (AERA, APA, & NCME, 2014). Some pertain to test administration conditions. According to the standards, variation in conditions and the presence of distractions in the environment need to be limited to prevent construct-irrelevant variance. Other standards concern general test security to prevent cheating on the part of test-takers, including false identification and the theft of test materials.

2.4 Security in an Online Test Environment

Security risks pose a significant threat to score validity. Where security is inadequate, scoring validity may be compromised, meaning the test itself may cease to be fit for high-stakes purposes. Thus, institutions may be accepting students on the basis of results obtained by illegitimate means – unreliable results which may be associated with significant later costs.

Online test security was a step into relatively unknown territory in 2020, certainly in comparison to the known risks of test centre administration. Many of the risks and methods of mitigation are outlined by Langenfeld (2020) and more generally by Ferrara (2017), who calls for cooperation and basic standards among test providers to create stronger security measures. However, little information is available on the extent of malpractice: unsurprisingly, test providers are reluctant to make public information which may reveal security flaws and help test-takers cheat undetected. Yet malpractice clearly occurs. Steger et al. (2020) found difference in scores and ability rankings of candidates in proctored and unproctored tests. Unproctored tests led to higher scores, suggesting the occurrence of malpractice in those conditions.

Remote proctoring and lockdown browsers are an attempt to control the home testing environment and prevent cheating. Different models of proctoring are available, with a combination of human or artificial intelligence on the one hand and real-time or post hoc 'record and review' monitoring on the other (Camara, 2020). Real-time monitoring, particularly by a human proctor, allows action to be taken during the test to identify suspicious behaviour and prevent further malpractice from occurring. Often a hybrid model is employed, where machine monitoring identifies potential undesirable behaviour for post hoc human review. Michel (2020) provides a framework for security and levels of invigilation, with live proctoring together with AI as the most secure, record and review technologies less secure, and pure AI monitoring the least secure proctoring option. While more secure systems are obviously desirable, these must be offset by cost and practicality, particularly with on-demand testing. However, the presence of proctoring can serve to reduce cheating (Karim et al., 2014).

There is no consensus at the time of writing on optimum test security procedures, but some principles of 'secure' practice can be employed. To deter item theft, large item banks are effective, but at a cost in terms of test design; some tests created as online tests from the outset have a design reflecting the ability to be generated and scored automatically (Wagner, 2020). Alternatively, content can be refreshed on a regular basis with fixed-session rather than on-demand tests. Computer-adaptive testing (CAT) is another preventive measure, though CAT is not immune to content theft (Cohen & Wollack, 2006). Post hoc statistical approaches (as in Cizek & Wollack, 2016) to detecting malpractice are important in discovering where cheating prevention measures have failed and how these can be adjusted to minimise both test-taker misconduct and prevent excessive content exposure in the future. In writing tests, plagiarism detection software is an effective response, while for speaking, raters can provide insight into detecting pre-prepared answers (Gates et al., 2020). However, with online at-home testing, by definition there is a diverse range of test-taking environments which are outside the control of administrators. In this context, the security of at-home tests was yet to be substantiated during the height of the pandemic. Despite widespread claims to the contrary, it could be said that no test was fully secure in 2020.

In terms of accessibility, online tests have basic technological requirements. These include minimum computer specifications, and hardware such as camera, microphone, and speakers or headphones. More of an issue may be access to an adequate internet connection (Green & Lung, 2021), particularly with regard to the requirements of continuous camera usage for remote proctoring as well as delivery of different modes of test content. Another issue of concern is privacy (Isbell & Kremmel, 2020) which is potentially reduced when using secure exam browsers or webcam monitoring, AI and (possibly unscrupulous) invigilators, and monitoring of test-taker computer activity. Such high levels of intrusion may have a significant impact on test-taker performance due to a potential increase in test anxiety, particularly from proctoring (Karim et al., 2014). Before a test, candidates are made aware that certain behaviours, such as disappearing from view of the camera or constantly looking away from the screen, may result in that behaviour being flagged as suspicious (by a human or AI proctor) and risk the withholding of test results. The effect of proctoring may be pronounced for candidates who are already prone to test anxiety as findings suggest such candidates perform worse remotely than in a test centre (Woldeab & Brothen, 2019). Thus, surveying test-taker views on the impact of privacy concerns is an essential piece of evidence in a validity argument.

The other major validity-related aspect is the addition of test administration features pertinent to remote online testing, such as the suitability or otherwise of the home environment for test-taking: it remains unclear what impact this may have on candidate performance. For example, candidates may suffer interruptions from other individuals in the household, or may be hampered by technological and connection issues, affecting concentration and triggering anxiety.

2.5 Mitigation – The Role of Existing Research

With these considerations in mind, existing IELTS research laid the foundations for the development decisions surrounding Indicator – looking at this research in more detail will help clarify how this was done.

2.5.1 Computer-Based IELTS (Writing, Listening, and Reading Skills)

Previous work on computer-based IELTS formed a significant basis of Indicator test development, with earlier validation studies effectively providing a link between the two. Investigating the viability of introducing technological innovations to test delivery is not new for IELTS, even if drawing on these simultaneously to deploy Indicator was unprecedented. One validity concern arising from differences in test conditions is the potential difference between traditional pen-and-paper and computer-delivered tests, i.e., the extent to which constructs are altered by delivery mode. Cambridge ran a series of early studies into the comparability between paper and computer-based IELTS in 2001, revealing that delivery mode had a negligible impact on item difficulty, and observing strong alignment between listening and reading test scores in both versions (Blackhurst, 2007). Subsequent larger-scale trials were conducted (2003, 2004) to overcome potential motivation effects on the previous sample (Maycock, 2004). These supported earlier findings, showing that test delivery mode had little bearing on rater agreement. For writing, another follow-up study (Green, 2004) indicated that response format – handwritten or typed – had no measurable impact on scores. This was further supported by commissioned work indicating that test scores and candidates' cognitive processing were comparable across paper and computer-based versions of IELTS Writing (Weir et al., 2007), though others (e.g., Chan et al., 2018) have found some small differences. Continual monitoring and internal Cambridge validation work ensures that the scoring and score comparability have remained under close scrutiny since computer-delivered IELTS was launched internationally in 2017.

Furthermore, as Fulcher (1999) reminds us, scoring is only one aspect of comparability; candidates' familiarity with technology (and attitudes towards it) should not be overlooked. Equality of digital literacy for the specific purpose of testing should not be assumed (Clark & Endres, 2021; Moore et al., 2018). Individual differences in how test-takers perceive varying delivery modes highlight the importance of accommodating their views (Yu, 2010) as a key part of the validation process (Brunfaut et al., 2018; Weir, 2005). For example, many test-takers reacted favourably to computer-delivered IELTS and felt quite capable of writing text onto a screen (Maycock & Green, 2005). How these findings compare to the experiences of IELTS Indicator candidates involved in at-home testing is of interest to investigate.

2.5.2 Extending Video-Call (Speaking) Technology Beyond Its Original Purpose

Although the basis for Indicator test validation already existed through research on computer-based IELTS (apart from the new at-home element instead of at a secure test centre), the use of video-call (VC) technology played a new and central role. Beyond computer-based delivery, a four-phase systematic trial (2016–2021) of the use of VC technology in a test centre to administer IELTS Speaking originally explored access for candidates unable to attend a face-to-face examiner session in locations affected by issues including conflict, disease, or a lack of suitable infrastructure.

Preliminary trialling compared test-taker and examiner behaviour between face-to-face and VC delivery modes, revealing that although scoring was similar overall, there were some differences in test management and rating behaviours (Nakatsuhara et al., 2016). Crucially, the speaking construct remained the same across the two modes. Phase 2 involved a larger-scale trial, looking at these issues in more depth. Findings indicated that scoring differences were minimal, supporting the earlier outcome (Nakatsuhara et al., 2017). Interestingly, test-takers asked more clarification questions in VC speaking mode; most (71%) preferred face-to-face delivery at that juncture, but some were slightly less anxious using remote delivery than in person. Examiners largely (80%) felt that candidates would be able to demonstrate their language proficiency across modes equally, and that rating was similarly straightforward in both cases. The third phase was a technical trial of a new platform for VC speaking, collating further evidence that earlier test administration issues around technology had been resolved, and that scoring validity was maintained (Berry et al., 2018). Recommendations for adapting the interlocutor frame were implemented for Phase 4 that additionally answered outstanding questions around timing and participant perceptions, all of which proved satisfactory (Lee et al., 2021).

By the start of the pandemic, these findings had been used as a basis for successful rollout of VC speaking at a number of locations globally, with candidates using VC technology at designated centres. However, although this extensive in-centre trialling provided an indication of expected viability, how VC speaking would work with at-home testing remained unclear. With the majority of test centres closed, this would form the principal delivery mode for the Speaking test, raising further questions. For test-takers participating at home, it should not be assumed that their environment is capable of providing them with the same opportunity to demonstrate their language proficiency as other candidates, for example (Papageorgiou & Manna, 2021).

2.6 Research Objectives of the Current Study

In sum, the studies outlined above provided a solid research basis to support the launch of IELTS Indicator. It should be highlighted that all aspects of scoring validity were continually monitored throughout the deployment of Indicator; a separate validation study investigating the implications of online assessment for IELTS scoring is underway, to be detailed in a forthcoming report. To narrow down the scope from some of the other validity-related questions raised, this chapter will focus on the experiences of two groups who are central to understanding Indicator post-rollout: candidates and examiners. Our overall preliminary inquiries are based on data gathered largely at the height of the pandemic in 2020, and a follow-up study in 2021 designed to investigate any potential changes over time. Lessons we have learned regarding online

TABLE 2.1 Data Collection Overview

Data collection method	Time period	Participants	Comments
Indicator Candidate Survey	April–September 2020	$N = 1{,}312$	Large-scale survey to inform **RQ 1**
Reports on incidents, dropout rates	April–September 2020	N/A	Collated documents to inform **RQ 1**
Examiner Focus Groups	August 2021	$N = 5$ (×2 groups)	**RQ 2, RQ 2b**
Follow-up Candidate Survey	January–September 2021	$N = 1{,}132$	Large-scale survey to inform **RQ 1b**

assessment practices will now be outlined, building on the previous findings around comparability described above.

2.6.1 Data Collection and Analysis

The following research questions were developed to guide the study:
Research Questions (RQs)

RQ 1: What were candidate experiences of using IELTS Indicator?
RQ 1b: Did these experiences change over time?
RQ 2: What were examiner experiences of using Indicator?
RQ 2b: Did these experiences change over time?

The following data collection methods were used, described in detail in Table 2.1. Two large-scale voluntary candidate surveys and two examiner focus groups were the main sources of data:

2.6.2 Indicator Candidate Survey (2020)

2.6.2.1 Participants (N = 1,312)

Survey responses came from test-takers across six test dates from 29th April to 5th June. The gender split was close to 50/50. Respondents' ages ranged from 15 to 63, with a mean of 27.5.

The largest proportion of respondents by far gave their nationality as Saudi Arabian ($N = 348$; 26.52%), with the next most common being Italian ($N = 87$; 6.63%), Chinese ($N = 86$; 6.56%), Indian ($N = 84$; 6.40%), and Emirati ($N = 66$; 5.03%). Most respondents currently resided in Saudi Arabia ($N = 313$; 23.86%), the UK ($N = 149$; 11.36%), UAE ($N = 88$; 6.71%), Italy ($N = 77$; 5.87%), or Germany ($N = 75$; 5.72%). Other locations were reported on a smaller scale.

2.6.3 Indicator Candidate Survey (2021)

2.6.3.1 Participants (N = 1,132)

Survey responses for the follow-up candidate questionnaire came from the period January to September 2021, a period of stability (and little change) in terms of Indicator test development. As before, the almost equal proportion of female and male students was noted. Respondents' ages ranged from 16 to 67, with a mean of 27.86.

There were 114 nationalities reported by respondents, with the largest number being Indian ($N = 240$; 21.20%), followed by Chinese ($N = 209$; 18.46%) and French ($N = 84$; 7.40%). About half of respondents were resident in India ($N = 214$; 18.90%), the UK ($N = 136$, 12.01%), China ($N = 116$; 10.25%), and France ($N = 104$; 9.19%), from a total of 77 locations. This reflects the fact that, geographically, Indicator users shifted over time, as test centres closed or reopened in different regions across the world, preventing straightforward comparisons of results from the two survey periods.

2.6.4 Examiner Experiences of Indicator (Focus Groups, August 2021)

We also carried out two semi-structured focus groups with examiners (Group 1, $N = 3$, Group 2, $N = 2$).

The examiners all had experience of examining in various formats, including Indicator since launch, and all except one had done substantial examining on the VC project. All were experienced test centre examiners.

The broad range of areas discussed included:

- Their experience of Indicator so far;
- Changes in Indicator over time;
- Comparison between Indicator, VC speaking, and face-to-face speaking examinations;
- Examiner support and training;
- Any areas requiring further improvement.

2.6.5 Data Analysis

2.6.5.1 Survey Responses

This analysis took three forms:

- All test-takers were offered a survey at the end of the test. Questions included overall perception of Indicator, ease of finding information about the product and procedures, and issues encountered. Data were

thematically coded, and basic statistical analysis carried out, including distribution frequencies and correlations. Open-text survey responses were thematically coded and common topics reported.
- Quantitative analysis of test-taker completion and dropout rates at different stages of the test-taker user journey, from registration to completion of the final component.
- Quantitative analysis of Incident Report Forms (i.e., the record of all user-reported issues), coded to categorise recurring issues and follow-up actions. Descriptive analysis was then carried out to examine patterns across session, country and broader geographical region.

For both surveys, results are described quantitatively, together with qualitative findings from thematic analysis of test-taker responses.

2.6.5.2 Focus Group Analysis

Transcripts were inductively coded by two researchers, and thematically analysed (using Braun & Clarke, 2006) with the coding framework subsequently unified. The following sections describe the emergent themes.

2.7 Results and Discussion
2.7.1 Indicator Candidate Survey Results

For brevity, results from both surveys are presented together. However, as mentioned above, any comparison should be treated with caution (Table 2.2).

Across both surveys, test-takers positively commented on the at-home environment (149 positive out of 161 total in 2020; 58 positive out of 69 total in 2021) with comfortable surroundings, a lack of distraction (from other test-takers) and the familiarity of the environment reducing stress noted as common factors. The convenience (60/69 in 2020; 47/55 in 2021) and the absence of travel were also commonly referred to. Example responses included (these are unedited to maintain authenticity):

2.7.1.1 2020

- 'Choose the opproiate [sic] time and test at home without the need to travel or go to a test place away far from my home'.
- 'Quiet environment and comfortable chair, there is no distraction from examiners [i.e. invigilators]'.
- 'Because I was alone in my room with a pin drop silence and no other distractions except vocal reminder of last 10 min for each module'.

TABLE 2.2 Test-Taker Perceptions

	Survey results 2020	Survey results 2021
Preferred Indicator	58.7%	70.4%
Preferred test centre (IELTS)	30.6%	20.0%
Mean average of agreement with each statement; 10 = strongly agree		
Taking Indicator was more relaxing than taking IELTS at a test centre	7.0	7.0
Booking the IELTS Indicator test was easy	8.1	7.9
Setting up and accessing the test was simple	7.3	7.2
The information and instructions for IELTS Indicator were clear	7.5	7.7
Finding information about IELTS Indicator was easy	6.9	7.1
Test questions were easy to read (LRW)/hear (S)	7.4; 7.5	7.5; 7.7
What I was required to do at each step of the test was clear	7.6	7.7
Disruptions		
No disruptions	60.1%	54.7%
Internet connection	13.2%	19.4%
Noisy environment	7.1%	12.5%
Interruptions from other people	6.8%	9.5%
Power supply	4.5%	7.0%
Of those who reported technological issues, these related to:		
Secure exam browser	32%	22.4%
Accessing the test	20%	18.1%
Submitting answers	19.1%	10.3%
Computer was too slow	7.9%	3.6%
Internet was too slow	7.9%	7.1%
Other	12.9%	36.3%
Of the total respondents, the following percentages reported issues with computer components:		
Sound	8%	6.7%
Microphone	4.3%	2.7%
Screen	2.9%	3.6%
Webcam	2.4%	4.7%

2.7.1.2 2021

- 'No stress to be on time for the exam (i.e. transport issues …) and less stress in a familiar environment'.

When Indicator was launched, one of our concerns with the online test environment was the extent to which test-takers could expect to be undisturbed if sitting a test at home. The survey results suggested a quiet environment was possible for most test-takers, with 60.1% of respondents in 2020 reporting no distractions, and 54.7% in 2021.

Both surveys revealed some preference for an in-centre test due to anxiety surrounding possible technological issues. In 2020, of the 30% of respondents who preferred test centre testing, the majority of related comments were concerned with this area:

- 'I was still very nervous, as I was worried about possible disconnection of the internet (even though I knew it wouldn't happen)'.

While in 2021 only nine (4%) mentioned technological problems as a discouraging factor, another nine respondents (4%) referred to the *anxiety* of possible technological problems, and two (1%) were worried that their behaviour in the test might inadvertently be tagged as cheating:

- 'Because you never know when someone could disturbed you and the environment is very not adapted to be fully concentrate'.
- 'I'm so worried about electricity shortage and internet instability during the test'.
- 'I always need to worry about my actions might be misinterpreted as cheating'.

2.7.2 Technology

2.7.2.1 2020

As can be seen above, technological issues were a key theme throughout the results of both surveys. As well as a worldwide unprecedented reliance on technological infrastructure and rapid user upskilling in new software, the necessary pace of release for Indicator in 2020 meant that some problems persisted.

In terms of technical issues, operational reports in 2020 show that the listening paper was the most affected component (dropout rates <22%; other components <4.5%); interviews suggested this may be related to the increased requirement for internet speed.

2.7.2.2 Geographical 2020

It is important to note the role of geographical variation. When trends in technical issues were analysed geographically, for countries classified as developing vs developed countries (based on UN categorisation), the two most common issues were audio and connectivity, as given in Table 2.3.

Percentages are of total reported issues for countries classified as developed/developing respectively. It may be an indication of the comparatively higher level of connectivity in developed countries that connectivity issues are almost

TABLE 2.3 Common Technology Issues

	Audio issues	Connectivity issues
Developed countries	17.3%	9.2%
Developing countries	9.4%	11.2%

half as common as audio issues, in stark contrast with developing countries where connectivity is most common. As further evidence of the role of connectivity in SEB[3] functionality, candidates in developing countries were more likely to report problems with installing the SEB, encountering a lock screen, as well as the SEB becoming unresponsive.

2.7.2.3 Communication with Test-Takers

Communication remained an important issue in both 2020 and 2021: many test-takers reported a lack of human assistance when they encountered difficulties. In 2020, this manifested as complaints about customer service response times, and sometimes test-takers did not receive key information on test/speaking dates until shortly before the test date itself. In 2021, many of these issues appear to have been resolved, comments instead centring around miscommunication in scheduling and rescheduling tests, particularly speaking:

- 'I was disconnected before the test and needed to reconnect. I'm not sure if that time was included in my test time'.
- 'Figure out a way to provide live support inside the test'.
- 'I had a concern with the request for re-scheduling of Speaking Test. They gave me 2 schedules. I got confused. I prepared for two given schedules'.

Another aspect for improvement across both surveys was the opportunity for test-takers to have breaks during the test. In 2020, there was some lack of understanding on how and when breaks would happen (average survey result: 5). In 2021, the average was 4.43, but the full range of ratings 0–10 was used in responding to this item, suggesting there was some confusion whether breaks were available. This came through in some of the comments:

- 'The systems are really good but it would be better if there is a 5 min break between sections…'
- 'A prompt indicating that we can take a break now (for mentioned minutes)… didn't take one because I thought I might be penalised for moving away from the screen'.

The second comment here is illustrative in that it raises three recurrent themes: the need for explicit directions to the candidate in an environment where help may not always be available; the need for candidates to take short breaks during what is still an intense test experience; and anxiety created by conscious avoidance of any behaviour that may be seen as suspicious.

2.7.2.4 Examiner Focus Group Results

Examiners generally had a very positive impression of Indicator, saying that 'the overall experience, I think is really good' (Fiona, Interview 2), that they felt 'students like taking these exams online' (Anne, Interview 1); and expressing a desire for it to continue. Martin also commented how online work and communication is becoming more normalised: 'I work online a lot so it's almost more natural to be meeting you like this than it would be in real life' (Interview 2). When comparing different formats for delivering speaking exams, participants noted that many test-takers appeared more relaxed with online testing formats (although this is 'not [true] for everybody' – Anne, Interview 1), and speculated that this may be due to the tiring and sometimes stressful nature of test centre procedures dictated by security protocols and heightened by the inclusion of COVID-related procedures. 'It's a long day' (Louise, Interview 1); 'they're nervous about when they can come into the room' (Martin, Interview 2); '[face masks cause worry that] you can't hear them, or they worry they can't be heard' (Steve, Interview 1).

As well as providing a more relaxing environment, Louise and Steve saw Indicator as being more convenient for the test-taker, Steve noting that 'people pick their own timeslot'. Louise also highlighted that Indicator has widened access to the test, as she 'tested a number of women with children – put them in the other room for a bit – allows them to access the exam'. All three examiners in Interview 1 highlighted that the experience they had gained with Indicator stood them in good stead for higher-stakes examining: 'It was good practice for VC speaking' (Steve, Interview 1); '[it] has made me a better examiner' (Anne, Interview 1).

A different theme from the interviews that mirrored the findings of the surveys was that online test-taking removes the support that test-takers are given at test centres, increasing the need for test-taker self-management and anxiety stemming from this. Examiners said that misunderstanding of test-day requirements was common, with test-takers either attending without necessities: 'at the beginning a lot of them would show up without a paper and pencil or without identification to show you' (Martin, Interview 2); '[I've had] cases where [the test taker] was a minor but the chaperone didn't turn up' (Anne, Interview 1); or presenting in inappropriate test environments: '[I couldn't] continue the test because somebody is actually driving [… or] they're sitting in a café' (Fiona, Interview 2). Presumably as an effect of this required self-management, candidates also appeared anxious to make sure that they had received all necessary information: 'They panic – when will the email turn up? They don't feel that reassured.' (Anne, Interview 1); 'That's the difference between the test centre – no one there to help you' (Louise, Interview 1).

Test-takers were also at the mercy of interruptions outside their control. While for the most part, speaking exams were not interrupted, internet connectivity and power cuts were sometimes experienced by a small minority. In these cases, Martin reported that he could compensate for any impact on candidate performance: 'if it did [impact performance], I stopped and started again' (Interview 2).

2.8 Conclusion and Post-Pandemic Lessons Learned

This chapter has outlined some of the major issues of relevance both to the IELTS Indicator test and to online testing in general. In the urgency to respond to the pandemic, validation may not have kept pace with the development of online delivery solutions. However, as experience in this field grows, it is incumbent upon testing organisations to provide evidence (Geranpayeh & Taylor, 2013) that online tests are fit for purpose, and to address issues which are found to raise concern. As noted earlier, the socio-cognitive framework that underpins IELTS validation activities requires continual data to be sought, both to inform best practice and react favourably to changing educational and testing landscapes.

In 2020, little support was available to substantiate claims for high-stakes uses of online at-home tests. It is within this context that the results of IELTS Indicator tests were recommended 'for indicative purposes only', despite a significant body of supporting research, particularly with regard to VC speaking. The present study represents an initial attempt to document the experience of online testing (Isbell & Kremmel, 2020), highlighting areas for investigation and shedding light on those issues as they impact IELTS Indicator. While these findings themselves are largely indicative, they do provide some useful insights. The candidates surveyed expressed a high degree of satisfaction with the test, its presentation online, and supporting candidate information. There was also a positive response to the home testing environment, with most seeming to prefer this option to a test centre.

Nevertheless, lessons can be learned for future generations of online testing. The variability of candidate home environments and resources presents a significant challenge to test reliability. For some candidates, a test centre may provide a more controlled environment. Similarly, as seen from operational reliability reports, dependence on the candidate's hardware and internet bandwidth can create problems for test delivery. Furthermore, it is essential to support candidates with clear communications and technical assistance. The attitudes expressed by IELTS candidates here suggest that online testing has now established itself as a permanent feature of the assessment landscape, even as a wider choice of delivery modes becomes available. It is now up to providers to learn from their experience during the pandemic and demonstrate the validity of their tests for their intended use.

Notes

1 IELTS Indicator test description here: https://www.ielts.org/about-ielts/ielts-indicator
2 A full test description is available here: https://www.ielts.org/about-ielts/what-is-ielts
3 Indicator made use of a Safe Exam Browser (SEB) to provide a basic level of security suitable for the indicative status of the scores, as this was the first iteration of this functionality.

References

AERA, APA, & NCME (2014). *Standards for educational and psychological testing*. American Educational Research Association.

Berry, V., Nakatsuhara, F., Inoue, C., & Galaczi, E. (2018). *Exploring the use of videoconferencing technology to deliver the IELTS speaking test: Phase 3 technical trial*. IELTS Partnership Research Papers, 2018/1. IELTS Partners: British Council, IDP: IELTS Australia and Cambridge Assessment English.

Blackhurst, A. (2007). Computer-based and paper-based versions of IELTS. In O. Alexander (Ed.), *New approaches to materials development for language learning* (pp. 265–274). Peter Lang.

Braun, V., & Clarke, V. (2006). Using thematic analysis in psychology. *Qualitative Research in Psychology, 3*, 77–101.

Brunfaut, T., Harding, L., & Batty, A. (2018). Going online: The effect of mode of delivery on performances and perceptions on an English L2 writing test suite. *Assessing Writing, 36*, 3–18.

Camara, W. (2020). Never let a crisis go to waste: Large-scale assessment and the response to COVID-19. *Educational Measurement: Issues and Practice, 39*(3), 10–18.

Chalhoub-Deville, M., & O'Sullivan, B. (2020). *Validity: Theoretical development and integrated arguments*. British Council Monograph Series 3. Equinox Publishing.

Chan, S., Bax, S., & Weir, C. (2018). *Researching participants taking IELTS academic writing task 2 (AWT2) in paper mode and in computer mode in terms of score equivalence, cognitive validity and other factors*. IELTS Research Reports Online, 4/2017. IELTS Partners: British Council, IDP: IELTS Australia and Cambridge Assessment English.

Chapelle, C. A. (2020, June 17). Discussion. In E. Voss (Chair), *Exploring the future of online language testing and assessment: Technological opportunities and challenges* [Webinar]. International Language Testing Association. Retrieved from: https://www.iltaonline.com/page/ILTAWebinar/Exploringthefuture

Cizek, G. J., & Wollack, J. A. (2016). *Handbook of quantitative methods for detecting cheating on tests*. Routledge.

Clark, T., & Endres, H. (2021). Computer-based diagnostic assessment of high school students' grammar skills with automated feedback – An international trial. *Assessment in Education: Principles, Policy & Practice, 28*(5–6), 602–632. https://doi.org/10.1080/0969594X.2021.1970513

Clark, T., Spiby, R., & Tasviri, R. (2021). Crisis, collaboration, recovery: IELTS and COVID-19. *Language Assessment Quarterly, 18*(1), 17–25.

Cohen, A. S., & Wollack, J. A. (2006). Test administration, security, scoring, and reporting. *Educational Measurement, 4*, 17–64.

Ferrara, S. (2017). A framework for policies and practices to improve test security programs: Prevention, detection, investigation, and resolution (PDIR). *Educational Measurement: Issues and Practice, 36*(3), 5–23.

Fulcher, G. (1999). Computerizing an English language placement test. *ELT Journal, 53*(4), 289–299.

Galaczi, E., & Taylor, L. (2018). Interactional competence: Conceptualisations, operationalisations, and outstanding questions. *Language Assessment Quarterly, 15*(3), 219–236.

Gates, G. E., Cox, T. L., Bell, T. R., & Eggington, W. G. (2020). Line, please? An analysis of the rehearsed speech characteristics of native Korean speakers on the English Oral proficiency interview—Computer (OPIc). *Language Testing in Asia, 10*, 1–20.

Geranpayeh, A., & Taylor, L. (Eds.) (2013). *Examining listening: Research and practice in assessing second language listening.* Studies in Language Testing volume 35. UCLES/Cambridge University Press.

Green, A. (2004). *Comparisons of computer and paper-based versions of IELTS writing: A further investigation of trial of data.* Cambridge ESOL Internal Validation Report 585.

Green, B. A., & Lung, Y. S. M. (2021). English language placement testing at BYU-Hawaii in the time of COVID-19. *Language Assessment Quarterly, 18*(1), 6–11. https://doi.org/10.1080/15434303.2020.1863966

He, L., & Jiang, Z. (2020). Assessing second language listening over the past twenty years: A review within the socio-cognitive framework. *Frontiers in Psychology, 11*, Article 2123.

Isbell, D. R., & Kremmel, B. (2020). Test review: Current options in at-home language proficiency tests for making high-stakes decisions. *Language Testing, 37*(4), 600–619.

Karim, M. N., Kaminsky, S. E., & Behrend, T. S. (2014). Cheating, reactions, and performance in remotely proctored testing: An exploratory experimental study. *Journal of Business Psychology, 29*, 555–572.

Langenfeld, T. (2020). Internet-based proctored assessment: Security and fairness issues. *Educational Measurement, Issues and Practice.* https://doi.org/10.1111/emip.12359

Lee, H., Patel, M., Lynch, J., & Galaczi, E. (2021). *Development of the video call speaking test: Phase 4 operational research trial and overall summary of a four-phase test development cycle.* IELTS Partnership Research Papers, 2021/1. IELTS Partners: British Council, IDP: IELTS Australia and Cambridge Assessment English.

Maycock, L. (2004). *CB IELTS: Report on the findings of trial A (Live Trial, 2003/04).* Cambridge ESOL Internal Validation Report 558.

Maycock, L., & Green, A. (2005). The effects on performance of computer familiarity and attitudes towards CB IELTS. *Research Notes, 20*, 3–8.

Michel, R. S. (2020). Remotely proctored k-12 high stakes standardized testing during COVID-19: Will it last? *Educational Measurement: Issues and Practice, 39*(3), 28–30.

Moore, R., Vitale, D., & Stawinoga, N. (2018). *The digital divide and educational equity: A look at students with very limited access to electronic devices at home.* ACT Center for Equity in Learning.

Muhammad, A. A., & Ockey, G. J. (2021). Upholding language assessment quality during the COVID-19 pandemic: Some final thoughts and questions. *Language Assessment Quarterly, 18*(1), 51–55.

Nakatsuhara, F., Inoue, C., Berry, V., & Galaczi, E. (2016). Exploring performance across two delivery modes of the same L2 speaking test: Face-to-face and video-conferencing delivery. A preliminary comparison of test-taker and examiner behaviour. *IELTS partnership research papers, 1.* IELTS Partners: British Council, IDP: IELTS Australia and Cambridge Assessment English.

Nakatsuhara, F., Inoue, C., Berry, V., & Galaczi, E. (2017). Exploring performance across two delivery modes for the IELTS speaking test: Face-to-face and video-conferencing delivery (phase 2). *IELTS partnership research papers, 3.* IELTS Partners: British Council, IDP: IELTS Australia and Cambridge Assessment English.

Papageorgiou, S., & Manna, V. F. (2021). Maintaining access to a large-scale test of academic language proficiency during the pandemic: The launch of TOEFL iBT home edition. *Language Assessment Quarterly, 18*(1), 36–41.

Spiby, R., & Clark, T. (forthcoming). Responding to a transformed assessment landscape: The example of IELTS. In E. Kantarcioglu et al. (Ed.), *Life after the pandemic: Revision and reform in EAP contexts* (in press). Cambridge Scholars Publishing.

Steger, D., Schroeders, U., & Gnambs, T. (2020). A meta-analysis of test scores in proctored and unproctored ability assessments. *European Journal of Psychological Assessment, 36*(1), 174–184.

Taylor, L., & Chan, S. (2015). *Reviewing the suitability of English language tests for providing the GMC with evidence of doctors' English proficiency.* The General Medical Council.

Wagner, E. (2020). Test review: Duolingo English test, revised version July 2019. *Language Assessment Quarterly, 17*(3), 300–315.

Weir, C. (2005). *Language testing and validation: An evidence-based approach.* Palgrave MacMillan.

Weir, C. J., & O'Sullivan, B. (2011). Test development and validation. In B. O'Sullivan (Ed.), *Language testing: Theory and practice* (pp. 13–32). Palgrave.

Weir, C. J., O'Sullivan, B., & Jin, Y. (2007). Does the computer make a difference? The reaction of candidates to a computer-based versus a traditional hand-written form of the IELTS writing component: Effects and impact. *IELTS research report, 7.* IELTS Partners: British Council, IDP: IELTS Australia and Cambridge Assessment English.

Woldeab, D., & Brothen, T. (2019). 21st century assessment: Online proctoring, test anxiety, and student performance. *International Journal of E-Learning & Distance Education, 34*(1), 1–10.

Yu, G. (2010). Effects of presentation mode and computer familiarity on summarization of extended texts. *Language Assessment Quarterly, 7*(2), 119–136.

3
EMERGENCY REMOTE ASSESSMENT (ERA) NARRATIVES FROM THE UK ENGLISH FOR ACADEMIC PURPOSES (EAP) SECTOR

Examining Validity and Longevity of Technology-Driven Solutions

Emma Bruce

BRITISH COUNCIL, MANCHESTER

Heléna Stakounis

UNIVERSITY OF DURHAM, DURHAM

3.1 Introduction

In March 2020, English for Academic Purposes (EAP) providers in the UK were forced to shift all operations and educational provision online as a result of the nationwide lockdown. In the very early days, Hodges et al. (2020) coined the term Emergency Remote Teaching (ERT), to describe the 'temporary shift in instruction which is provided in the immediate aftermath of a crisis or pandemic and which will return to the original format'. While Hodges et al. (2020) focus on the 'short-term' and suggest that once the crisis is over, things will return to the status quo, data from research funded by The British Association of Lecturers of English for Academic Purposes (BALEAP) reveal that in the case of EAP, changes may not be temporary but rather long-lasting, particularly in terms of assessment. In the ERT context, emergency remote assessment (ERA) also emerged, which we define as 'emergency assessment policies, procedures and instruments adopted in an Emergency Remote Teaching context' (Bruce & Stakounis, 2021), notably moving away from Hodges et al.'s (2020) notion of the 'temporary'.

DOI: 10.4324/9781003221463-4

Within the UK higher education sector, EAP providers were on the frontline as they were often the first in their institutions to take their programs entirely online. In this sudden pivot, they were forced to work at pace to implement contingency measures to administer remote EAP assessments for students sitting in their homes all around the world. This resulted in many EAP institutions moving towards innovative, digital, and more authentic forms of EAP assessment, as highlighted by our BALEAP-funded research (Bruce & Stakounis, 2021). The study adopted three research questions:

1. What changes were made to the delivery of EAP provision to enable the programs to proceed?
2. How did key operations such as administration, admissions, and progression change or adjust during this period?
3. Were the changes considered successful? What key challenges and opportunities emerged?

Data were collected by questionnaire ($n = 240$) and interview ($n = 14$) from EAP professionals in academic, managerial, and administrative positions in 63 universities and 8 private providers in the UK. Semi-structured interviews were carried out with five EAP teachers, two co-ordinators, three managers, two administrators, one subject lead, and one curriculum developer during the period November to December 2020. A collaborative approach to data analysis was adopted to produce 'an agreed interpretation' (Cornish et al., 2014); this included consensus coding (Richards & Hemphill, 2017) to enhance validity and reliability.

In this chapter, we discuss the challenges, strategies, and opportunities which emerged during the period of ERA in the UK EAP sector in the immediate aftermath of the COVID-19 pandemic. We share insights from research participants and draw on validation models, such as the socio-cognitive validation framework (SCF) (Weir, 2005) and Chalhoub-Deville and O'Sullivan's (2020) integrated argument approach to validation, to evaluate the approaches adopted. We also argue that while delivering valid assessments during this period was understandably not 'easy', long-lasting and positive developments in assessment have emerged out of this crisis (Muhammad & Ockey, 2021).

3.2 UK EAP Assessment Pre-Pandemic

Most UK universities and many UK private education providers offer EAP programs. In both contexts, this may take the form of pre-sessional courses in advance of a student's main undergraduate or postgraduate degree program, in-sessional support throughout the academic year, or pathway or foundation programs (Bell, 2016). Assessment forms an integral part of all such EAP courses, and is often high stakes as it determines whether students progress onto their degree program or not (Seviour, 2015). Brindley and Ross (2001) highlight the dual purpose of EAP assessment in sampling 'the specific skills or knowledge which form the basis of the course objectives' (i.e., achievement assessment), while also assessing language proficiency, 'to establish the extent to which learners can use the language for their intended purposes' (p. 149). In addition to its function as a gatekeeper to main degree programs, EAP assessment is sometimes used to validate students' language level for obtaining a Tier-4 student visa, according to the UK government's immigration requirements (Home Office, 2021a, 2021b). UK EAP assessment is thus a critical aspect of any EAP program and this did not cease to be the case in the ERT context.

Pre-pandemic, there had been calls for EAP assessment to evolve. Schmitt and Hamp-Lyons (2015), for example, suggested a move away from large-scale proficiency style exams towards more classroom-based and coursework style achievement assessments which, instead of testing language proficiency, would test the content covered on the course. In addition, Bruce (2020), with specific reference to EAP assessment, and Sambell and Brown (2020) in the wider UK Higher Education (HE) context, highlighted the limitations of the unseen, time-controlled exam. However, any change to EAP assessment would be constrained by the need to satisfy the UK government requirement to provide discrete scores for reading, writing, speaking, and listening, and this is something that has held back developments in language assessment more generally (Alderson et al., 2017), as well as in EAP specifically. Pearson (2021) argues that this has led to a product-oriented approach to EAP assessment as opposed to a focus on the process of learning, a notion supported by Seviour (2015) in reference to the essay style assessment. He (ibid), in contrast to Brindley and Ross (2001), views the dual role of EAP assessment as a tool for ascertaining students' readiness for degree programs and as a vehicle for learning.

EAP practitioners also called for increased authenticity in EAP assessment and for tasks more closely mirroring the kinds of assignments students would face on their degree programs. In some contexts, this led to more integrated assessment tasks, such as reading-into-writing or listening-into-speaking (Cumming, 2013). Roche (2017), in the Australian EAP context, argued that EAP assessment should assess a wider range of skills beyond language if it is to successfully prepare students for today's university and the world beyond. According to Roche (2017), EAP programs 'should embed and design assessments which explore the intersection between six literacies' (p. 84), namely English language, critical, socio-cultural, academic, institutional, and digital literacies. In the wake of the pandemic, it is now clear how pertinent digital literacy skills in particular have become as students could not even gain access to their course content or assessments without some recourse to the digital. Incidentally, the call for more technology-integrated approaches to EAP assessment had also already been made many years prior (Brindley & Ross, 2001).

Another aspect recognised as an area in need of attention was practitioners' language assessment literacy (Manning, 2016; Taylor, 2009). While some EAP providers have a dedicated team responsible for testing and assessment, others rely on individual teachers, who may have varying levels of assessment literacy. This is in addition to digital assessment literacy. Eyal (2012) argues that teachers and assessment developers should have knowledge and skills 'adapted to the digital environment and tailored for the pedagogical approaches of the 21st century' (p. 37).

In short, there was a desire for renewal in the field of EAP assessment, yet external factors often prevented this from happening (Pearson, 2021), such as Home Office regulations, and perhaps also, a lack of assessment literacy. However, the COVID-19 pandemic and the panic around whether students would be able to travel to the UK led to a relaxation in rules around government endorsed secure English language tests (SELTs) in summer 2020 (Home Office, 2021a, 2021b). This prompted a shift in direction for many EAP providers with the development of new in-house assessments for program entry and a less-constrained look at the assessments for progression onto degree programs (Bruce & Stakounis, 2021). Other providers simply seized the opportunity to embrace the digital and explore new ways of assessment. As Sambell and Brown (2020) emphasise, this was not only a chance to make adaptations to assessment in crisis conditions but rather to improve it for the long term.

3.3 Approaches to Validation

In the past, validity was seen as dichotomous in the sense that it was an all or nothing, and a test was either valid or not. However, conceptualisations of validity have evolved over time. It is acknowledged that the notion of validity refers to interpretations and use of scores, and not an assessment instrument itself. Validity is thus a matter of degree rather than an absolute and a validation argument is built on many different kinds of validity evidence.

The socio-cognitive framework (SCF) (Weir, 2005, revised by O'Sullivan & Weir, 2011 and O'Sullivan, 2016) was the first systematic attempt to create a practical framework for developing a validity argument drawing on social, cognitive, and evaluative aspects of language use. The SCF is a useful model to inform test development, research and validation of large-scale tests, and those developed in-house for local purposes. The model highlights the ongoing nature of validation and specifies the kinds of a priori and a posteriori evidence to be collected at each stage of the test development, trialling and administration process. The test-taker is at the heart of the model since, as the name implies, the construct resides in the interaction between the test-taker's cognitive abilities and the context of use. According to Weir (2005), 'the more evidence collected on each of the components of this framework, the more secure we can be in our claims for the validity of a test' (p. 47).

Chalhoub-Deville and O'Sullivan (2020) suggest an integrated argument-based approach to validation which includes four integrated arguments: development, measurement, theory of action, and communication engagement. This model looks beyond traditional validation frameworks, which predominantly focus on test development and measurement arguments, and emphasises the impact that tests and assessments have on *all* stakeholders (i.e., test-takers, test-developers, teachers, test-users, and society as a whole) and the need for communication with these stakeholders.

Both of these models highlight that the extent to which a testing instrument can be said to be valid is specific to a particular use, context, and group of test-takers. In other words, EAP tests and assessments designed pre-pandemic for face-to-face, paper-based administration in controlled conditions may not have been suitable for remote administration in the ERA context, even to the same group of learners. O'Sullivan (2011) reminds us of the necessity of considering the context: 'Tests developed for use in a particular domain or context with a particular population are far more likely to work if the population and domain are taken into account at all stages of design and development' (p. 7).

Online delivery of a test intended to be paper-based may impact the validation claims in different ways. For example, students may seek external help, which poses a threat to the scoring validity, or the time allowance may affect test-takers in such a way that their cognitive processing behaviour is different in the two contexts, resulting in a different construct (Bruce, 2020). In addition, a lack of familiarity with the testing instrument and delivery platform as well as inadequate computer literacy may also affect test-taker performance. Consequently, regardless of the trust placed in established assessment instruments through iterative development, repeated use and ongoing validation before COVID-19, confidence in the inferences made from test scores could no longer be assumed owing to a new context of use.

In short, validation frameworks provide useful guidelines for designing, developing, and delivering valid tests and assessments, yet during ERA, in the panic to find solutions, there was insufficient time to engage in usual validation activities. Existing assessments had most likely not been developed by building a validity argument for remote delivery and there was certainly no validation model specifically for ERA purposes. Practicality and logistics were the overriding considerations in the initial months of the pandemic when the main objective was to continue to assess students in geographically diverse locations and different time zones. The most pressing question was whether the demands of an existing specification could be met within the limits of the available resources. EAP practitioners often had no choice but to make hurried decisions, and in the following section, we present the general approaches taken.

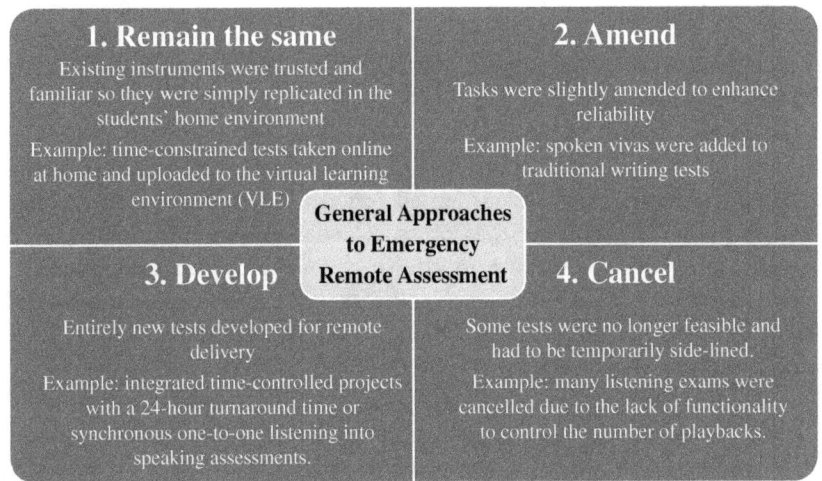

FIGURE 3.1 Approaches to EAP emergency remote assessment (ERA).

3.4 General Approaches to Emergency Assessment of EAP

Thematic analysis of questionnaire and interview data collected for our BALEAP-funded research highlight four broad classifications for the approaches adopted to emergency assessment of EAP in the first six months of the pandemic, as shown in Figure 3.1.

Although certain validation frameworks, such as the SCF, lay out the temporal sequencing of what should happen at each stage of the validation process, the model was not intended for an ERA context. When operationalising the first three decisions above, there was limited or no time for a priori validation to evaluate context and cognitive validity, and most likely insufficient time for a posteriori validation of scoring, consequential and criterion-related validity. However, as test development is iterative and validation is an ongoing process drawing on validity evidence from the whole life of a test, evaluations of assessment from the first six months of the pandemic are invaluable for ensuring the validity of future iterations of EAP tests and assessments.

3.5 Challenges

Once EAP providers had decided which of the aforementioned four approaches to take, they were faced with additional challenges. The three main challenges identified from our BALEAP data (Bruce & Stakounis, 2021) were technology, academic integrity, and assessment literacy, all of which will now be discussed.

3.5.1 Technology

Although technology was undoubtedly the saviour, being the main facilitator for ensuring ERA could go ahead, it was also a limiting factor in terms of delivering existing EAP assessments. Listening tests in particular proved to be very challenging. The inability to control the number of playbacks and the possibility of generating captions, raised concern over the meaning of scores since important elements of the construct could not be measured through existing instruments, resulting in construct underrepresentation (Messick, 1989). A number of EAP providers had to abandon existing listening assessments as there was no feasible solution. Interview data from the BALEAP study reveal this:

> We didn't do listening assessment at all, we just didn't do it because we couldn't work out how to do it online ... so that was a loss.
>
> *(ManagerF2)*

Connectivity was also a major concern, mentioned by almost half of the participants. This is particularly significant given that 70% claimed they were using live online exams. Any brief interruption to connectivity could have had adverse consequences for test-takers, adding significant levels of stress, especially in time-controlled situations. One EAP coordinator stated:

> I mean in China they still did their presentations in groups online, but then they had to be recorded and we then watched them and marked them. But the Internet in China is so poor and sometimes their recordings didn't work and sometimes the recordings worked, but the sound quality was so poor it was hard to mark.
>
> *(CoordinatorF1)*

In addition to poor connectivity, the Chinese firewall caused access issues for students located in China and this issue was often discussed in relation to the technology being mandated by those higher up the institutional hierarchy. EAP providers were often instructed to make use of software or Virtual Learning Environments (VLE) which the institution had already invested in, yet these particular packages may have been unsuitable for the desired assessment purposes. As a consequence, some EAP units switched to a familiar or preferred technology, often without the support of the institution or IT support services. Inevitably, this created additional challenges for EAP practitioners who were left to face technological problems alone.

Another significant issue was digital literacy. Many participants mentioned that digital literacy, which had not been part of the intended construct, became an essential skill for students to access and complete the assessment task. This is referred to as construct irrelevance or the introduction of uncontrolled variables, which means a significant proportion of score variation can be traced to an irrelevant factor (Messick, 1989). In this case, students' digital skills were being assessed alongside the language and study skills covered in their EAP program. In addition, a certain level of digital literacy was required for those developing and delivering assessments to successfully complete the necessary tasks, but this was not always sufficient.

3.5.2 Academic Integrity

Academic integrity was being discussed pre-pandemic and was an issue of rising concern in the UK Higher Education sector in general (Morris, 2018). The International Center for Academic Integrity (2014) defines the term as 'a commitment, even in the face of adversity, to six fundamental values: honesty, trust, fairness, respect, responsibility, and courage'. The Quality Assurance Agency (QAA) for Higher Education in the UK states that assessment practices should be reliable, fair, and transparent and thus, academic integrity is not only a responsibility that rests with students but is a joint responsibility of the whole academic community, meaning education providers and learners have a mutual commitment to good and fair academic practice. However, the ERA context presented adverse circumstances for all stakeholders and in the new online environment, academic integrity emerged as one of the principal concerns among respondents of the BALEAP survey, with over half specifically listing it as a challenge. Even though 70% of participants mentioned that their institutions were using live online exams to assess students during this period, there was a general lack of awareness of proctoring solutions in relation to both makeshift and commercially available resources. In fact, only 30% of participants were monitoring students' screen activity and only 10% were using a lockdown browser. Perhaps more concerning in terms of academic integrity is that less than 40% were verifying student IDs. Consequently, only 62% of respondents felt that measures adopted were adequate with many echoing the view that fairness could not be guaranteed due to the difficulty with monitoring students in remote settings. One interviewee explained:

> [Students] do that [listening to note-taking assessment] by hand so they watch a video and then they make notes by hand. Normally, they just hand that in at the end of the assessment. We didn't really have time to come up with a whole new assessment, so we did that online and we just kind of asked them, keep your camera on and, trusted them not to cheat. We said you can't have a phone and so on.
>
> *(CoordinatorF1)*

3.5.3 Assessment Literacy

Kremmel and Harding (2020) define assessment literacy as the skills, knowledge, and abilities that test stakeholders need to carry out assessment-related activities. This includes an awareness of the steps involved in validation of assessments and the factors which may threaten the inferences drawn from the scores awarded. In other words, assessment literacy and validity cannot be separated; they are interdependent. Yet, as aforementioned, assessment literacy in the EAP context was already an area identified as being in need of attention (Manning, 2016).

BALEAP (2008, p. 9) claims that all EAP teachers may be responsible for assessment and therefore need some level of assessment literacy. Our data revealed that some EAP staff had developed their assessments over time through a combination of intuition, knowledge of assessment theory, insights from the literature, empirical experience, and contextual requirements, while others had simply inherited their processes from previous program leaders. The varying levels of assessment literacy could explain the differing approaches to assessment during the period March to September 2020, with some having the confidence to take the earlier mentioned option 3 to develop entirely new assessments while others preferring option 1, a repeat of the same but simply online (see Figure 3.1). Indeed, owing to the emergency situation, sometimes those tasked with adapting, designing, and delivering the online assessments were teachers who had not previously been involved in assessment. Many found themselves thrust into this role without warning and often without prior experience or knowledge of assessment practices, and especially not digital assessment.

Eyal (2012) explains that digital assessment literacy requires: 'the awareness and ability to cope with the risks and inherent ethical issues associated with the use of digital assessment tools'; 'the use of a variety of methods and digital tools to gather information on the progress of learners'; and, 'the ability to diagnose and assess a range of study and developmental areas using performance tasks that incorporate various technological tools' (p. 45). However, the BALEAP survey participants recognised that they did not always have such skills, with 40% of managers and 46% of coordinators stating that they would have liked more training in carrying out online assessment. In addition, 45% of managers and 35% of coordinators said they would have liked more training in ensuring the integrity of online assessment. One manager in the interview explained:

> We replaced things like more traditional listening-into-writing exams which had IELTS-like multiple choice dimensions because we didn't think there would be a way to do that securely with the numbers of students we had and we didn't have the kind of familiarity with some of the things that tech would allow us to do with regard to test security.
>
> *(ManagerM1)*

Coombe et al. (2020) remind us of the need to take the current 'knowledge base' and the 'context of practice' into account when designing assessment literacy training and to make connections between them. They highlight the important considerations of time and context, and this feels particularly apt in an emergency situation. Unfortunately, for most EAP providers there simply was not the time to dedicate to assessment literacy nor to the more specific need of digital assessment literacy in the ERA context.

The three challenges mentioned may have compromised the validity claims of EAP assessments in the ERA context, and some interviewees in the study alluded to this:

> I'm not sure in terms of how we assessed whether we were assessing in exactly the same way as we would normally have done.
>
> *(ManagerF1)*

> Really all the assessments were more challenging. And less reliable in a way, I felt like I had a bit less confidence that we were being fair. And then you know, the marks were they a true reflection of what the students could do?
>
> *(CoordinatorF1)*

Owing to this, the lack of time to adopt usual practices and quality assurance measures such as trialling, meant that behaviours, which perhaps could have been avoided, were not pre-empted. In fact, even highly experienced colleagues with high levels of EAP assessment literacy were unable to anticipate and prepare for some of the unexpected outcomes which were brought about by the sudden move to digital assessment during this time of crisis.

3.6 Strategies

With the challenges established, we turn now to the strategies and innovative solutions adopted for EAP assessment in the ERA context. Table 3.1 provides a summary of some of the key strategies and some illustrative narratives from the Bruce and Stakounis (2021) data.

In terms of technology, there were many creative low-tech solutions to proctoring and security in the form of behavioural controls, such as monitoring breakout rooms, requesting students to scan their camera around the room, requiring use of a whiteboard instead of notepaper and using a wider variety of questions. These compare to the commercially available high-tech tools to detect misconduct adopted by a small number of participants, such as lockdown browsers and online proctoring. The most popular tool was Turnitin or similar plagiarism checkers, tools already widely used pre-pandemic. Many institutions had insufficient funds to invest in these proctoring solutions and

TABLE 3.1 ERA Strategies and Illustrative Narratives

Strategy	Illustrative narrative
Amending the weighting of formative and summative assessment to mitigate the possible bias being introduced by students working in unmonitored conditions	We also just changed the balance of assessment, increasing the significance of coursework and adjusting the nature of coursework tasks and increasing the number of coursework tasks to reflect their new importance. (ManagerM1)
Personalised or contextualised tasks with bespoke briefs to deter students from contract cheating (e.g., reports/presentations including prescribed content or based on students' personal university context)	We put levels of contextualisation in place for exams that discouraged fraudulent behaviour (knowledge of specific content presented during the course was required). (Questionnaire respondent)
Self-reflective writing focussing on students' particular learning context	Students were encouraged to record their own progress by making a list of achievements/ completing self-assessment tasks. (Questionnaire respondent)
More frequent, lower-stakes assessments with less reliance on scores from final exams and time controlled tasks (e.g., mini continuous assessment tasks)	We monitored performance carefully with weekly formative assignments. (Questionnaire respondent)
A greater focus on the process of learning as opposed to the traditional product-oriented exam formats (e.g., portfolio/process-oriented assessment tasks)	Moving away from summative exams meant that students could focus on learning and developing skills not on just getting through the final exam. Much less sense of teaching them to get through a test and meet the marking criteria. Without summative assessments, students could set their own learning goals which was more motivating and their portfolio provided evidence of them achieving these goals. It gave students more autonomy and ownership of their learning. It allowed for an ongoing feedback dialogue between teachers and students which was one of the successes of the course based on student and teacher feedback. (Questionnaire respondent)
Enhanced learner training/support, e.g., training videos, familiarisation, practice, live troubleshooting through online chat, particularly to mitigate a lack of digital literacy skills among students	We gave several practice runs of the assessment throughout the course so that students could become accustomed to the procedure and the protocol for recording their screen and submitting their video. We also had a mock viva so that students could receive feedback on their performance and be advised against reciting memorised scripts and more towards interaction and communication that meets the needs of the interlocutor. (Questionnaire respondent)

(Continued)

TABLE 3.1 ERA Strategies and Illustrative Narratives (*Continued*)

Strategy	Illustrative narrative
Vivas, especially for listening	We assessed listening through an extended viva following the speaking assessment. We also assessed language through the viva so that we could know it was the student's own language. (Questionnaire respondent)
Back-up plans for technological issues	Back-up exam formats for students who couldn't access the main exam platform. (Questionnaire respondent)
Opportunity for students to give feedback/transparent and honest communication/dialogue	Student focus groups to collect feedback on assessment processes, to reassure them and manage their expectations. (Questionnaire respondent)

even in instances where institutions did, there was much dissatisfaction surrounding their efficacy. Some reported technology issues and service failure during live tests and others mentioned that due to the tight turnaround time for grades it was almost impossible to look through the recordings and reports. Consequently, remote proctoring became a deterrent rather than a means of detection.

3.7 Opportunities

The COVID-19 pandemic was clearly a catalyst for rethinking EAP assessment and many respondents mentioned the welcome opportunity for evaluating existing assessment constructs and reflecting on levels of satisfaction. In this way, assessment became more current and authentic with innovative and original ways of doing things, which promoted digital literacy skills and better preparedness for the wider world of work. As one questionnaire respondent mentioned, there was 'the opportunity to experiment with different styles and formats of assessments to both allow for more authentic assessment and to encourage positive washback on the course'. Others explained how they welcomed the opportunity to place more focus on the learning process rather than just the outcomes, as they adopted fewer time-controlled tests and moved towards assessment processes they considered to be more relevant and humane. Examples included the creation of spaces for students to engage in peer feedback prior to live presentations, inclusion of feedback on drafts in writing assessments, and open-book exams to be completed over several days.

Another opportunity identified by research participants was enhanced feedback. Although many teachers initially reported feeling overwhelmed when attempting to provide feedback on all asynchronous work, once they streamlined their processes, they discovered innovative ways of providing feedback, such as through audio or video recording or through shared documents. They were also able to provide automated feedback using technology such as online quizzes or forms, further freeing up teacher time and giving students instant feedback. Almost 90% of participants were satisfied with the quality and extent of feedback they were able to provide remotely. This may have been further facilitated by the adoption of a flipped learning approach. Time spent synchronously with students provided more opportunities for feedback as less time was required for input. Pre-pandemic, much of the feedback was one-way teacher to student, but in the online environment there was a feeling that digital solutions facilitated more dialogic feedback between teachers and students as well as among students. In addition to this, students often provided more extensive, specific, and honest feedback during peer review as they perhaps felt more comfortable critiquing others' work in the online arena than they do when face-to-face, a notion supported by other scholars (e.g., Arasaratnam-Smith & Northcote, 2017).

Some participants mentioned that digitalisation led to more accessible data, which could be used to reflect on the quality of the emergency assessments. For example, item-level statistics are automatically produced by many online assessment platforms and this helps staff who do not know how to conduct those analyses themselves, providing them with useful insights to make improvements. These data provide valuable validity evidence and also contribute to EAP practitioners' digital assessment literacy (Eyal, 2012).

On reflection, although there were immense challenges, ERA offered an opportunity to tip the balance towards more learning-oriented and sustainable assessment, which is something that many institutions had been hoping to move towards prior to the pandemic. As one interviewee commented:

> We converted all assessments to online forms. This was a challenge but also offered an opportunity to review our previous assessment practices. We have developed a stronger suite as a result.
>
> *(Questionnaire respondent)*

Ockey (2021) optimistically predicts that the success stories which have emerged, in spite of the technological limitations, will help 'to shuttle in a new era of technology-driven language assessments'. As the industry moves out of survival mode, there is a need now to evaluate the quality of the measures adopted during ERA to determine which show promise for the future.

3.8 Validity Issues

Time pressure in the ERA context made it very challenging to implement pre- and post-live test validation procedures (such as those recommended by models like the SCF). However, the need to provide scores or a pass/fail status remained essential for students' progression onto main degree programs. EAP staff therefore had to work flexibly, quickly, and often without the necessary skillset or technological know-how. The particular aspects of validity relevant to the ERA context, which were predominantly highlighted through our data, are context validity, scoring validity, and test-taker characteristics. In addition, conversations around the success and challenges of emergency assessment procedures have focused on the impact and washback of new types of assessments for both teaching and learning and also for preparing students for their post-university endeavours.

Context validity was emphasised by the research participants in the data as this relates to the physical conditions which define the testing or assessment event such as the planning time, setting, and delivery mode. One example from our data concerns a private EAP provider offering pre-degree and pre-masters programs. Since their usual timed paper-based exams could not be administered, they switched to a four-part integrated task which was administered over two days with a number of deadlines for individual tasks during that period. The major issue with this integrated assessment concerned the listening task, which involved listening to a lecture once and taking notes in order to complete a guided summary.

The task was designed to be livestreamed and centrally controlled with a single playback. However, many students experienced connectivity issues which prevented this. In such instances, the lecture had to be uploaded to the VLE for students to access and control themselves. This resulted in a change to the construct as the intention was for students to listen *once* and simultaneously take notes, yet the students accessing the recording through the VLE were able to rewind and play individual sections numerous times and also complete the guided summary *while* listening rather than just relying on their notes to complete it. A strict 30-minute time allowance was introduced to discourage multiple playbacks and students were required to submit their notes, but these measures were merely a deterrent. As well as introducing construct irrelevant variance this connectivity issue threatened equity and fairness as the conditions were not the same for all test-takers. All such instances were carefully documented and reported during exam boards where members made decisions as to the most appropriate action.

Owing to the absence of summative exams conducted in controlled conditions, and the resulting reduction in the number of measurement points used to inform final grades, our data show that many institutions adopted extraordinary measures to enhance scoring validity. These included teacher provision of additional evidence about students such as results of mock tests, predicted grades and qualitative insights about performance and special, extended moderation boards to scrutinise results and consider this information.

Changes to one part of a test can have far-reaching implications for the different aspects of validity since they are interdependent. Thus, it is not surprising that the changes to the listening exam mentioned above also impacted scoring validity. Threats to the reliability of the scores arose from the lack of consistency in the administration, the unintended test-taker behaviours elicited by the inability to control the playback of the lecture and connectivity/technology issues experienced by certain test-takers. Again, careful documentation of such instances was encouraged, but in cases where scores could not be generated or could not be relied upon, a listening score had to be generated by an algorithm which included the teacher's predicted score and exam scores in the other three skills. Although far from ideal, this was regarded as a consistent approach to deal with these instances. Teachers were consulted to confirm the scores based on their first-hand insights of student performance.

In terms of the validity implications of test-taker characteristics, even though the population of EAP test-takers remained stable in the emergency context, the fact that tests were being delivered remotely gave rise to variables which may not have been part of the original test design. Our data show that these included: increased anxiety owing to a lack of familiarity with the platform or testing instrument; lack of confidence due to poor digital literacy; and general unease about online testing.

Consequential validity, including the washback impact of a test on learning and teaching should be a guiding principle which informs the whole test-development cycle, yet in the rush to administer assessments and generate scores, minimal attention was paid to this in the context of ERA. In this context, decisions were usually made post-hoc rather than with the intention of informing teaching and learning. However, what has since arisen, and what was apparent in our data, is the beneficial impact of the kinds of changes which were adopted. The following example highlights this.

With the shift to online EAP assessment, one university pre-sessional program took the opportunity to make the changes to assessment that had long been discussed. The four week pre-sessional program did not require a pass/fail score on a test for progression onto main degree programs but rather acceptable completion of coursework assignments. This included an individual written essay of 1,200–1,500 words and a group presentation of 8–10 minutes in length. For several years, coordinators of the program had wanted to move to a more process-oriented approach to writing, with students working on one essay over the four weeks as opposed to several different essays, as had previously been the case. With the chance to reinvent the course structure in the move to online delivery, coordinators made this change to assessment a priority and a core driving force of the new course design. The majority of input was delivered asynchronously with only a 40 minute synchronous session per week. Tutors provided a mixture of spoken and written feedback to individuals, groups, and the whole class. They received individual feedback on their essay submission each week. Teachers were extremely satisfied with the alternative kinds of feedback that technology enabled as well as the opportunities for peer feedback and audio feedback to be repeatedly accessed. One teacher on the program explained:

> The feedback was definitely effective for the students who engaged with it because instead of being always teacher-led it became very much a group thing with the teacher as the monitor and in that sense, the learning experience was rather richer than it might have been had we only been relying on face to face work in the classroom because the words have gone, then there's no record of them. Flip grid …. proved to be the single most effective thing, you know, little 2 minute presentations and the students could monitor them again and again so that you could see that they'd watched their own video or someone else's video 25 times.
>
> *(TeacherF1)*

With the focus on one main essay built up over time, the cognitive and context validity of the assessment were potentially enhanced, providing a more authentic format which more closely reflected what many of the EAP students would go on to do on their main degree programs. The need to engage in digital literacy also prepared students both for university and the world of work beyond, as called for pre-pandemic by Roche (2017). Scoring validity was also ensured for the essay marking, as previous years' essays could be provided for standardisation purposes as the title and structure remained largely unchanged. For the presentation, however, the scoring criteria had to be hastily adjusted to reflect online delivery, something which was novel for the context and for the teachers.

The examples in this section provide insights into how extremely different approaches were taken by two EAP providers. Such experiences can now be built upon, enhancing the validation processes of the newly designed digital assessments to move beyond the ERA situation.

3.9 Final Comments

To return to the title of this chapter and our intention to evaluate the validity and longevity of EAP testing and assessment practices adopted in the first six months of the pandemic, it is evident that there were immense challenges which posed a threat to validity, but the ERA narratives highlight the valuable lessons which were learnt and which can enhance quality assurance and invigorate EAP assessment practices. Validity is a balancing act between a number of factors, as highlighted throughout this chapter, and there is never a 'perfect' balance. Nevertheless, the unprecedented contextual parameters during this emergency period augmented the quest to find a balance which EAP practitioners could be comfortable with. Perhaps because they were no longer able to rely on long-standing, traditional, and trusted measures, such as time-constrained tests in controlled conditions, other aspects of assessment which may have previously seemed aspirational, such as learner-centredness, feedback, and flexibility, were forced to take centre-stage and allowed to thrive. Consequently, methods of assessment which had previously been viewed with mistrust were implemented.

Validity is developmental so all lessons learnt in the first six months of the pandemic are invaluable to the EAP sector's future planning of digital assessment, and perhaps also to similar contexts. We now have essential experience and empirical evidence of the innovative contingency measures which were adopted during this emergency period. ERA was a live trial of sorts, and we can build on the lessons learnt to enhance the quality of digital assessments. More than ever, as Chalhoub-Deville and O'Sullivan (2020) comment, there is a need for a flexible approach to validity which considers the 'context of use'. As they acknowledge, in the UK, EAP assessment is 'participant-driven' and therefore training and upskilling, particularly in the area of digital assessment literacy, are certainly required.

We recommend that the next phase in terms of validity is to evaluate and refine the assessments introduced during ERA using more stringent processes. O'Sullivan and Weir (2011) advise that test specifications should be based on a validation model which determines the kinds of validity evidence which will be collected at the various stages to build up the validity argument. EAP providers therefore need to continue to collect evidence throughout the whole assessment process in order to determine quality and appropriateness of their newly designed assessments. O'Sullivan and Weir (2011) further explain that, 'a theory of validity is only of practical value if it is translatable into a coherent theory or "model" of validation, which can then be operationalised through a set of validation procedures' (p. 26). The SCF may thus be a starting point but this will need to be further developed to account for technology-driven assessment formats. If, as Chalhoub-Deville and O'Sullivan (2020) state, 'validity is demonstrated by showing that the test task has indeed resulted in the elicitation from successful learners of the expected language performance/task', academic integrity issues need to be addressed to ensure that the language is being elicited from the students in question.

To capitalise on the positive changes already made in terms of enhanced feedback, authenticity, relevance, and compassion, there is a need to engage with stakeholders. This includes discussions with students, EAP teachers, parent departments and so on to collect further feedback on measures adopted and to gather needs analysis data from their new post-COVID contexts. This validity evidence can be fed back into the cycle to enhance the quality of future assessments. In this sense, ERA has made a significant contribution to the cycle of validation, even if some of the practices became a 'lesson learnt' and were ultimately abandoned.

The EAP sector now needs to look beyond the traditional validation frameworks to those which place more emphasis on context relevance, impact, and engagement with stakeholders. In the absence of time to implement usual validation processes, EAP staff embarked on a different kind of validation, one that takes a broader view. It is important that this change does not become a 'temporary shift … which will return to the original format' (Hodges et al., 2020) when the crisis subsides. This momentum must be harnessed to ensure that lessons are not lost from this ERA period, and to make sure EAP assessment is fit for purpose for 21st century students.

Acknowledgements

With thanks to BALEAP for the research funding and to all those in the UK EAP sector who took part in the research.

References

Alderson, C., Brunfaut, T., & Harding, L. (2017). Bridging assessment and learning: A view from second and foreign language assessment. *Assessment in Education: Principles, Policy and Practice, 24*(3), 379–387.

Arasaratnam-Smith, L. A., & Northcote, M. (2017). Community in online higher education: Challenges and opportunities. *Electronic Journal of e-Learning, 15*(2), 188–198.

BALEAP. (2008). *TEAP working party: The competency framework for teachers of English for Academic Purposes*. Retrieved from www.baleap.org

Bell, D. E. (2016). *Practitioners, pedagogies and professionalism in English for Academic Purposes (EAP): The development of a contested field* (Doctoral dissertation). University of Nottingham.

Brindley, G., & Ross, S. (2001). EAP assessment: Issues, models, and outcomes. In J. Flowerdew & M. Peacock (Eds.), *Research perspectives on English for Academic Purposes* (Cambridge Applied Linguistics, pp. 148–166). Cambridge University Press. https://doi.org/10.1017/CBO9781139524766.013

Bruce, E. (2020). *The impact of time allowances in an EAP reading-to-write argumentative essay assessment* (PhD thesis). University of Bedfordshire.

Bruce, E., & Stakounis, H. (2021). *The impact of Covid-19 on the UK EAP sector during the initial six months of the pandemic*. BALEAP-funded report. Retrieved from https://www.baleap.org/wp-content/uploads/2021/06/BALEAP-Report-Covid-and-EAP-May-2021.pdf

Chalhoub-Deville, M., & O'Sullivan, B. (2020). *Validity: Theoretical development and integrated arguments*. British Council Monographs.

Coombe, C., Vafadar, H., & Mohebbi, H. (2020). Language assessment literacy: What do we need to learn, unlearn, and relearn? *Language Testing in Asia, 10*, 3. https://doi.org/10.1186/s40468-020-00101-6

Cornish, F., Gillespie, A., & Zittoun, T. (2014). Collaborative analysis of qualitative data. In U. Flick (Ed.), *The sage handbook of qualitative data analysis* (pp. 79–93). Sage.

Cumming, A. (2013). Assessing integrated writing tasks for academic purposes: Promises and perils. *Language Assessment Quarterly, 10*, 1–8.

Eyal, L. (2012). Digital assessment literacy—The core role of the teacher in a digital environment. *Educational Technology & Society*, 15(2), 37–49.

Hodges, C. B., Moore, S., Lockee, B. B., Trust, T., & Bond, A. M. (2020). The difference between emergency remote teaching and online learning. *Educause Review*, March 27, 2020. Retrieved from https://er.educause.edu/articles/2020/3/the-difference-between-emergency-remote-teaching-and-online-learning

Home Office. (2021a). *Covid-19: Guidance for student sponsors, migrants and short-term students, temporary concessions in response to Covid19*. First published April 2020. Retrieved from https://assets.publishing.service.gov.uk/government/uploads/system/uploads/attachment_data/file/966653/Student_Guidance_-_Covid19_response_03032021_FINAL.pdf

Home Office. (2021b). *Guidance: Prove your English language abilities with a secure English language test* (SELT). Retrieved from https://www.gov.uk/guidance/prove-your-english-language-abilities-with-a-secure-english-language-test-selt

International Center for Academic Integrity. (2014). *Fundamental Values Project*. Retrieved from https://www.academicintegrity.org/fundamental-values/

Kremmel, B., & Harding, L. (2020). Towards a comprehensive, empirical model of language assessment literacy across stakeholder groups: Developing the language assessment literacy survey. *Language Assessment Quarterly*, 17(1), 100–120. https://doi.org/10.1080/15434303.2019.1674855

Manning, A. (2016). *Assessing EAP: Theory and practice in assessment literacy*. Garnet.

Messick, S. (1989). Validity. In R. L. Linn (Ed.), *Educational measurement* (3rd ed., pp. 13–103). Macmillan.

Morris, E. J. (2018). Academic integrity matters: Five considerations for addressing contract cheating. *International Journal for Educational Integrity*, 14(1), 1–12.

Muhammad, A. A., & Ockey, G. J. (2021). Upholding language assessment quality during the COVID-19 pandemic: Some final thoughts and questions. *Language Assessment Quarterly*, 18(1), 51–55. https://doi.org/10.1080/15434303.2020.1867555

O'Sullivan, B. (2011). Introduction. In B. O'Sullivan (Ed.), *Language testing: Theory and practice* (pp. 1–12). Palgrave.

O'Sullivan, B. (2016). Validity: What is it and who is it for? In Y.-n. Leung (Ed.), *Epoch making in English teaching and learning: Evolution, innovation, and revolution* (pp. 157–175). Crane Publishing Company Ltd.

O'Sullivan, B., & Weir, C. (2011). Language testing and validation. In B. O'Sullivan (Ed.), *Language testing: Theory and practice* (pp. 13–32). Palgrave.

Ockey, J. (2021). An overview of COVID-19's impact on English language university admissions and placement tests. *Language Assessment Quarterly*, 18(1), 1–5. https://doi.org/10.1080/15434303.2020.1866576

Pearson, J. (2021). Assessment of agency or assessment for agency?: A critical realist action research study into the impact of a processfolio assessment within UK HE preparatory courses for international students. *Educational Action Research*, 29(2), 259–275.

Richards, K. A. R., & Hemphill, M. A. (2017). A practical guide to collaborative qualitative data analysis. *Journal of Teaching in Physical Education*. https://doi.org/10.1123/jtpe.2017-0084

Roche, T. B. (2017). Assessing the role of digital literacy in English for Academic Purposes university pathway programs. *Journal of Academic Language and Learning*, 11(1), A71–A87.

Sambell, K., & Brown, S. (2020). *The changing landscape of assessment: Some possible replacements for unseen, time-constrained, face-to-face invigilated exams*. Retrieved from https://sally-brown.net/kay-sambell-and-sally-brown-covid-19-assessment-collection/

Schmitt, D., & Hamp-Lyons, L. (2015). The need for EAP teacher knowledge in assessment. *Journal of English for Academic Purposes, 18*, 3–8.

Seviour, M. (2015). Assessing academic writing on a pre-sessional EAP course: Designing assessment which supports learning. *Journal of English for Academic Purposes, 18*, 84–89.

Taylor, L. (2009). Developing assessment literacy. *Annual Review of Applied Linguistics, 29*, 21–36. https://doi.org/10.1017/S0267190509090035

Weir, C. (2005). *Language testing and validation: An evidence-based approach*. Palgrave Macmillan.

4
LANGUAGE TESTING AND ASSESSMENT IN COVID-19 PANDEMIC CRISIS

Hossein Farhady

YEDITEPE UNIVERSITY, ISTANBUL, TURKEY

4.1 Introduction

Language testing/assessment is agreeably a critical component of any educational endeavour. Testing seems to be the common denominator of almost all education fields regardless of philosophical schools, geographical locations, governing bodies, and teachers' attitudes (Farhady & Tavassoli, 2018). One reason for the significance of testing is that test scores lead to making decisions on people's lives, especially in the context of high-stakes tests for admission or certification purposes. Another reason is the value of the information that tests can provide about students' learning and the efficacy of instructional programs. Unfortunately, the dominance of psychometric culture in many parts of the world has turned testing into a source of anxiety and stress for the test-takers. This may be because most decisions about achievement that depend on obtaining higher scores have often overshadowed obtaining information about the students' abilities. Since testing is at the centre of the intersection of learner, learning, and decision-making, modifications in any of these fields usually lead to some changes, and sometimes-drastic ones (Bachman, 2014; Farhady, 2021). However, despite all changes, its main purpose of measuring the construct of language ability has not changed.

In any instructional context, we often think of a teacher who teaches and expects someone to learn. To demonstrate that someone has learned, we need to offer some sort of evidence that most often comes from the application of some sort of testing. Based on the evidence, we decide on the performance of the learners that often influence their personal or educational lives. This cycle, from teaching to decision-making, is not as simple as it looks. Moving from teaching to decision-making involves a multitude of construct-relevant

DOI: 10.4324/9781003221463-5

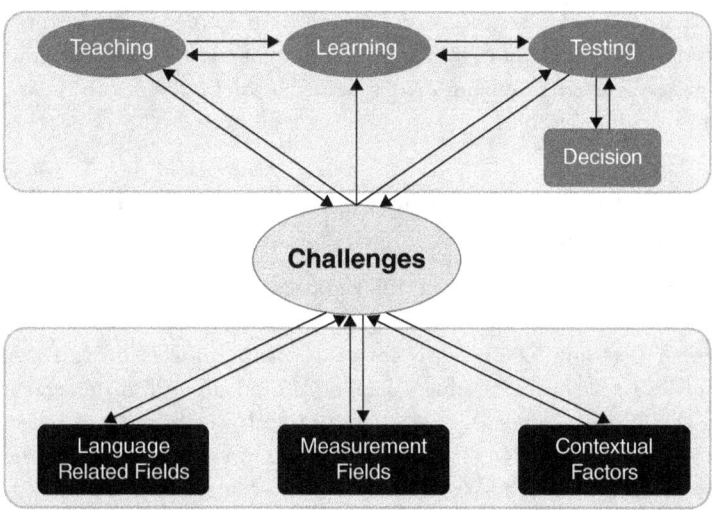

FIGURE 4.1 Interaction of factors in the process of teaching and learning.

and irrelevant factors that make the process quite complex and complicated. What we observe on the surface, and we may call it the bright side of our profession, includes the teacher, the process of teaching that leads to learning, providing evidence by giving tests, and eventually making a decision. The direct path from teacher to decision-making is quite straightforward and consistent. However, what makes the field challenging, is the hidden factors that influence the processes of teaching, learning, and assessment (Bachman, 2014) because stakeholders either are not aware of or do not pay due attention to the factors on this side. The roots of most of the challenges we face are in this side that we may call the dark side of our profession (Figure 4.1). These challenges usually stem from innovations in the treatment of the language ability construct, measurement of the ability, and context-related factors and the interactions among them.

Innovations in the language-related fields have changed our treatment of the nature of language, learning, and assessment (Brown & Lee, 2015). First, the definition of the language ability construct has changed from the ability to describe the rules of grammar to the ability to communicate in real contexts. Second, the definition of the concept of learning has changed from memorising words and grammar rules to a self-regulated, active, and dynamic process.

Therefore, the process of measuring language ability has followed these developments and has changed from a focus on discrete elements of language such as phonemes, morphemes, and structures to measuring the overall communicative effectiveness of the utterance. Third, the COVID-19 pandemic has changed the context of teaching from face-to-face classes to online ones where neither appropriate infrastructures nor well-trained teachers were available to deal with it. Although the focus of this chapter is on the developments in language assessment during the pandemic, a brief reference to the interactions of teaching, learning, and assessment seems necessary.

4.2 Product-Oriented Testing vs. Process-Oriented Assessment

The educational reform in the late 1980s and early 1990s led to a paradigm shift from psychometric testing focusing on the product of learning to edumetric assessment (Farhady, 2005, 2021) focusing on the process of learning. The change from testing to assessment happened gradually within several stages. Along this process, scholars have offered several classifications based on the functions that tests serve in different contexts. For instance, just before the turn of the century, many scholars divided tests into categories such as prognostic, placement, achievement, diagnostic, etc. Later, Cumming (2014) categorised tests based on the interpretations of test scores such as normative, summative, and formative. In addition to classifications in the testing and assessment field, categorisations in the teaching area have also been helpful in the conceptualisation of the changes in the field of testing and assessment. For instance, although Kumaravadivelu (2006) classified teaching methods and practices into two main periods of method and post-method eras without mentioning testing practices, we can apply this classification to the testing field as well.

Method and post-method classification seems to go along with the principles of assessment (Assessment Reform Groups, 2002) that led the field to change from testing to assessment (Farhady & Tavassoli, 2018). Teaching and testing in the method era, which dominated the field for a long time, focused on the product of learning. The product-oriented approach to measurement concerned itself with the outcome of learning with little or no attention to the processes that lead to learning. Post-method era, on the other hand, focused on the processes of teaching, learning, and testing (Gipps, 1994). Following the principles of the process-oriented approach, criticisms began to rise on the appropriateness of product-oriented tests including international and local standard tests used as external criteria as indicators of achievement.

In a product-oriented approach, learning refers to some sort of accumulation of knowledge that may come from a variety of sources such as teachers, books, lectures, and media. Very naturally, tests following this approach would attempt to measure the extent of accumulated knowledge. Such tests, whether high or low stakes, lend themselves to normative interpretation because their purpose is to provide benchmarks for admission to educational institutions or certification for degrees. One could fairly assume that all testing practices in the method era were of product-oriented types. For example, Lado's discrete point approach in the 1950s and 1960s (Lado, 1961) and Oller's integrative testing in the 1960s and 1970s (Oller, 1983) were in this category since they attempted to measure the outcome of learning. Even the rise of the communicative approach in the 1970s (Canale & Swain, 1980), followed by functional testing in the 1980s (Farhady, 1983), the comprehensive language ability model of the 1990s (Bachman, 1990), and the four-skill models in early 2000s (De Jong, 2004) were also product-oriented. This implies that regardless of the fundamentally different frameworks they followed, the underlying construct of measuring language ability did not change very much. Of course, every theoretical framework claimed improvements over its predecessors since each emphasised different aspects of language ability. However, they did not lead to a substantial change in the procedures for measuring it.

With the growing attention to the process of language learning and testing, the product-oriented normative testing system gradually lost its momentum and failed to meet the requirements of the new paradigm for a few reasons. First, scholars believed that such tests created a strong negative washback that often led to test-driven curricula focusing on boosting learners' scores on the test with little or no attention to the processes learners go through (Bailey & Jakicic, 2011; Conrad & Donaldson, 2004; Wylie, 2020). Second, some scholars believed that such tests exercise power on the learners (Hamp-Lyons, 2007; Shohamy, 2001) and are all operating in a nondemocratic context and an authoritarian manner. This meant that stakeholders including the learners, teachers, and administrators had no voice in the development, administration, and score interpretations of this system of testing. Testing organisations often had control over other stakeholders and made decisions on the applicants without their involvement. Third, other scholars believed that such tests undermine students' role in the assessment, especially their capacity to judge their performance (Boud & Falchikov, 2006). Of course, some of the criticisms made on normative standard tests seemed justified not because of the quality of the tests but because of misuses of such tests around the world, especially when they served as criteria for decision-making in instructional contexts. Such criticisms were also valid and probably more important for summative and formative assessments since they were also following the product-oriented approach to teaching and testing.

With the emergence of the post-method era and the shift of attention from the product of learning to the process of learning (Kumaravadivelu, 2001), a new perspective emerged in the conceptualisation of learning. Learning came to be not the extent of knowledge teachers transmit to the learners to store, but the knowledge the learners create through active and constructive processes that Dewey (1916) mentioned more than a century ago. He claimed that learning is a highly intellectual process that occurs when learners are involved in many cognitive and metacognitive activities to get a sense of achievement and self-confidence and to move towards self-regulation and autonomy. Figure 4.2 illustrates the processes that contribute to the learning process.

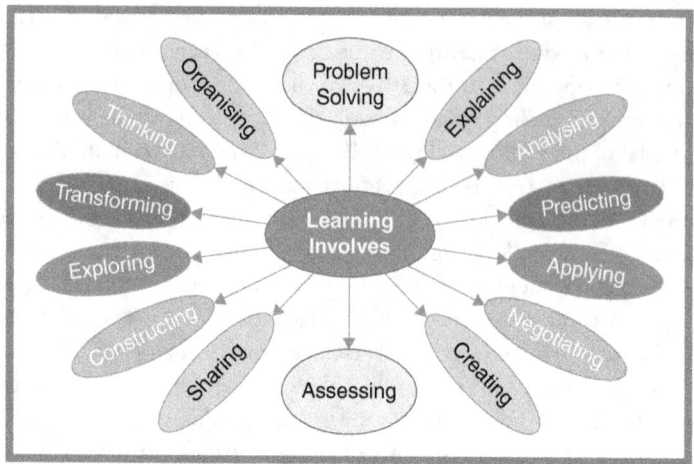

FIGURE 4.2 Processes involved in learning.

With the developments in the areas of teaching and learning, testing in general and instruction-based testing, in particular, needed to accommodate the changes as much as possible. Therefore, when the process of 'testing' and the practice of 'test' did not satisfactorily meet the new challenges, the field turned to use the more comprehensive term 'assessment'. Assessment refers to the measurement of students' status by far more than paper-and-pencil instruments. It embraces diverse kinds of tests and measurements (Popham, 2004). Similarly, Green (2013) claims that language assessment involves obtaining evidence to inform inferences about a person's language-related knowledge, skills, or abilities. Indeed, neither definition does justice to the underlying nature of assessment as a dynamic process. In such contexts, assessment means measuring an individual's performance by obtaining data from multiple sources such as tests, quizzes, interviews, written samples, observations, etc. It pictures more of 'Multiple Testing' rather than 'Assessment'. We may call these types of assessments 'Psychometrically Oriented Assessments' (Farhady, 2021).

4.3 The Emergence of LOA

The word 'assessment' has become a frequently mentioned term in the field in the last few decades. New terms flourished with the word 'assessment' such as performance, authentic, alternative, formative, summative, classroom-based, dynamic, diagnostic, assessment of, for, and while learning (Conrad & Donaldson, 2004; Volante, 2010). Scholars have used some of these terms sometimes synonymously, sometimes slightly differently, and sometimes erroneously. For instance, performance assessment often refers to measuring test-takers' ability in production skills of writing and speaking. In general, it refers to any assessment that attempts to measure the produced language. The question may arise about the difference between what they called 'performance assessment' and the traditional oral interview or rating of a piece of writing. For the same reason, the term 'diagnostic assessment' does not seem to be different from diagnostic tests to identify the strengths and weaknesses of the learners. Of course, certain shades of similarities exist among these assessment types. For instance, they all intend to measure students' ability on using language in as authentic contexts as possible. Most of them also require teachers to provide feedback, but the purpose of feedback is not always to enhance learning (Black & Wiliam, 1998; Stiggins et al., 2004; Wiliam & Thompson, 2007).

It was certainly a desirable move to collect data on applicants' performance from multiple sources since it would most likely improve the quality of educational decisions (Gipps, 1994). This was also a start to avoid making decisions on the students' performance with one midterm and one final test. Therefore, improvements in the treatment of the concept of assessment led to definitions that are more comprehensive and could accommodate the changes in the field. For instance, no later than a decade from the early definitions of assessment, Green (2017) almost redefined assessment as the systematic process of evaluating collected data and information on students' language knowledge, understanding, and ability *to improve their language learning and development by providing "feedback"* (italics mine). A fundamental principle of this definition is that assessment and learning are interrelated and influence each other through the process of feedback. I call this type of assessment that, by definition, assists learning, 'Edumetrically Oriented Assessment' (Farhady, 2021).

There are significant differences between psychometrically oriented and edumetrically oriented assessments. The differences do not lie in the superficial treatment of the terms but lie deep in their purpose, process, and implementation. First, while testing is retrospective, i.e., measuring what students have already learned, assessment is prospective, i.e., attempts to guide learning. Second, while testing reveals learners' existing knowledge, i.e., the product of learning, the assessment shows the learners' changing state of the knowledge, i.e., the process of learning. Third, while testing is often teacher-controlled where learners have no voice in its planning, development, and administration, assessment occurs in cooperation between the teacher and the learners. Fourth, while testing occurs once or on multiple occasions, assessment is an ongoing process. Finally, testing rarely provides feedback to the learners, while assessment heavily focuses on feedback.

Carless (2007, 2009) formulated a working framework in a series of papers, introduced the concept of learning-oriented assessment (LOA) as an umbrella term, and claimed that the goal of LOA is to promote the learning component of assessment, either summative or formative. Many applied linguists such

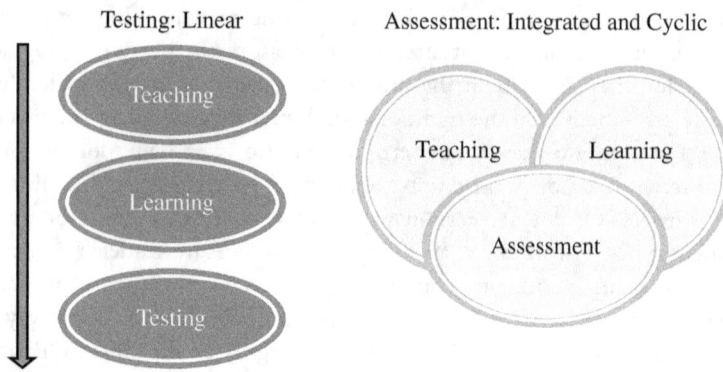

FIGURE 4.3 Changes from testing to assessment.

as Purpura and Turner (2014a, 2014b), and Green (2017) popularised it as a promising alternative to the traditional testing system.

The emergence of LOA had a pleasant consequence of integrating teaching, learning, and assessment as a unified process rather than treating them linearly. Figure 4.3 illustrates the interrelation of teaching, learning, and assessment in testing and assessment contexts.

Considerable attention to LOA by both applied linguists and practitioners led to the formulation of certain principles to distinguish it from similar types of assessment. First, in the LOA context, the learner, learning processes, and learning outcomes are integrated and stand at the centre of attention (Purpura, 2015). In other words, assessment tasks serve as learning tasks to facilitate and promote learning interactively. In addition, learners need to have access to detailed instructions for the assignments, criteria, and rubrics for evaluating their assignments so that they would have a better understanding of learning goals. One of the students reflected on this issue and wrote, 'The brief explanation of the assignment was beneficial in understanding the nature of the assignment. As I always mention, I feel a lot better when I know what I am supposed to do'. The hidden outcome of sharing the criteria with the learners (teaching learners indirectly how to use assessment criteria) is to motivate learners for more discussion, involvement, and eventually learning (Carless et al., 2006; Falchikov, 2005).

Second, the assessment should provide appropriate and timely feedback that would serve as feedforward for further improvement, i.e., a feedback loop (Boud & Molloy, 2013). The purpose of establishing a feedback loop is not to see how the teacher provides the feedback but to see what learners can do with the feedback to support current and future student learning (Gibbs & Simpson, 2005). Considering the feedback loop, we may envisage a process similar to scaffolding in Vygotsky's (1978) Zone of Proximal Development (ZPD) where negotiation with peers and mentors enhances learning. In Vygotsky's sense, scaffolding is the process that refers to the role of teachers and others in supporting the learner's development and providing support to help learners improve (Horstmanshof & Brownie, 2013). Nassaji and Swain (2010), indeed, highlighted that negotiated help provided within the learners' ZPD is more effective than help provided randomly. The process of leading the learners through a feedback loop to improve learning in LOA resembles the practice of scaffolding in the constructivist approach. Hattie (2009) and Hattie and Timperley (2007) synthesised the findings of 800 meta-studies of 52,637 papers that included over 200 million students from different age groups and language ability levels and reported the significant role of feedback in the LOA context. Their studies revealed that among ten factors that would improve learning, providing feedback was marked as one of the top-ranked features that positively influenced student learning.

Third, LOA enables both teachers and learners to move some of the learning activities from inside the class to outside the classroom, which is intensified during the pandemic. Although learners might have received education in a predominantly lecture-based environment and may prefer a passive role in class, LOA enhances negotiations between both teachers with students and students with students. The process raises awareness and encourages learners to a smooth and gradual shift of their learning from in-class to outside class. The teacher then acts as an assisting member who leads the learners by directing them into the feedback loop. Reinders (2020) claims that moving part of the learning from in-class to outside class will not only increase learner autonomy but also offer diverse opportunities that enhance learning.

Research on various aspects of LOA also offers strong support for the effectiveness of LOA in various instructional contexts. For instance, Keppell et al. (2006) reported the positive effect of LOA in a technology-enhanced environment. This indicates that, even during the COVID-19 pandemic where instruction went to an online system, LOA was effective and could help learners achieve their goals. Ashton et al. (2012) also reported the effectiveness of LOA in primary and secondary school contexts. Ibrahim (2013) and Carless (2014) reported the positive role of LOA in increasing learner involvement in the process of learning. Hamp-Lyons (2017) suggested that LOA improved the speaking skills of teaching assistants. In a different context, Green (2017) demonstrated the effectiveness of using LOA in developing instructional materials, and Saygili (2021) showed through experimental research that LOA significantly improved students' academic writing performance.

4.4 LOA Practice during the COVID-19 Pandemic

LOA enjoys a multitude of tasks that teachers can implement in class. Of course, some tasks are more practical than others due to their complexity, the number of students involved, and the context. I will address the issue using data from reflections of an undergraduate class of 35 and a graduate class of 10 students at Yeditepe University during the COVID-19 pandemic. Most of them experienced a test-oriented system of midterm and final exams throughout their education. Therefore, they needed to make two adjustments: first to understand and implement the ongoing assessment system of LOA, and second to cope with the new experience of online instruction. Following the principles of LOA, they performed several weekly tasks individually, in pairs, or group work. An examination of one of the tasks, namely a weekly reflective essay about the class management, their learning processes, and problems revealed an important issue. The learners did not think that online education due to COVID-19 made any significant difference either in their study habits or in their learning rates. Since most of the tasks in an LOA system enhance students' learning outside the class environment, students did not feel any pressure. For instance, students reflected that in lecture-based courses, the instructors increased homework load considerably assuming that the volume of assignments would improve the learning rate in an online system. They also claimed that the processes and procedures of LOA-based instruction did not change very much except for the medium. However, certain issues need attention for the effective implementation of the LOA framework, especially during online classes.

First, teachers need to open a channel of communication with the students to share all the instructions, rubrics, and procedures for in and out of class tasks and assignments. One way to open this channel is by asking students to write reflective essays that would provide opportunities for both learners and teachers to share their thoughts. Through reflections, learners receive a chance to contribute to classroom procedures when they reflect on each session and write about their perceptions of what went on in the class. The teacher shares frequently mentioned issues and suggestions with the class. When the learners feel that they have a voice in class procedures, they become motivated to participate more in class management. Besides, they practice writing without conscious focus on writing but by communicating their thoughts to the teacher. The following statement seems to demonstrate the significant contribution of reflections to students' learning.

> While writing RE, I have a chance to evaluate my performance, revise my knowledge, and see what I have learned so far. I always feel that I am listening to my inner voice and reading my thoughts while writing.

Second, the teacher needs to create a context for collaboration among the students, as either pair work or group work. In many contexts, the culture of self, peer, and collaborative assessment may not be common to students. Peer- and self-assessment are two effective tasks in LOA that contribute to students' involvement in their learning process (Stiggins, 2005). When they are not concerned with grades, they assess themselves fairly because they understand that the purpose is to see how much they learned rather than what score they can get. A considerable majority of the students claimed, '*We learned a lot by assessing our performance and sharing it with a peer*'. Some teachers may have concerns about the students' overrating or underrating themselves. However, when the teacher shares the purposes, principles, and rubrics of the tasks, students try to observe the rubrics and pay close attention to the instructions of the assignments. Most of the learning happens in the process of performing the task since they need to learn and use their knowledge in self and peer assessment (Saito, 2008).

For instance, a good number of students did not appreciate either pair work or group work claiming, '*Group members do not contribute their fair shares and the load falls on one or two other members*'. It may be true on some occasions, but as they continue performing these tasks, the same students claim,

> I did not value group work before. My attitudes towards group work changed, and we not only learned from one another but also enjoyed the within-group discussion and negotiations.

Third, the teacher needs to direct the learner through the feedback loop. It is important to note that the main objective of the tasks and pushing the learner through the feedback loop is often a hidden agenda that would enhance student learning. As an example, in performing a group task, the instructions require students to observe certain steps. First, group members perform the task individually and then exchange their tasks within the group. Second, each member performs a peer assessment, provides feedback, and returns it to the other members (this is the first stage of the feedback loop that functions as feedforward for the next stage of performing the task). Third, each member examines the feedback before the group members get together and discuss the feedback until they get to a consensus on the single group performance (the second stage of the feedback loop for each member to improve the task). They send their original draft, group members' feedback, the revised drafts, and final group work to the instructor. Finally, the instructor provides further feedback and requires revision and improvement (the last stage of the feedback loop that serves as a feedforward to improvement and finalising the task). This process usually takes a few weeks while learners are moving along through the multiple stages of the feedback loop. A few students mentioned in their reflections that they mastered the content of the session through receiving feedback and feedforward. The following is what some of the students said:

> As I always mention, whenever you give us feedback, it is helpful in many ways and complements the feedback from group members.
>
> We are learning through experience how to be an observer, questioner, planner, and organizer.

Fourth, one of the major concerns of online instruction for teachers has been the validity and reliability of online assessment of student achievement. The feeling of academic dishonesty (often inappropriately called cheating) has created a tense atmosphere between teachers and learners. Of course, it may be possible for a few students to get help from others that is acceptable if the assistance leads to learning. Besides, when students need to complete assignments in multiple stages within the feedback loop, it would be difficult to manage help from others for all stages (Palloff & Pratt, 2009). Therefore, the potential for unethical behaviour on the students' side reduces to almost zero, especially if there are multiple stages of delivery for the assignments.

The point is not to downgrade undesirable effects of the COVID-19 pandemic on the instructional procedures since it is not easy to ignore some major negative effects of imprisonment at home. Students', as well as teachers', attitudes and motivation in addition to their boredom, mental peace, and sometimes health, changed due to lack of socialisation (Saladino et al., 2020). However, teachers and students could mitigate most of the negative effects of online instruction by employing appropriate instructional procedures. Some points from students' reflections indicate that the LOA system alleviated some of the difficulties they experienced with other courses during the pandemic.

4.5 Conclusions

The purpose of this chapter was to present the principles of LOA and demonstrate that it could serve as a desirable framework to mitigate the negative effect of the COVID-19 pandemic. Experience with both graduate and undergraduate students and examining their reflections, I believe LOA made several significant changes in the instructional behaviours of the learners. First, it helped students to develop self and peer assessment skills as activities to enhance their learning process. In most cases, learners claimed, *'When I try to assess my peer's task, I try to learn what I need to know to assess'*. This is an indication of indirect learning and maybe acquisition.

This implies that they did not feel much stress through self-assessment, peer assessment, or other weekly tasks. They considered all tasks as learning assistance while peers and teachers assessed their performance.

Second, the process of online LOA encouraged self-assessment, peer-assessment, and group cooperation. Some may rightly argue that a student's assessment may not provide a valid outcome, but the important point in these activities is not grading but learning. Of course, we do not expect perfection from students' assessment, self or peer, though Matsuno (2009) suggested that peer assessment could be an effective means of awarding grades in university classes. Although the majority of research reports support the agreement between peer assessment and teacher assessment (Asaba & Marlowe, 2011;

Wakabayashi, 2008), Mahoney (2011) reported significant differences between peer and teacher grading.

A note is in order here that the main underlying purpose of self and peer assessment is not to grade the tasks but to engage students in the learning process (Brown & Abeywickrama, 2018). Since they need to work as a team, they need to self-regulate themselves and observe certain within-group deadlines for completing the assignments. The advantage of such an approach to performing the tasks is that students engage in the process of learning without any pressure from the teacher. Sometimes acting as a group coordinator gives them a sense of leadership that improves their self-confidence.

Third, and maybe the most important, LOA online reduced the extent of academic dishonesty to almost zero. With a class atmosphere of trust, students consider the tasks, as an opportunity to assess themselves and see the extent to which they have accomplished the learning objectives of the course. They claimed, 'They did not feel doing anything unethical because it would have been a self-deception'.

I would like to end this chapter by highlighting the challenges that persist in implementing LOA, particularly in the pandemic and post-pandemic era. Probably the major challenge is teachers' professional knowledge about the new developments in TEFL. Research on teachers' level of professional knowledge is not promising. Numerous research projects on the issue consistently report that teachers do not have the necessary opportunities to improve their professional knowledge that would enable them to cope with the fast-growing field (Farhady & Tavassoli, 2021; Popham, 2011). Another challenge is changing the learners' mindset from having a traditionally passive role to exercising an active and dynamic role in their learning journey. In some cases, teachers may face strong resistance from the learners since they feel they are moving away from the comfort zone of a peaceful learning environment where they have been practicing for a long time. Although quite challenging at the beginning, they change their attitudes and claim that the new learning atmosphere helps them develop a sense of self-evaluation and motivation.

References

Asaba, M., & Marlowe, J. P. (2011). Using peer assessment in the language classroom. *The Language Teacher*, 35(1), 29–33. https://doi.org/10.37546/JALTTLT35.1-4

Ashton, K., Salamoura, A., & Diaz, E. (2012). The BEDA impact project: A preliminary investigation of a bilingual program in Spain. *Research Notes*, 50, 34–41. University of Cambridge ESOL Examinations.

Assessment Reform Groups. (2002). *Assessment for learning: 10 principles*. University School of Education.

Bachman, L. F. (1990). *Fundamental considerations in language testing*. Oxford University Press.

Bachman, L. F. (2014). Ongoing challenges in language assessment. In A. J. Kunnan (Ed.), *The companion to language assessment, Vol. 3: Evaluation, methodology, and interdisciplinary themes* (pp. 1586–1603). John Wiley & Sons.

Bailey, K., & Jakicic, C. (2011). *Common formative assessment: A toolkit for professional learning communities.* Solution Tree.

Black, P., & Wiliam, D. (1998). Assessment and classroom learning. *Assessment in Education: Principles, Policy, and Practice, 5*(1), 7–74.

Boud, D., & Falchikov, N. (2006). Aligning assessment with long-term learning. *Assessment & Evaluation in Higher Education, 31*(4), 399–413. https://doi.org/10.1080/02602930600679050

Boud, D., & Molloy, E. (2013). What is the problem with feedback? In D. Boud, & E. Molloy (Eds.), *Feedback in higher and professional education* (pp. 1–10). Routledge.

Brown, H. D., & Abeywickrama, P. (2018). *Language assessment: Principles and classroom practices* (3rd ed.). Pearson.

Brown, H. D., & Lee, H. (2015). *Teaching by principles: An interactive approach to language pedagogy* (4th ed.). Pearson.

Canale, M., & Swain, M. (1980). Theoretical bases for communicative approaches to language teaching and testing. *Applied Linguistics, 1*(1), 1–47.

Carless, D. (2007). Learning-oriented assessment: Conceptual bases and practical implications. *Innovations in Education and Teaching International, 44*(1), 57–66. https://doi.org/10.1080/14703290601081332

Carless, D. (2009). Learning-oriented assessment: Principles, practice, and a project. In L. H. Meyer, S. Davidson, H. Anderson, R. Fletcher, P. M. Johnston, & M. Rees (Eds.), *Tertiary assessment and higher education student outcomes: Policy, practice, and research* (pp. 79–90). Ako Aotearoa.

Carless, D. (2014). Exploring learning-oriented assessment processes. *Higher Education, 69*, 2–5. https://doi.org/10.1007/s10734-014-9816-z

Carless, D., Joughin, G., & Liu, N. (2006). *How assessment supports learning: Learning-oriented assessment in action.* Hong Kong University Press.

Conrad, R. M., & Donaldson, J. A. (2004). *Engaging the online learner: Activities and resources for creative instruction.* Jossey-Bass: A Wiley Imprint.

Cumming, A. (2014). Linking assessment to curricula, teaching, and learning in language education. In D. Qian, & L. Li (Eds.), *Teaching and learning English in East Asian universities: Global visions and local practices* (pp. 2–18). Cambridge Scholars Publishing.

De Jong, J. H. A. L. (2004). Relating tests to the Common European Framework. *Language Testing Update, 35*, 80–83.

Dewey, J. (1916). *Democracy and education: An introduction to the philosophy of education.* MacMillan.

Falchikov, N. (2005). *Improving assessment through student involvement.* Routledge Falmer.

Farhady, H. (1983). On the plausibility of the unitary language proficiency factor. In J. W. Oller Jr (Ed.), *Issues in language testing research* (pp. 11–28). Newbury House.

Farhady, H. (2005). Language assessment: A linguametric perspective. *Language Assessment Quarterly, 2*(2), 147–64.

Farhady, H. (2021). Learning-oriented assessment in virtual classroom contexts. *Journal of Language and Communication, 8*(2), 121–132.

Farhady, H., & Tavassoli, K. (2018). Developing a language assessment knowledge test for EFL teachers: A data-driven approach. *Iranian Journal of Language Teaching Research, 6*(3), 79–94. https://doi.org/10.30466/ijltr.2018.120602

Farhady, H., & Tavassoli, K. (2021). EFL teachers' perceptions and practices of their language assessment knowledge. *Language Testing in Asia, 11*(17), 1–19. https://doi.org/10.1186/s40468-021-00135-4

Gibbs, G., & Simpson, C. (2005). Conditions under which assessment supports students' learning. *Learning and Teaching in Higher Education, 1*, 3–31.

Gipps, C. V. (1994). *Beyond testing*. Falmer Press.

Green, A. (2013). *Exploring language assessment and testing: Language in action*. Routledge.

Green, A. (2017). Learning-oriented language test preparation materials: A contradiction in terms? *Papers in Language Testing and Assessment, 6*(1), 112–132.

Hamp-Lyons, L. (2007). The impact of testing practices on teaching: Ideologies and alternatives. In J. Cummins, & C. Davison (Eds.), *The international handbook of English language teaching* (Vol. 1, pp. 487–504). Springer.

Hamp-Lyons, L. (2017). Language assessment literacy for language learning-oriented assessment. *Papers in Language Testing and Assessment, 6*(1), 88–111.

Hattie, J. (2009). *Visible learning: A synthesis of over 800 meta-analyses relating to achievement*. Routledge.

Hattie, J., & Timperley, H. (2007). The power of feedback. *Review of Educational Research, 77*(1), 81–112.

Horstmanshof, L., & Brownie, S. (2013). A scaffolded approach to discussion board used for formative assessment of academic writing skills. *Assessment & Evaluation in Higher Education, 38*(1), 61–73.

Ibrahim, H. A. (2013). In search for implementing learning-oriented assessment in an EFL setting. *World Journal of English Language, 3*(4), 12–14.

Keppell, M., Au, E., Ma, A., & Chan, C. (2006). Peer learning and learning-oriented assessment in technology-enhanced environments. *Assessment & Evaluation in Higher Education, 31*(4), 453–464. https://doi.org/10.1080/02602930600679159

Kumaravadivelu, B. (2001). Toward a post-method pedagogy. *TESOL Quarterly, 35*(4), 537–560. https://doi.org/10.2307/3588427

Kumaravadivelu, B. (2006). *Understanding language teaching: From method to post method*. Lawrence Erlbaum Associates.

Lado, R. (1961). *Language testing: The construction and use of foreign language tests: A teacher's book*. McGraw-Hill.

Mahoney, S. (2011). Exploring gaps in teacher and student EFL error evaluation. *JALT Journal, 33*(2), 107–130. https://doi.org/10.37546/JALTJJ33.2-1

Matsuno, S. (2009). Self-, peer-, and teacher assessments in Japanese university EFL writing classrooms. *Language Testing, 26*(1), 75–100. https://doi.org/10.1177/0265532208097337

Nassaji, H., & Swain, M. (2010). A Vygotskian perspective on corrective feedback in L2: The effect of random versus negotiated help on the learning of English articles. *Language Awareness, 9*(1), 34–51.

Oller, J. W. Jr. (Ed.). (1983). *Issues in language testing research*. Newbury House.

Palloff, R., & Pratt, K. (2009). *Assessing the online learner: Resources and strategies for faculty*. Jossey-Bass.

Popham, W. J. (2004). Why assessment illiteracy is professional suicide. *Educational Leadership, 62*(1), 1–2.

Popham, W. J. (2011). Assessment literacy overlooked: A teacher educator's confession. *The Teacher Educator, 46*(4), 265–273.

Purpura, J. E. (2015). *Learning-oriented assessment in second and foreign language classrooms*. Paper presented at LTRC, Toronto, Canada.

Purpura, J. E., & Turner, C. E. (2014a). *A learning-oriented assessment approach to understanding the complexities of classroom-based language assessment.* Presentation at the Roundtable on Learning Oriented Assessment in Language Classrooms and Large-Scale Contexts, Teachers College, New York, Columbia University.

Purpura, J. E., & Turner, C. E. (2014b). *Learning-oriented assessment in language classrooms: Using assessment to gauge and promote language learning.* Routledge.

Reinders, H. (2020). A framework for learning beyond the classroom. In M. Raya, & F. Vieira (Eds.), *Autonomy in language education: Theory, research, and practice* (pp. 1–9). Routledge.

Saito, H. (2008). EFL classroom peer assessment: Training effects on rating and commenting. *Language Testing, 25*(4), 553–581. https://doi.org/10.1177/0265532208094276

Saladino, V., Algeri, D., & Auriemma, V. (2020). The psychological and social impact of COVID-19: New perspectives of well-being. *Frontiers in Psychology, 11*, 577684. https://doi.org/10.3389/fpsyg.2020.577684

Saygili. (2021). *The effect of learning-oriented assessment on EFL learners' academic writing ability* (Unpublished Ph.D. dissertation). Yeditepe University, Istanbul, Turkey.

Shohamy, E. (2001). *The power of tests: A critical perspective on the uses of language tests.* Longman.

Stiggins, R. (2005). *Student-involved assessment for learning.* Prentice-Hall. https://doi.org/10.1080/09588221.2019.1667831

Stiggins, R. J., Arter, J. A., Chappuis, J., & Chappuis, S. (2004). *Classroom assessment for student learning: Doing it right – Using it well.* Retrieved from https://www.researchgate.net/publication/268441382.

Volante, L. (2010). Assessment of, for, and as learning within schools: Implications for transforming classroom practice. *Action in Teacher Education, 31*(4), 66–75.

Vygotsky, L. S. (1978). *Mind in society: Development of higher psychological processes.* Cole, M., Jolm-Steiner V., Scribner S., & Souberman E. (Eds.). Harvard University Press.

Wakabayashi, R. (2008). The effect of peer feedback on EFL writing: Focusing on Japanese university students. *OnCUE Journal, 2*(2), 92–110.

Wiliam, D., & Thompson, M. (2007). Integrating assessment with learning: What will it take to make it work? In C. A. Dwyer (Ed.), *The future of assessment: Shaping teaching and learning* (pp. 53–82). Lawrence Erlbaum Associates.

Wylie, C. (2020). Digital module 20: Classroom assessment standards. *Educational Measurement: Issues and Practice, 39*(4), 135–136. https://doi.org/10.1111/emip.12407

5
ARGUMENT-BASED VALIDATION IN THE TIME OF THE COVID-19 PANDEMIC

Erik Voss

TEACHERS COLLEGE, COLUMBIA UNIVERSITY, NEW YORK, NY, UNITED STATES

5.1 Introduction

The global pandemic which began in 2019 disrupted assessment practices around the world. As language tests were administered remotely, the notion of validity and threats to validity were soon discussed. Because many language tests were administered by adapting to remote contexts which are different from the intended planned administration procedures, any prior validation efforts were called into question. Although some language test administrations were attempted by following safety protocols with social distancing, masks, and other personal protective equipment (PPE) requirements, the assessments that were most susceptible to validity threats were in online, remote contexts. This chapter will first point out the extent to which validation frameworks have been utilized in appraising online assessment. The chapter will then discuss the application of an argument-based approach to validation (Chapelle et al., 2008; Kane, 2006, 2013) and how it can be applied to the evaluation of language assessment in remote assessment contexts.

5.2 Approaches to Language Assessment Validation during the Pandemic

During the pandemic, language assessment was reimagined in many ways as administration was adapted or cancelled due to the requirements to administer assessments at a distance. Validation efforts are intended to justify interpretations based on score meaning and score uses. A variety of validation frameworks directed the type and amount of evidence to collect to justify interpretations of intended score meanings. Among these frameworks were Weir's (2005) socio-cognitive framework applied to English for Academic Purposes (EAP) assessments (Bruce, this volume) and IELTS Indicator assessment (Clark et al., this volume), Bachman and Palmer's (1996) test usefulness framework applied to e-portfolio assessments (Lam, this volume) and measuring second language pragmatic competence through videoconferencing technology (Zhang & Isaacs, this volume), Kunnan's (2008) test fairness framework, which was applied to the evaluation of an English placement test (Neiriz et al., this volume), and an argument-based approach (Chapelle et al., 2008; Kane, 2006, 2013) used to support claims about the TOEFL iBT Home Edition (Papageorgiou & Manna, 2021). Yet, other research has only mentioned validity or made claims about score meaning interpretations and collected evidence in areas such as test construct, fairness, and test security, and effectiveness of assessments delivery though digital platforms without specifying a particular framework. Although many approaches seek evidence to support interpretation of intended score meaning and uses, the argument-based framework discussed in this chapter is based on the work by Kane (2006, 2013).

5.2.1 Argument-based Validation Framework

Although many of the chapters in this volume have adopted other validation frameworks, the application of an argument-based approach to validation has been increasingly explored as a validation framework in the field of language assessment (Chapelle & Voss, 2013) and online language education (Voss, 2018). The argument approach supports the notion that validity is a characteristic of test score interpretations and uses and not a property of the test. The argument structure is based on Toulmin's (2003) informal or practical argument structure. Theoretical and empirical evidence is collected about a test that either support or weaken the claims resulting in a degree of validity for the interpretation and uses of test scores for the intended purpose of the test.

The framework for the argument structure (presented in Figure 5.1) guides the collection of evidence to support the plausibility of seven types of inference in a sequence (Chapelle et al., 2008; Kane, 2006). The framework consists of two steps and begins with an *interpretation/use argument* (I/UA) that presents a detailed proposal for potential interpretations and uses of the scores (Kane, 2013). This step in the framework specifies the claims, warrants, and assumptions for each inference that provide the foundation for score interpretation. A claim is a statement about the interpretation of an intended score meaning or use. Claims are further specified through warrants and assumptions that provide theoretical rationale for the claim and guide the selection of backing needed to support the inference. Once the I/UA has stated the claims to be made about the assessment, research is conducted to collect evidence to support those claims. The second step in the framework is the *validity argument* (VA) which presents the degree to which theoretical

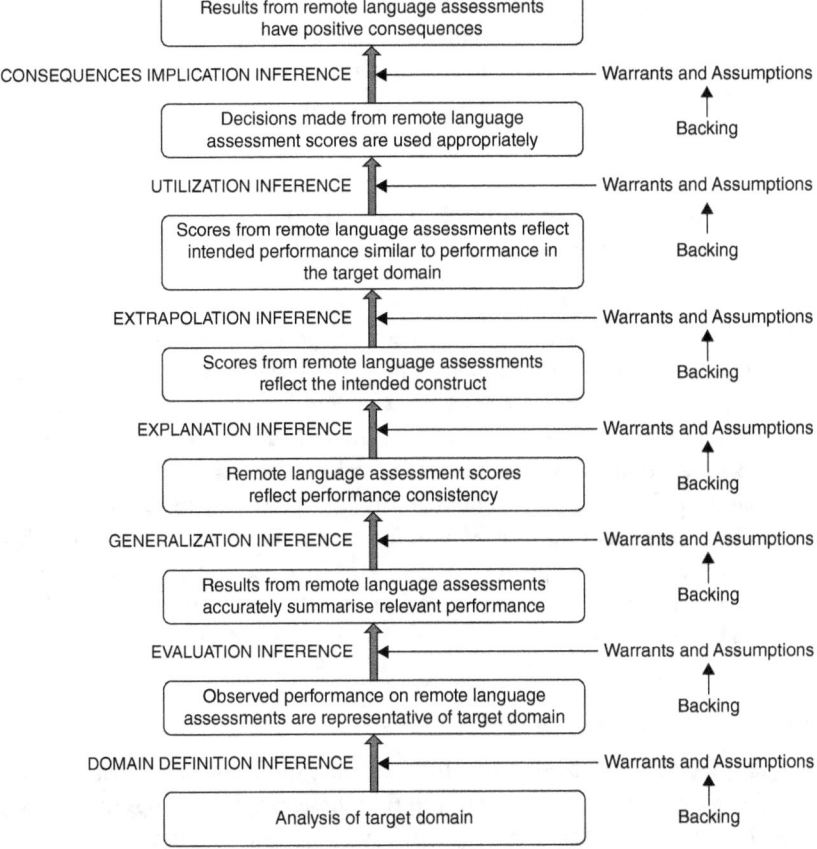

FIGURE 5.1 Structure of validity argument for remote language assessments.
Adapted from Chapelle (2021).

and/or empirical evidence collected in the intermediate stage has supported each inference. In order to progress through the argument, an interpretation must be supported. The conclusion for that inference becomes the grounds for the next inference. Figure 5.1 presents the structure for the VA beginning with the domain definition inference and concluding with the consequences implication inference.

While a debate has occurred regarding whether consequences should be included as part of validity (O'Sullivan & Chalhoub-Deville, 2020), the I/UA includes both consequences and uses of test scores when developing VAs (Chapelle, 2021). The I/UA begins by stating claims about a test for its intended purpose. Each claim is a conclusion for an inference. Preceding the consequences implication and utilization inferences related to score use are five inferences stating claims about score interpretation.

The VA presents judgements about the degree of support from each inference. These evaluatory conclusions are determined by the theoretical and empirical evidence collected though both quantitative and qualitative methodology.[1] The next section will present examples of inferences, claims, warrants, and assumptions for developing an I/UA for remote language assessments.

5.2.2 Argument-based Validation for Remote Language Assessments

In general, the argument should seek to collect evidence for claims that are weaker in the argument and test alternative hypotheses to reduce doubts and enhance robustness of the argument (Fulcher & Davidson, 2007). This is also true, in this chapter, where in-person assessments have been adapted to online administration and, as a result, may have altered various facets of the assessment. Special attention should be paid to collect validation evidence to support claims in these instances. On the other hand, assessments that were easily adapted to remote administration would not require as much backing. This section will present examples of inferences, claims, warrants, and assumptions that are relevant to remote assessment in the developmental stage of the VA, an I/UA. The first two inferences state claims about assessment score use.

5.2.2.1 Consequences Implication Inference

Test developers and providers usually claim that results from language assessment scores are used appropriately and that these results have positive consequences (Chapelle, 2021). Therefore, the consequences implication inference leads to the claim that the use of the assessment has beneficial consequences for the purpose of the assessment. The warrants supporting this claim can explicate the support for positive impact on the user or society.

The claims made about remote tests should take into account the beneficial consequences afforded by the use of technology. Examples of warrants and assumptions related to claims about remote assessments to support the consequences implication inference are presented in Table 5.1.

Claims for beneficial consequences impact test takers and other stakeholders such as current and future instructors and future employers. A positive benefit from a remote assessment during the pandemic, for example, was the ability to take a remote test that might otherwise be impossible due to lockdowns and restricted travel. For instance, students who have the opportunity to take a remote assessment such as the Secure English Language Test (SELT) will benefit from the opportunity to apply for a visa to enroll in degree programs in the UK (see Bruce, this volume). Backing for this warrant would collect evidence for the assumption that test takers were able to take the required English language assessment successfully at home or in a remote context.

TABLE 5.1 Claim, Warrants, and Assumptions for the Consequences Implication Inference for Remote Assessments

Claim: Results from remote language assessment scores have positive consequences		
Warrant 1: Remote assessment allows users to complete an assessment that might otherwise be impossible under some circumstances such as lacking funding to travel, limited seating at testing facilities, or travel restrictions during a pandemic. A.1 Test takers were able to take a test at home or in a remote context.	*Warrant 2:* Remote assessment can supplement remote teaching to align teaching and testing delivery methods. A.2 Assessment methods are similar to instructional methods and contexts and are appropriate and beneficial for assessment and learning.	*Warrant 3:* Remote assessment can prepare students to use technology that they may use in an academic or work setting. A.3 Similar technology-based tasks are used and knowledge of such technology is beneficial in the target domain.

A second type of warrant supporting consequences of remote assessments would demonstrate an alignment between remote assessment and remote teaching. This warrant would be supported by backing from the assumption that remote assessment and teaching are similar enough to be appropriate and beneficial for learning. Finally, the ability to complete a remote assessment may be similar to completing remote training for a potential employer. Therefore, backing for this warrant could demonstrate that knowledge of technology to complete online tasks in the real-world has prepared test takers for future study or employment that may require knowledge of and ability to use similar technology. The grounds for this inference that are used appropriately come from the conclusion of the next inference, Utilization.

5.2.2.2 Utilization Inference

The utilization inference begins with the claim that the assessment is used appropriately for a specific proposed purpose. The warrants underlying this claim can support the inference about the utility of the assessment. That is to say that the assessment scores are being used appropriately for the intended purpose of the assessment or that decisions based on the assessment scores are appropriate. Such decisions can take many forms such as diagnostic and educational, depending on the decisions that stakeholders intend to make. Examples of warrants and assumptions to support the utilization inference for remote assessments are presented in Table 5.2.

Warrants for remote assessments supporting the claim that a remote assessment is useful for producing scores for the intended purpose of the assessment

TABLE 5.2 Claim, Warrants, and Assumptions for the Utilization Inference for Remote Assessments

Claim: Results from remote language assessment scores are used appropriately	
Warrant 1: A remote assessment is useful for producing scores for the intended purpose of the assessment.	Warrant 2: Decisions made from remote assessment scores are used appropriately.
A.1 Test scores are used for the intended purpose for which the assessment was designed.	A.2 Decisions are made from assessment scores that are appropriate and useful.

is not necessarily different from most testing contexts assuming that score use is interpreted based on the intended purpose of the assessment. Backing for this warrant can be supported by evidence that demonstrates the use of scores for the intended purpose for which the assessment was designed. This warrant has been particularly relevant during the pandemic when assessment scores were accepted as evidence of English proficiency for English-medium university admission decisions for convenience rather than for their intended purpose. For instance, Isbell and Kremmel (2020) and Wagner (2020) point out that the Duolingo English Test (DET) does not indicate that the assessment was designed to measure language proficiency in academic contexts. Yet, during the pandemic when many secure test centers closed, university admissions offices began accepting DET and other at-home test scores as a measure of academic English language proficiency for admission purposes (Isbell & Kremmel, 2020; Papageorgiou & Manna, 2021). Evidence would need to be collected to provide backing for this inference in order to support the use of scores from these assessments for university admission decisions.

A second type of warrant for this inference would support decisions made based on remote assessment scores. Backing for this warrant would indicate that the decisions were appropriate and useful. Assumptions could be supported by collected evidence that placements were correct, admission decisions were correct, or students were placed correctly into appropriate language courses. This inference is based on support from the next inference, Extrapolation. The conclusion from the extrapolation inference that scores from remote assessments reflect intended performance similar to performance in the target domain forms the grounds for the utilization inference.

5.2.2.3 Extrapolation Inference

This inference explores the extent to which scores from remote assessments reflect intended performance similar to performance in the target domain. Stated another way, it explores the degree to which performance on the assessment is reflective of performance on similar tasks in the real world.

TABLE 5.3 Claim, Warrants, and Assumptions for the Extrapolation Inference

Claim: Scores from remote assessments reflect intended performance similar to performance in the target domain
Warrant 1: Remote assessments use technology that reflects technology used in the target domain tasks. A.1 Performance on assessment tasks is similar to performance on real-life tasks with equivalent technology in the target domain context.

Warrants supporting this inference would include observations of the comparison between technology use on an assessment and technology use in the real world. Evidence is collected through analysis and observation of real-life tasks to determine the strength of the relationship and the amount of support for this inference. Table 5.3 provides an example of a warrant and assumption for the extrapolation inference for remote assessments.

A warrant for the claim that scores from remote assessments reflect intended performance similar to performance in the target domain would seek evidence to support the use of technology on the test tasks that is similar to technology used in real-world tasks. An assumption outlines the type of evidence to collect to support this warrant. Thus, backing for this warrant could collect evidence that may present results indicating similar performance on technology-based tasks in the real-world and on the technology-based test tasks. Strong support for this inference can also support the claim that having the knowledge of certain technology can have positive implications as stated in the consequences implication inference.

Tasks for some assessments may have changed during the transition to remote delivery. For instance, a paper-based writing assignment needed to be presented as a computer-based writing assignment during the pandemic, changing the original intended task of replicating an in-person, classroom hand-written writing assignment. There were, however, other assessments that were designed to replicate real-life target language tasks that included the use of technology. An example is Jun's (2021) source-based writing task which requires students to use sources from the Internet to complete their text. This task was initially intended to replicate a real-life source-based writing assignment. This inference begins only if the next inference has been supported. The conclusion from the explanation inference forms the grounds for the extrapolation inference.

5.2.2.4 Explanation Inference

The explanation inference focuses on the relationship between task performance and an underlying trait or construct. This inference seeks support for a claim that scores from assessments reflect the intended construct. The use of

TABLE 5.4 Claim, Warrants, and Assumptions for the Explanation Inference

Claim: Scores from remote language assessments reflect the intended construct	
Warrant 1: Technology required for tasks on remote assessment is part of the construct.	Warrant 2: Test takers have the technological knowledge to operate the hardware and software that is required to complete the remote assessment.
A.1 Description of the construct being measured includes technology knowledge and/or ability required to complete a task.	A.2.1 Test takers are able to complete the test task without technological interference. In other words, technology was transparent. A.2.2 Test takers have the technological knowledge or ability to begin and complete the task.

technology in remote assessments creates the need to reexamine the language constructs measured by language assessments because any changes to the tasks can have implications for the meaning of the test scores (Chapelle & Voss, 2021b). The underlying construct measured with the assessment needs to be clearly defined in order to determine the appropriate type of evidence to collect to support this inference. Warrants and assumptions for the explanation inference for remote language assessments can be seen in Table 5.4.

The explanation inference seeks evidence that scores from remote assessments reflect the intended construct. There are two types of warrant indicating content-related technology. The first warrant states that any technology used for a test task is part of the construct. Backing for this warrant would provide a detailed description of how the technological knowledge and/or ability is part of the construct. For example, writing ability will include the ability to use keyboarding skills. Speaking ability will include the ability to coordinate turn taking in a remote environment. This type of evidence is construct-relevant and should be included in the construct definition.

A second warrant states that test takers have the technological knowledge to operate the hardware and software that is required to begin and complete the remote assessment. In other words, the technology does not interfere with the ability to complete the test tasks. Backing to support this warrant would state how there were no technological issues that hindered task completion. Transparent technology would include, for example, reliable internet connection with no noticeable latency, and adequate hardware to complete the tasks. A second assumption for this warrant is that test takers had the technological knowledge to begin and complete the remote assessment without delays or seeking assistance. For example, test takers would need to know how to allow a browser to access a web camera, how to log into a testing platform, or how to navigate through the assessment. Technological troubleshooting has become part of the construct being measured in most remote assessments. This type of technology knowledge needed to navigate the platform, while just as important, is different from the technological knowledge required to complete a task but just as important. This inference is warranted only if the generalization inference has sufficient support.

5.2.2.5 Generalization Inference

This inference seeks confirmation of performance consistency across occasions and contexts. Reliability estimates are calculated as a measure of consistency of a testing instrument. Measurement of high reliability of test scores indicates a high probability that test takers would perform similarly and receive similar scores if they took the test a second time. In other words, high reliability of test scores is an indication that the test is measuring the intended language ability or construct. Table 5.5 provides examples of warrants and assumptions for the generalization inference for remote language assessments.

This inference is based on the claim that remote assessment scores reflect performance consistency. Warrants supporting this inference identify potential sources of error reflected in test scores. Assumptions reflect the claims of the remote assessment. One type of warrant focuses on the analysis of automated scoring, which is becoming more common and more complex in language assessment. Backing for this assumption underlying the first warrant would provide reliability estimates for the automated scoring algorithm.

A second warrant is supported by backing that compares consistency on remote administration with face-to-face administration of the same assessment. Backing for this mode comparison can be provided by comparing reliability estimates from assessment scores from both modes. Clark et al. (this volume) express concern over how differences between the controlled environment of a test center administration and a variable at-home administration can affect reliability of an assessment. The justification for this inference depends on sufficient support from the evaluation inference. If scores from remote assessments do not accurately summarize relevant performance, any claims about reliability are vacuous.

TABLE 5.5 Claim, Warrants, and Assumptions for the Generalization Inference

Claim: Remote language assessment scores reflect performance consistency	
Warrant 1: Automated scoring is equally consistent as scoring by human raters.	*Warrant 2*: Total test scores from remote administrations are equally as consistent as to face-to-face administrations.
A.1 Reliability estimates for the automated scoring algorithm are adequate.	A.1 Reliability estimates for remote administrations are similar to face-to-face administrations.
A.2 Reliability estimates from automated scoring systems are similar to or outperform reliability estimates from human scoring.	

5.2.2.6 Evaluation Inference

The evaluation inference seeks evidence to support the claim that scores from remote assessments accurately summarize relevant performance. For most assessments, this inference evaluates the extent to which scoring rubrics and scales reflect appropriate target language, skills, and abilities. This inference is also supported by an examination that assessments were presented uniformly to all test takers. Additional support can be collected by surveying test takers about the use of technology to deliver the assessments. Finally, analysis of test scores can show how well individual items are at appropriate levels of difficulty or if the items are able to distinguish among test takers at disparate levels of ability. Table 5.6 shows two warrants related to remote language assessments that would support the claim that scores from remote assessments accurately summarize relevant performance.

Two types of warrant are stated to support the claim for this inference. The first warrant attends to the standardization and security of remote assessments. This issue has been a major obstacle during the recent pandemic. Test takers have been attempting to complete language courses and assessments on tablet computers and mobile devices rather than a laptop or desktop computer. The first assumption provides support if evidence is found that test takers had adequate and appropriate computer hardware to complete the assessment tasks.

A second assumption provides backing for this inference if procedures are implemented to enhance the security of a remote assessment. Low security has been another major obstacle during this pandemic. Backing can be provided with evidence that proctoring or other security measures have been implemented and are adequate for the assessment. An attempt to mitigate this situation and provide support for this assumption has included the use of remote proctoring software that utilized artificial intelligence to monitor test takers (Purpura et al., 2021). However, even with such software, there are concerns about test takers finding ways to cheat the system.

Research should also be conducted to ensure that human scoring procedures are not influenced by remote assessment and scoring. Backing for this warrant would investigate the interaction if an interlocutor is involved in the

TABLE 5.6 Claim, Warrants, and Assumptions for the Evaluation Inference

Claim: Scores from remote assessments accurately summarize relevant performance	
Warrant 1: Remote test administration ensures a high level of standardization and security.	*Warrant 2*: Automated scoring evaluates responses similar to a trained human rater.
A.1.1 Computer hardware is sufficient to deliver a remote test appropriately.	A.2. Automated scoring systems are designed to evaluate language and award a score similar to a human rater.
A.1.2 Procedures are in place to prevent cheating and test security.	

assessment task. According to Zhang and Isaacs (this volume), the degree to which an interlocutor is able to use the required technology may influence the scores awarded and subsequently the reliability of the assessment. Likewise, the ability of a human rater to make a judgement about language performance in a remote setting cannot be influenced by the failure of technology (e.g., dropping out, latency issues) without potentially affecting reliability of the assessment.

A second type of warrant is relevant if the remote assessment utilizes automated scoring. In such a case, additional assumptions are needed to evaluate the performance of the automated scoring system in relation to a human judge. Backing for this assumption would detail the design of the automated scoring system and collect statistical evidence that an automated score is similar to a human score. Sufficient support is needed for the next inference, domain definition, in order to justify support for the evaluation inference. For example, if observed performance is not representative of the target language domain, the evidence collected to support the evaluation would have little or no meaning.

5.2.2.7 Domain Definition Inference

This inference relates to the content and context for the language assessment through an analysis of the target language domain. For example, assessments measuring academic language would draw from language in a specific academic discipline. Whereas, an assessment for air traffic controllers would be designed by sampling language from the target language domain of air traffic controlling. The language would differentiate these two assessment contexts.

Evidence to support this inference can include analysis of documentation, expert's views of language needs, surveys, and applying a corpus linguistic methodology to a corpus of authentic language sampled from the domain. Table 5.7 shows two warrants related to remote language assessments that would support the claim that observed performance on remote assessments is representative of the target domain.

TABLE 5.7 Claim, Warrants, and Assumptions for the Domain Definition Inference

Claim: Observed performance on remote language assessments is representative of the target domain	
Warrant 1: The target domain that the remote assessment is intended to assess is described appropriately for the test purpose. A.1: The content and expected responses are appropriate for the target domain and include language necessary to complete tasks in the digital context.	Warrant 2: The content of machine-scored assessments is the same as human-scored assessments. A.2. Automated scoring does not change the test content or test takers' responses and is appropriate.

Two types of warrant are provided as examples for this inference to support the claim that observed performance on remote assessments is representative of the target domain. The first warrant states that the target domain the remote assessment is intended to assess is appropriate for the test purpose. Each language assessment is unique for a specific purpose and would document and present the analysis that is appropriate. Backing for this assumption is based on an analysis for language in the target domain. The content of an assessment may not change when adapted to a remote administration. In this case, the content may reflect the target domain regardless of delivery mode, which may be the case for standardized assessments. In a low-stakes context, however, the process of adapting a task to reflect online communication may alter the content of the task. Remote delivery of assessment tasks may introduce new vocabulary that was not included in expected responses. For example, language about sharing screens, muting, or video latency and troubleshooting technological difficulties may be introduced to synchronous communication.

A second warrant states that the content of machine-scored assessments is the same as human-scored assessments. Backing for this warrant would collect evidence that the content is appropriate for the task and is not different. One example of content that varies is a computer-adaptive test (CAT) such as the assessment suggested by Clark et al. (this volume) as an attempt to mitigate content theft. However, this type of assessment typically draws from a bank of items that have been developed and vetted by humans. A second type of assessment that is more challenging to collect supportive evidence for is assessments that automatically generate items. Because the human in the loop is minimal in these situations, more care must be taken to curate an appropriate corpus from which the items are generated. Backing for this inference would rely on an analysis for automatically generated items to determine if they are appropriate for the assessment purpose. In addition, if a task requests students to use online resources, the language will differ based on websites that the test taker visits. For example, since Jun (2021) included the ability to find and evaluate sources on the Internet for a writing task as part of the construct, the language from relevant sources would be included in the target domain for that task. This inference begins with an analysis of the target domain; however, that domain may be defined for the particular language assessment.

5.3 Post-Pandemic Lessons

The considerations made for administering language assessments during the challenge of a pandemic will have lasting effects on how we view the use of technology to support delivery, scoring, and reporting of language assessments and how adaptations using technology may affect language test score interpretation and use. During this time, instructors and test providers experienced a range of situations from searching for technological solutions for emergency adaptations to the implementation of planned online assessments. Both individual teachers as well as language testing companies implemented these changes for their particular purpose. The success of these implementations is still under investigation although we might agree that those with more technological literacy were better prepared to address the needs of administering remote assessments.

One lesson we should learn from this experience is that the best solution is by identifying technology that supports the planned language assessment for its intended purpose. This was, however, not easy for many language teachers who were unfamiliar with the range of existing technological solutions or unable to find a solution that would support the intended construct for their particular assessment. For example, a business conferencing platform was quickly adapted both for online education as well as language assessment administration. Today, post-pandemic, despite the obvious drawbacks to the platform for supporting education, the company has been slow to adapt to the needs of teachers. This is also true for most learning management systems that were designed to support learning with less consideration about how to support evolving forms of assessment. The I/UA presented in this chapter is one method for identification of claims about the degree to which the use of technology supports a language score interpretation and score use.

A second lesson is the realization that technology is becoming an integral part of language assessment even after the effects of the pandemic have passed. Automatic test generation and scoring will become more common as well as new forms of interaction through advances in artificial intelligence. Many people have experienced remote language assessment and are more familiar with the technology, which lowers the barrier for entry for such emerging products and tools. The acceptance of new forms of assessment using technology will grow when the tools are more widely used.

A final lesson is the need to understand the range of technological knowledge necessary for teachers, administrators, and test takers. The introduction of technology may require the knowledge to use technology to complete the assessment. This type of technology is related to the construct. Additional technological knowledge may be needed if web cameras and microphones are used in the assessment. Consequently, a test taker may be required to change the permission settings in the browser to allow the camera and microphone to record. This is a different type of technological knowledge that is not related to the construct but acts as a gatekeeper to access the assessment. Furthermore, additional types of construct-unrelated technological knowledge may require the test taker to be able to troubleshoot infrastructure in the environment such as Wi-Fi connectivity issues, using a virtual private network, or latency.

Overall, the lessons from administering remote assessments during a pandemic are driven by technology and technological knowledge needed by the instructors and test providers as well as the test takers. The range of technological knowledge includes construct-related as well as construct-unrelated knowledge. These considerations are fundamental when developing and I/UA and a validation argument for remote language assessments.

5.4 Conclusion

The chapter began by identifying frameworks that have been identified to collect validity evidence for remote language assessments during the pandemic. The variety of chosen frameworks shows the diversity of approaches. In addition, many language assessment documentation efforts during this time collected validity evidence without an identified framework. This chapter presented an argument-based approach to validity that focused on inferences, claims, warrants, and assumptions that are relevant to remote assessment. The development of an I/UA stated claims unique to each assessment for the intended assessment purpose. The claims developed for specific remote assessment range from identified positive consequences and uses to claims that support score meaning within the unique digital context of use including the language necessary for remote administration.

The final step in the VA would present a judgement for each inference based on the collected theoretical and empirical evidence. The degree to which the evidence supports each inference would either support or weaken the interpretation of the claims about score use and score meaning. While this approach is flexible and comprehensive, it is structured as an argument. This means that the type and amount of evidence collected depends on the requirements by the stakeholders. Low-stakes classroom assessments would require less evidence than high-stakes language assessments. This overall practicality issue is specific to each individual assessment context. A benefit of this argument-based approach is the ability of the assessment specialist to identify areas where evidence is lacking or does not sufficiently support the intended inference. This is particularly relevant when language assessments were quickly adapted to remote assessment situations. Additional consideration can be given to these areas in the VA to reconsider the claims being made or plan for additional data to be collected.

Note

1 For case studies demonstrating the argument-based validation framework in practice, see Chapelle and Voss (2021a).

References

Bachman, L. F., & Palmer, S. A. (1996). *Language testing in practice*. Oxford University Press.
Chapelle, C. A. (2021). *Argument-based validation in testing and assessment*. SAGE.

Chapelle, C. A., Enright, M. K., & Jamieson, J. (2008). *Building a validity argument for the test of English as a foreign language*. Routledge.

Chapelle, C. A., & Voss, E. (Eds.). (2021a). *Validity argument in language testing: Case studies of validation research*. Cambridge University Press.

Chapelle, C. A., & Voss, E. (2021b). Introduction to validity argument in language testing and assessment. In C. A. Chapelle, & E. Voss (Eds.), *Validity argument in language testing: Case studies of validation research* (pp. 1–16). Cambridge University Press.

Chapelle, C. A., & Voss, E. (2013). Evaluation of language tests through validation research. In A. J. Kunnan (Ed.), *The companion to language assessment* (Vol. 3, pp. 1–17). Wiley-Blackwell.

Fulcher, G., & Davidson, F. (2007). *Language testing and assessment: An advanced resource book*. Routledge.

Isbell, D., & Kremmel, B. (2020). Test review: Current options in at-home language proficiency tests for making high-stakes decisions. *Language Testing, 37*(4), 600–619.

Jun, H. (2021). Justifying the interpretation and use of an ESL writing final examination. In C. A. Chapelle, & E. Voss (Eds.), *Validity argument in language testing: Case studies of validation research* (pp. 235–263). Cambridge University Press.

Kane, M. T. (2006). Validation. In R. Brennen (Ed.), *Educational measurement* (4th ed., pp. 17–64). Greenwood.

Kane, M. T. (2013). Validating the interpretations and uses of test scores. *Journal of Educational Measurement, 50*(1), 1–73.

Kunnan, A. J. (2008). Towards a model of test evaluation: Using the test fairness and wider context frameworks. In L. Taylor, & C. Weir (Eds.), *Multilingualism and assessment: Achieving transparency, assuring quality, sustaining diversity* (pp. 229–251). Cambridge University Press.

O'Sullivan, B., & Chalhoub-Deville, M. (2020). *Validity: Theoretical development and integrated arguments*. Equinox Publishing.

Papageorgiou, S., & Manna, V. F. (2021). Maintaining access to a large-scale test of academic language proficiency during the pandemic: The launch of TOEFL iBT Home Edition. *Language Assessment Quarterly, 18*(1), 36–41.

Purpura, J. E., Davoodifard, M., & Voss, E. (2021). Conversion to remote proctoring of the community English language program online placement exam at Teachers College, Columbia University. *Language Assessment Quarterly, 18*(1), 42–50.

Toulmin, S. E. (2003). *The uses of argument* (updated edition). Cambridge University Press.

Voss, E. (2018). Argument-based approach to validation in online language education. In S. Link, & J. Li (Eds.), *Assessment across online language education* (pp. 239–256). Equinox Publishing.

Weir, C. (2005). *Language testing and validation: An evidence-based approach*. Palgrave Macmillan.

Wagner, E. (2020). Duolingo English Test, revised version July 2019. *Language Assessment Quarterly, 17*(3), 300–315.

6
ASSESSMENT WITHOUT BORDERS

Modernising Placement Tests for Diverse Contexts

Mahmoud Amer and María J. Cabrera-Puche
WEST CHESTER UNIVERSITY OF PENNSYLVANIA, WEST CHESTER, PA, UNITED STATES

6.1 Introduction

The COVID-19 pandemic made crystal clear two key needs for language educators: the need to adapt quickly to a changing educational landscape and the need to quickly onboard learners in our language programs. We realised that many students relied on technology not available to them outside of the university setting. We realised that remote learning seemed far more challenging for both learners and teachers; we also realised that remote learning is not going away anytime soon; and most importantly, we realised that the placement exam we had in place was not assessing students' proficiency level appropriately and their placement relied on the extra human interaction between instructors and students. This required us to shift our focus to the nature of and the philosophy of our assessment practices, including how we place students in language courses. While some of the issues existed prior to the pandemic, COVID-19 gave us the opportunity to reflect on our assessment practices and, in this chapter, we showcase our proposal for assessment practices in a post-pandemic world using a software that we designed in response to these needs.

6.2 Aligning Teaching and Assessment

Language programs should have a direct alignment of teaching, learning, and assessment practices. Following a backwards-design proposal, language programs should establish their desired program goals, and set the specific student learning outcomes (SLOs) to be met through the different courses that form each program. One can assure those SLOs are met at the course and

DOI: 10.4324/9781003221463-7

program-level through different forms of assessment (formative and summative assessments, low-stakes and high-stakes exams, etc.). Ultimately, attainment of the SLOs at the course and program level will be a reflection that the teaching and the assessment tools used are appropriate. Since many language programs rely on placement exams to place students with prior language experience in their courses, these programs need to consider how placement exams align with their course and program goals. A perfect alignment will enhance the language learning experience of students (and consequently help in student retention efforts), and the attainment of such goals. Therefore, assessment routines and placement exams should be placed within the context of the programs and institution goals (Dunkel, 1999).

6.2.1 Current Context of Placement Exams

Most departments offering language study invariably use some form of web-based testing for their placement needs. The efficiency and reliability of conducting exams via technology rendered paper-based tests obsolete:

> Web-based language testing offers several benefits, including automatic scoring and autonomy in testing location and time for test takers. These benefits have prompted the spread of the web as a tool for language testing from low-stakes testing situations—originally advised by Roever (2001)—to medium-stakes testing contexts (Shin, 2012). One such medium-stakes testing context that has witnessed an increased use of the web as a means for test delivery is the university-level foreign language (FL) placement exam.
>
> *(Long et al., 2018; p. 137)*

In addition, many of the commercially available placement exams are adaptive, meaning the technology selects items for students based on their response and performance to previous ones, thus creating a quick and effective way of placing students into a particular language level. Our students use the WebCAPE placement exam, a test designed to provide individualised testing by identifying the student's ability level with a combination of grammar, reading, and vocabulary questions. The exam uses an adaptive testing algorithm which selects and displays items based on the examinee's previous responses. Students seeking language placement in our programs use WebCAPE if they want to place in any of the following languages: Chinese, French, German, Russian, Spanish, and Italian. However, there are some limitations to WebCAPE: it does not measure the aural or oral (listening/speaking) ability of test takers, it is not available in all the languages we offer, and does not address the needs of heritage language learners. Thus, WebCAPE relies on grammar and vocabulary, as well as reading comprehension questions to place students, not placing any role in the aural/oral skills, which is a limited way to assess language proficiency, the ultimate base of our proficiency-based program. We understand that assessing specific points of the linguistic competence of students (in the form of grammar-centred assessment) can be relevant to some programs, even when the general focus is on language proficiency (Larson & Hendricks, 2013). As mentioned above, there are several limitations to placement via WebCAPE for our programs, chiefly the limited language options for placement. WebCAPE does not offer assessment for several of our language programs; nor does it address diverse populations, like heritage learners. Moreover, the assessment model varies from the way our students are taught and assessed in language courses. In other words, there is a gap between what the WebCAPE placement exam measures and the learning goals of our language programs. Before COVID-19, our students were first placed in a course based on the results from WebCAPE, but this placement was frequently overridden by instructors in those courses who could personally assess that a student' proficiency level was not in accordance to specific course expectations. Thus, before COVID-19, the placement exam we used (WebCAPE) needed an extra step (human interaction with expert instructors) to place students appropriately. However, during and after COVID-19, and due to the pandemic situation, this human interaction was limited, which led us to address the need to create an innovative, web-based placement exam that targeted our proficiency learning goals. Our approach in this chapter is to present a model of placement that addresses these limitations, drawing on the accelerating trend of modernising assessment in education, especially after COVID-19. We believe this approach will allow us to provide placement experiences that address a range of learner backgrounds, an approach to *assessment without borders* that includes the language options we offer, the students we teach, and the pedagogical model we follow.

6.2.2 Rethinking the Role of Placement Exams

One of the most important elements of properly designed placement exams first and foremost is the pedagogical dimension. Placing students in the most appropriate language level sequence is one of the most important conditions of ensuring proper development of their skills. Curricular and pedagogical decisions are supposed to be driven by the philosophy of the pedagogy, but they are also affected by the technology (Goetler, 2018). Language placement exams should be informed by the curricular and pedagogical approaches of the department. Within this framework of matching the learning context, placement exams would work the same way as other assessment practices. Specifically, since our language programs strive to appropriately assess given course SLOs, placement exams would be seen as an extension of the assessment practices taking place in each class. Current pedagogical trends in language classrooms focus on communicative and proficiency-based language teaching, consistent with ACTFL (American Council on the Teaching of Foreign Languages) World-Readiness Standards. Therefore, both course SLOs and its assessment practices as well as placement exams should be aligned with these national standards. Specifically, the program goals are proficiency-based and are achieved through a focus on a communicative methodology that targets proficiency in the language. Although the regular assessment practices used in our courses and programs align with our goals, our WebCAPE placement exam assessment practices are mainly grammar/vocabulary-centric. To fill the gap, our proposal presents a placement tool that assesses our proficiency-oriented curriculum and addresses a variety of learners (including transfer students, and heritage learners) and languages, utilising modern advances in existing technology.

6.3 Modernising Assessment: Computer-based Testing and Computerised Adaptive Tests (CATs)

6.3.1 Computer-based Assessments

Chapelle and Voss (2016, 2017) argue that there is room for creating innovative tests used for learning and teaching. The versatility and ability of computerised adaptive tests (CATs) to tailor exams have made assessment both specific, and more level focused. Computerised exams (and most specifically, CATs) have come a long way since the 1970s. Yet, despite the advances made in technology and assessment, the use of technology in assessment has been mostly limited to assessing grammar and vocabulary, and when applicable, limited assessment in aural skills. This is the case despite research in assessment that shows that CAT can be made more communicative (as the software model proposed in this chapter), and less form focused (Zabaleta, 2007).

Additionally, despite the unprecedented innovation in apps and games, and the social turn of mobile device use, little innovation has taken place in designing: (1) assessment around game-based problem solving (Zourou, 2014) and (2) mobile language assessment. According to Burston (2013), while research on mobile-assisted learning is still early, there has been a steady interest in mobile applications for language research, and interest in the study of how mobile-assisted learning can be implemented. In a review of 575 studies done on mobile-assisted language learning, only two studies in that body of literature dealt with investigating the extent to which assessment can be done on mobile devices (Burston, 2013). This is a significant limitation considering the success of several apps that exist for students and which teach and assess their language of choice (*Duolingo*, *Memrise*, etc.). The dearth of studies in this area can be attributed mainly to the high-stakes culture around assessment generally.

6.3.2 Mobile Devices for Assessment

Despite the ubiquity of mobile devices (Kétyi, 2015; Kukulska-Hulme & Shield, 2008; Stockwell & Hubbard, 2013), and the fact that more learners are accessing a variety of learning resources via such devices, research and experimentation with assessment on mobile devices remain limited (Burston, 2013), partly due to the typical logistics involved in these types of tests, where proctoring, test items security, and other elements make the mobile implementation a less attractive (and sometimes less feasible) option. However, not all assessments that can be completed via mobile devices fit this type. This is especially the case for low-stakes exams that students can complete on their own, without the need for proctoring (both our current WebCAPE placement exams, and the ones we created are adaptive to students' responses, can be completed online and are not proctored). However, our placement exam proposal establishes an extra security step: students need to register using their university email, where a confirmation code as well as their score are sent. Even though mobile devices have been growing in their ability to handle processing-intensive computing routines, they traditionally lacked the bells and whistles available in traditional (computer-based and web-based) testing. Additionally, their screen real-estate, until recently, remained limited compared to a typical computer screen (be it a laptop or a desktop), which limited the type of question formats that can be accomplished. Yet, despite all of this, mobile devices are quite capable when it comes to language assessment. If one thinks of the games that can be played on mobile devices, the resource-hungry features of these apps are no match to predictable type assessment questions routinely present in these exams.

Mobile devices have been gradually making their way into the learning and teaching arena. There are obvious reasons why most practitioners agree that they have the potential to transform learning. They are ubiquitous, and capable, and, generally speaking, appear to be more affordable. However, the resources afforded by mobile devices have not been fully utilised in the field of language assessment, and to a lesser extent mobile learning that goes beyond simple form-function drill type activities. However, mobile devices have inherent advantages both at the usability and availability levels. They present an option to offer *assessment without borders*, since they reduce the need for specific computer literacy, an issue other programs face to a varying degree. Purpura et al. (2021), for example, encountered difficulties associated with their conversion of an in-person lab-administered placement exams to online proctoring. Some of the difficulties encountered pertained to computer literacy, proctoring logistics, and the technical infrastructure. These issues are not typically present in mobile-based assessment experiences, as learners tend to have higher rate of mobile-app literacy. In the case of our placement exam, despite being a low-stakes exam, our proctoring solution using the university webmail as a confirmation tool provides an extra layer of security compared to the placement exam we used. Additionally, the technical infrastructure of our placement exam is effective and compatible with all mobile devices.

6.3.3 Online and Remote Exams Are Becoming the Norm

While some might balk at the idea of moving assessment practices online (with a host of issues including security, exam integrity, and the higher possibility of fraud), it needs to be mentioned that a majority of *high-stakes* exams are actually administered online. During the COVID-19 pandemic, where the majority of courses shifted to remote and online modalities (also known as alternative modalities), assessment practices shifted to an online medium. While the shift to online instruction was made fertile because of the pandemic, the reality is that the trend in online learning was on the rise before the pandemic. With instructors relying on project-based assessment, it is not uncommon to observe that exams and quizzes are increasingly being allocated less course grade weight than before, and are not seen as high-stakes assessment tools as they once were.

6.4 Description of and Rationale for the Project

We designed a mobile responsive placement exam software that addresses our program goals and utilises modern technologies. The software, named Alvl (A-Level), is a computer-adaptive software that assesses, in addition to vocabulary and grammar, reading and listening comprehension skills, with a proficiency-based goal in mind. The exam features different types of questions, including multiple selection, multiple choice, and True and False type questions, matching, and drag-and-drop assessment types. A high percentage of students at our academic institution have a language requirement for their majors, which ranges from one to four semesters of language study. Therefore, incoming, transfer, and current students usually complete a language placement exam to assess their language proficiency. The score obtained in the placement exam is intended to help the Department place students in the appropriate language course. However, as outlined earlier, our current placement exam is not aligned with our program goals, centred on proficiency (our majors are assessed with the ACTFL Oral Proficiency Interview and Writing Proficiency Test), and does not offer the range of languages needed.

6.4.1 Placement Is Critical to Language Recruitment and Retention

Many of the students entering our programs have some background knowledge in a given language, most commonly Spanish. We have noticed that student placement is critical to their retention for a minor or a major. If students are misplaced, they would be more likely to feel behind, or feel they are not being challenged in the classroom, which may not encourage them to continue beyond the required language courses. Beaudrie and Ducar (2012) note that placement exams should look beyond the score to help with students' retention and success. Additionally, students who score highly on the placement exam might be surprised if they feel the level in the respective class is not indicative of the score they received; thus, they might be put off by this mismatch, and may not continue with more advanced language not continue with more advanced language courses. In our case, the proficiency-based programs goals were not properly assessed with the placement exam used. Furthermore, pre-COVID-19, instructors played an important role in re-assessing and advising placed students who were not at the proficiency level of the course. This face-to-face interaction between students and instructors to re-assess their placement based on their actual proficiency level became difficult during COVID-19.

6.4.2 Current Data from Our Local Placement Context

Over 3000 students have taken our placement exam in the last two years; over 500 of whom have taken the placement exam during the last three months. While most students place in the lower-level sequence (Figure 6.1), in some languages, a significant number of students place in the mid- and higher-level courses (200–300). If students are placed in lower-level courses after studying a given language for some years, some may be disinterested in the language, and thus recruitment may not be possible. Since the placement exam is the first interaction between the students and the language programs, our approach is to identify a more cohesive and better-aligned exam with our prospective students utilising modern technology.

6.4.3 Discerning Heritage Speakers and Addressing Their Needs

According to our placement exam records, about 14% of our test takers indicate that the language they are placing into is spoken at home. However, some of these placement exams (including WebCAPE, the one used in our programs) do not address the distinct language ability heritage learners possess. Fairclough (2006) addresses these challenges explaining that there are no norms specific to heritage learners. According to Valdés (1989), the proficiency guidelines that undergird proficiency tests make it clear that 'these standards or descriptors were never intended for use with native speakers of ethnic or heritage languages, or indeed with a broad sample of native speakers of varying socioeconomic and educational background' (p. 394). The reality of the linguistic situation however is that language variation in real-life situations has

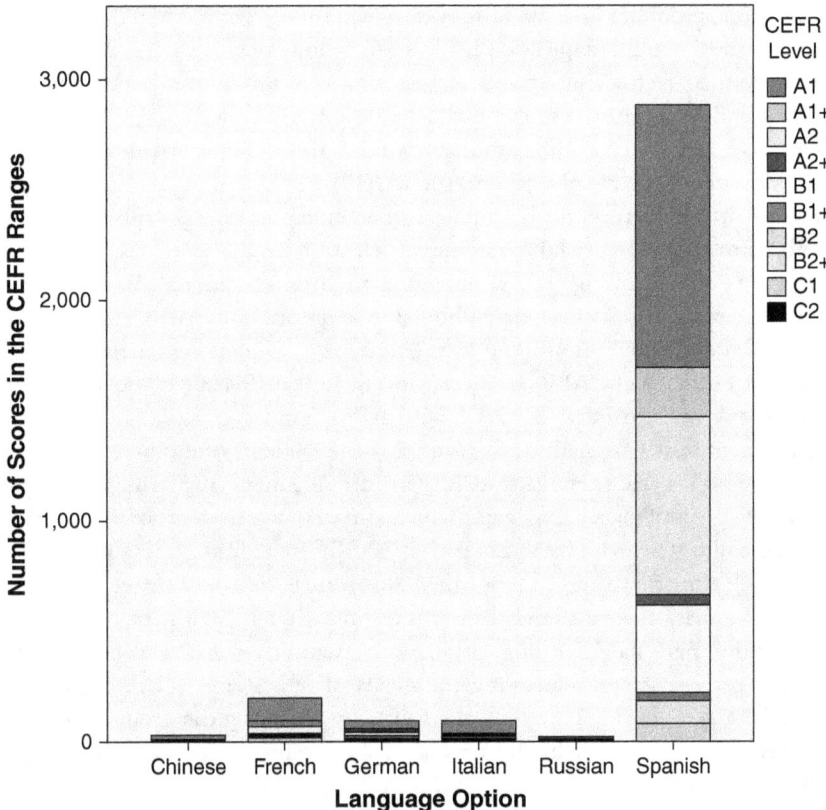

FIGURE 6.1 Language placement by level and area (fall 2019–fall 2021).

challenged concepts of standardised dialects. Nonetheless, foreign language instruction, and by extension assessment of that instruction, is still based on the idea of a standardised language construct, and neglect of multi-language constructs (Barnwell, 1996; Gutierrez & Fairclough, 2006; Savignon, 1985; Shohamy, 2011; Villa, 1996).

6.5 Heritage Language Learners and Placement Exams

There has been a steady increase in enrollments of Latino and Hispanic students at our institution (31% increase between 2015 and 2018), an increase reflected in the make-up of students in our Spanish courses, where both traditional Spanish language students learn side-by-side with Spanish Heritage Language Learners (SHLLs), a common situation already noted in other schools by several scholars (e.g., Campbell & Rosenthal, 2000; Sohn & Shin, 2007; Valdés, 2000). Our SHLLs necessitate not only specific pedagogical implementations but also appropriate assessment tools to place them, which we did not have. Our definition of heritage language learners follows that of Valdés (2000, p. 2) who defined such a learner as someone who was 'raised in a home where a non-English language is spoken, who speaks or only understands the heritage language, and who has some proficiency in English and the heritage language'.

Although we have always had some SHLLs in our classrooms, the population has only recently become large enough to enhance our focus and efforts for recruitment and retention, which we have addressed via curricular changes and addressing the placement exam currently offered. Recruitment and retention cannot happen without the appropriate curricular and pedagogical tools. Our in-house software (Alvl) for placement is needed since the current exam (WebCAPE) is not a good fit for our SHLLs (a move echoed by others, i.e., Beaudrie & Ducar, 2012). As Sohn and Shin (2007) argue 'placement tests designed for foreign language students often do not test the language skills that heritage students have trouble mastering' which conflicts with the goals of placement exams which aim to group students of similar language ability (Brown, 1989; Long et al., 2018). In addition, these placement tests lack construct validity (Shohamy, 2011) since they only target standardised grammatical forms, and do not recognise students with stronger BICS (Basic Interpersonal Communication Skills) (Cummins, 1999). While we are in the early stages of addressing the needs of our SHLLs (planning a specific language track and better placement), we are laying the groundwork for inclusive practices to help all our students make the most of their language experience.

6.5.1 Lessons from the Pandemic

Nascent research and reports on ways the pandemic reshuffled our priorities and changed our practices point to two keywords: flexibility and adaptability (Rilliard, 2020; Rossomondo, 2020; Urlaub, 2020). The COVID-19 pandemic created a need to shift the delivery of existing computerised exams to remote settings, as is the case with Community English Language Program (CELP) at Teachers College (Purpura et al., 2021). Our approach to the placement software in this study is meant to be an approach in modernising assessment, and thus utilise the full range of available technology that provides assessment and placement options for students beyond the limitation of time and space. The concept of innovation in assessment includes offering the placement test experience via a variety of tools, including a mobile-option. The gaps beyond ability in digital literacy to technology 'haves and have-nots' (Puckett & Rafalow, 2020; Vegas, 2020) exposed by the pandemic underscore the need to address this digital divide. Those who relied primarily and heavily on technology for education (Anderson & Perrin, 2018), i.e., populations that lack access to libraries, tutoring services, and other types of services available to more affluent countries and societies were mostly affected by the pandemic, since technology was the only means by which they can access educational services. Especially in resource-strapped countries and economies, more users have access to mobile devices than they do computer equipment (Richter, 2013). Additionally, mobile users are best positioned to receive the latest device updates compared to computer users. Thus, our (mobile-friendly) placement software addresses the digital divide (in the local and global sense). Modernising placement assessment means technology should not only adapt to student's ability; it should not privilege a group against another, especially those who lack access to computing equipment and resources, especially as we witnessed during the COVID-19 pandemic. In addition to addressing unequal access, the software we proposed is designed to provide access for assessment in all languages offered by our department, including Arabic, Japanese, Chinese, American Sign Language (ASL), and Latin, languages not typically offered in commercially available placement exams. The software also includes the ability to offer placement exams and tailor them for heritage learners. Additionally, providing not only reading but also listening skills options in the exams provides better conditions for placing students in the appropriate courses by measuring their language ability more fully. Utilising a mobile device to take a placement exam is a familiar activity for students who routinely utilise their mobile devices for a variety of tasks. Not only will this make the assessment process seem more familiar, but it will also make it more accessible for students to take the placement exam, without additional hoops and links, and compatibility issues. Furthermore, our software (Alvl) provides a proficiency-based placement, aligning this exam with the student learning goals in our program.

6.6 Description of the Project

The current beta version of the placement software (Alvl) we developed exists as a standalone application compatible with both Windows and Mac, Android, and iOS. It can currently place students in both Arabic and Spanish, with a library of questions that exceeds 450 question items across six levels of language proficiency (Novice-Low, Novice-Mid, Novice-High, Intermediate-Low, Intermediate-Mid, and Intermediate-High). The beta version of the software includes a section that collects information pertaining to students' previous language experiences, length of time they studied the language, and the context of their language use (formal schooling, home language, study abroad, etc.). Once the user answers these questions, they are asked to provide an email address where the results will be sent. Upon entering their email information, they receive a confirmation code to authenticate through their university email using a computer-generated code that expires at the conclusion of the session. Once the email is verified successfully, the users are presented with a screen listing the language options available to them. While the software currently lists all of our language options (our ultimate goal is to have all the languages taught represented), currently the only two functional language options are Spanish and Arabic, which we are developing for purposes of testing and piloting the software. The software features all question-types, including multiple choice, multiple selection, True/False, short answer, image selection, and matching, which assess grammar, vocabulary, reading, and listening comprehension. The software begins to pick question items at the lower-end of difficulty, and as users respond, the test adapts to their ability, either picking items at the next stage of language, or going back to easier items. The app keeps track of the scores and once plateaus, it shows a results screen and sends the score to the email on file.

6.7 Software Interface

Once the Alvl placement exam software is installed, and the students have entered their information (name, email and language use), the software will prompt an ethical pledge and a terms of use screen to inform students to not rely on outside material or help while they are completing the exams. The process can be quickly completed, and once the user submits the information, an access code is sent to their email for validation. The student/user then can provide the access code to login to the placement screen. The email contains a unique access code to help ensure the email provided is valid since the results of the exam will be sent to that email. Once users confirm their email, they are presented with the screen to choose a language for placement. The final version of the software will offer our vision of assessment as holistic, and adaptive to the languages we offer in our program.

6.7.1 Item Selection

Development of language and intercultural proficiency are among the main SLOs in our programs. By 'language proficiency', we refer to the ACTFL Proficiency Guidelines definition 'a description of what individuals can do with language in terms of speaking, writing, listening, and reading in real-world situations in a spontaneous and non-rehearsed context', and by 'intercultural communicative competence (ICC)' we refer to 'the ability to interact effectively and appropriately with people from other language and cultural backgrounds' (ACTFL). To achieve those outcomes, we developed a common assessment plan for all our programs, based on ACTFL proficiency standards and other high-stakes accreditation bodies. Our courses target different SLOs to achieve the overall program goals, and our curriculum targets the continuous development of language and intercultural competency. We

TABLE 6.1 [Audio, Matching] Escucha los audios. Une los audios con las respuestas apropiadas.

Audio	Written
¿Cómo te llamas?	Me llamo Álex.
¿Cómo estás?	Estoy bien, gracias.
¿Cuándo es tu cumpleaños?	El treinta de enero.
¿Cuántos años tienes?	Tengo veinte años.
¿Cómo eres?	Soy baja y rubia.
¿De dónde eres?	Soy de Estados Unidos.

encourage courses to follow the 2017 National Council of State Supervisors for Languages (NCSSFL) and the ACTFL Can-Do Statements to set up specific communicative learning goals, so that students can self-assess their progress in their development of language and intercultural proficiency. Our placement exam (AlvI) was created considering those overarching proficiency goals and the NCSSFL-ACTFL Can-Do Statements, so that incoming students entering our program would be placed in the appropriate course. Our placement exam assesses language proficiency without the implication of human scoring. The examples in Table 6.1 show a selection of questions that target the Novice proficiency level. The first example requires students to listen to each one of the simple questions (on very familiar topics, such as name, age, birthday, etc.) and select an appropriate answer to the listened question, from the list of possible answers. In the example in Table 6.1, the questions appear at random, and students need to click on each individual audio to listen to the question, so that they can link it to the answer.

The activity in Table 6.2 expects students to understand the direction line and the different possible options and select the appropriate clothing for the weather. This is a drag and drop activity where students select the labels of the clothing they would need to pack (Table 6.2).

The activity in Table 6.3 requires students to read and comprehend some sentences and indicate if they are true or false.

TABLE 6.2 [Selection/Drag and Drop] Voy a esquiar en los Pirineos y hace frío. Selecciona **ocho** prendas de ropa necesaria.

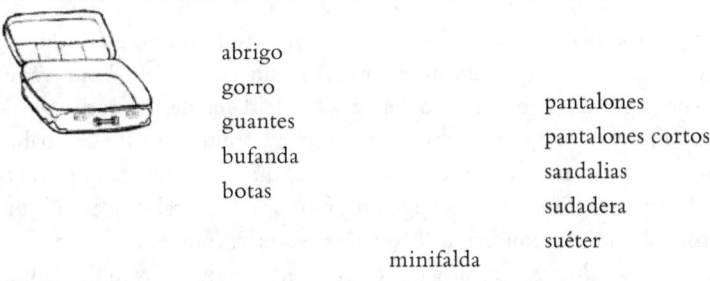

abrigo
gorro
guantes
bufanda
botas

pantalones
pantalones cortos
sandalias
sudadera
suéter

minifalda

TABLE 6.3 [True/False] Indica si son lógicas estas oraciones.

a	Cuando hace calor, llevo una bufanda. F
b	Cuando llueve, llevo botas de agua. C
c	En verano, las personas llevan gorro y guantes. F
d	Cuando hace buen tiempo, mi hermana lleva falda. C
e	Cuando hace frío, mi mamá lleva sandalias. F

6.8 Conclusion and Post-Pandemic Lessons

There is clear evidence that modernising assessment efforts should be implemented for low-stakes placement exams. Creating placement exams that utilise a broader spectrum of language assessment, reading comprehension, form-function mappings, and listening skills, areas that can be easily integrated via web and mobile apps, is an area of language assessment that need to be examined. Web and mobile apps are being utilised for virtually all high-profile tasks (banking, medicine, communication, among other), and many educational activities are being completed by mobile users. The current ubiquity of mobile technologies (Kukulska-Hulme & Shield, 2008; Stockwell & Hubbard, 2013) and the increasing affordability of data plans and connections (Palomo-Duarte et al., 2014) require us to think of ways in which these resources can be utilised in language assessment. Additionally, placement exams must embrace the reality of teaching and assessment, especially as the pandemic made it incumbent upon stakeholders to think about *assessment without borders*. The COVID-19 pandemic clearly forced thinking about adaptability, and social responsibility. Placement exams ought to be adaptable to a variety of language learners, including heritage language learners, and other learners in diverse contexts using available resources, while appropriately targeting language proficiency outcomes. The pandemic fashioned education without borders. *Assessment without borders* is an exercise in reflective practice, brought upon by the COVID-19 global pandemic. Schools across the world had to shut down and scramble to take advantage of available resources. The teaching and assessment during COVID-19 were mobile, and if not done on mobile devices, were at least completed in a mobile fashion, away from desks and proctoring centres. *Proctorio, Examity*, and other remote-assessment services became key players as institutions shifted their labour remotely. However, assessment on the go has always had fertile ground. As mobile devices (and technology generally) continue to improve in their capabilities, they have also been turned into devices of choice for a myriad of functional tasks. Placement exams for language programs are a logical stop at this journey of transformation of education. Most importantly, mobile assessment creates affordances that do not typically exist with other devices. From their ability to seamlessly record audio, to the myriad of touch-enabled behaviours, gestures, and taps, mobile devices have unique built-in tools to transform assessment. While utilising mobile devices is necessary for emphasising adaptability, it must be noted that placement exams should look beyond the basic task of identifying which class a student should place next in. They must embrace the culture of the program, and the culture of the institution, in addition to utilising existing technology. Additionally, these must be paired with a philosophy of placement: should a placement exam place a student in the next course, or should it additionally allow the student to identify their place in the language program? Having students understand the concept and the value of proper placement will help students understand the rationale for placement and its link to recruitment. As noted by Beaudrie and Ducar (2012), placement exams should look beyond the score of the placement exams to help with students' retention and success.

Creating low- and high-stakes mobile and adaptive exams that focus on the creation of proficiency-based questions, that represent different language varieties, and target all types of learners, including heritage language learners, would benefit language programs globally.

References

Anderson, M., & Perrin, A. (2018, May 30). *Nearly one-in-five teens can't always finish their homework because of the digital divide*. Pew Research Center. Retrieved October 30, 2021, from https://www.pewresearch.org/fact-tank/2018/10/26/nearly-one-in-five-teens-cant-always-finish-their-homework-because-of-the-digital-divide/

Barnwell, D. P. (1996). *A history of foreign language testing in the United States: From its beginning to the present*. Bilingual Press.

Beaudrie, S., & Ducar, C. (2012). Language placement and beyond: Guidelines for the design and implementation of a computerized Spanish heritage language exam. *Heritage Language Journal, 9*(1), 77–94.

Brown, J. D. (1989). Improving ESL placement tests using two perspectives. *TESOL Quarterly, 23*(1), 65–83.

Burston, J. (2013). Mobile-assisted language learning: A selected annotated bibliography of implementation studies 1994–2012. *Language Learning & Technology, 17*(3), 157–224. Retrieved from http://llt.msu.edu/issues/october2013/burston.pdf

Campbell, R., & Rosenthal, J. (2000). Heritage language education. In J. Rosenthal (Ed.), *Handbook of undergraduate second language education* (pp. 165–184). Lawrence Erlbaum.

Chapelle, C. A., & Voss, E. (2016). 20 years of technology and language assessment in language learning & technology. *Language Learning & Technology, 20*(2), 116–128. Retrieved from http://llt.msu.edu/issues/june2016/chapellevoss.pdf

Chapelle, C. A., & Voss, E. (2017). Utilizing technology in language assessment. In E. Shohamy & L. Or (Eds.), *Encyclopedia of language and education, Vol. 7. Language testing and assessment* (pp. 149–161) Springer International Publishing. Retrieved from https://doi.org/10.1007/978-3-319-02261-1_10

Cummins, J. (1999). *BICS and CALP: Clarifying the distinction*. ERIC. Retrieved from https://files.eric.ed.gov/fulltext/ED438551.pdf

Dunkel, P. A. (1999). Considerations in developing or using second/foreign language proficiency computer adaptive tests. *Language Learning & Technology*, *2*(2), 77–93.

Fairclough, M. (2006). Language placement exams for heritage speakers of Spanish: Learning from students' mistakes. *Foreign Language Annals*, *39*(4), 595–604.

Goetler, S. (2018). Normalizing online learning. In N. Arnold, & L. Ducate (Eds.), *Engaging language learners through CALL* (pp. 51–92). Equinox.

Gutierrez, M. J., & Fairclough, M. (2006). Incorporating linguistic variation into the classroom. In R. Salaberry, & B. Lafford (Eds.), *The art of teaching Spanish* (pp. 173–192). Georgetown University Press.

Kétyi, A. (2015). Practical evaluation of a mobile language learning tool in higher education. In F. Helm, L. Bradley, M. Guarda, & S. Thouësny (Eds.), *Critical CALL – Proceedings of the 2015 EUROCALL conference* (pp. 306–311). Research-publishing.net. Retrieved from https://doi.org/10.14705/rpnet.2015.000350

Kukulska-Hulme, A., & Shield, L. (2008). An overview of mobile assisted language learning: From content delivery to supported collaboration and interaction. *ReCALL*, *20*(3), 271–289. https://doi.org/10.1017/S0958344008000335

Larson, J. W., & Hendricks, H. H. (2013). A context-based online diagnostic test of Spanish. *CALICO Journal*, *26*(2), 309–323.

Long, A. Y., Shin, S.-Y., Geeslin, K., & Willis, E. W. (2018). Does the test work? Evaluating a web-based language placement test. *Language Learning & Technology*, *22*(1), 137–156. https://doi.org/10125/44585

Palomo-Duarte, M., Berns, A., Dodero, J. M., & Cejas, A. (2014). Foreign language learning using a gamificated APP to support peer-assessment. In. F. J. García-Peñalvo (Ed.), *Proceedings TEEM'14. Second international conference on technological ecosystems for enhancing multiculturality* (pp. 381–386). ACM. Retrieved from https://doi.org/10.1145/2669711.2669927

Puckett, C., & Rafalow, M. (2020). COVID-19, technology, and implications for educational equity (sociology of education). *Footnotes: A Publication of the American Sociological Association*, *48*(3), 34–35.

Purpura, E., Davoodifard, M., & Voss, E. (2021). Conversion to remote proctoring of the Community English Language Program online placement exam at Teachers College, Columbia University. *Language Assessment Quarterly*, *18(1)*, 42–50. https://doi.org/10.1080/15434303.2020.1867145

Richter, F. (2013, September 30). *Infographic: 5 billion people to use mobile phones by 2017*. Statista Infographics. Retrieved October 1, 2021, from https://www.statista.com/chart/1517/worldwide-mobile-phone-users/

Rilliard, M. (2020). Adaptability 2.0: Tackling the challenges of the COVID-19 crisis. *Second Language Research & Practice*, *1*(1), 179–182. http://hdl.handle.net/10125/69853

Roever, C. (2001). Web-based language testing. *Language Learning & Technology*, *5*(2), 84–94. https://doi.org/10125/25129

Rossomondo, A. (2020). Flexibility is the watchword. *Second Language Research & Practice*, *1*(1), 164–167. http://hdl.handle.net/10125/69850

Savignon, S. J. (1985). Evaluation of communicative: The ACTFL proficiency guidelines. *Modern Language Journal*, *69*, 129–134.

Shin, S.-Y. (2012). Web-based language testing. In C. Coombe, B. O'Sullivan, P. Davidson, & S. Stoynoff (Eds.), *The Cambridge guide to language assessment* (pp. 274–279). Cambridge University Press.

Shohamy, E. (2011). Assessing multilingual competencies: Adopting construct valid assessment policies. *The Modern Language Journal*, *95*(3), 418–429. https://doi.org/10.1111/j.1540-4781.2011.01210.x

Sohn, S., & Shin, S. (2007). True beginners, false beginners, and fake beginners: Placement strategies for Korean heritage speakers. *Foreign Language Annals*, *40*(3), 407–418.

Stockwell, G., & Hubbard, P. (2013). *Some emerging principles for mobile-assisted language learning. The international research foundation for English language education* (pp. 1–15). Retrieved from http://www.tirfonline.org/english-in-the-workforce/mobile-assistedlanguage-learning/some-emerging-principles-for-mobile-assisted-language-learning

Urlaub, P. (2020). It takes a village: Digitizing domestic summer programs to confront COVID-19. *Second Language Research & Practice*, *1*(1), 149–154. http://hdl.handle.net/10125/69847

Valdés, G. (1989). Teaching Spanish to Hispanic bilinguals: A look at oral proficiency testing and the proficiency movement. *Hispania*, *72*, 392–401.

Valdés, G. (2000). Introduction. In L. A. Sandstedt (Ed.), *Spanish for native speakers. AATSP professional development series handbook for teachers K-16* (Vol. 1) (pp. 1–2). Harcourt College Publishers.

Vegas, E. (2020). *School closures, government responses, and learning inequality around the world during COVID-19*. The Brookings Institution.

Villa, D. (1996). Choosing a "standard" variety of Spanish for the instruction of native Spanish speakers in the U.S. *Foreign Language Annals*, *29*(2), 191–200.

Zabaleta, F. (2007). Developing a multi-media, computer-based, Spanish placement test. *CALICO Journal*, *24*(3), 675–692.

Zourou, K. (2014). Review of Assessment in Game-Based Learning: Foundations, Innovations, and Perspectives by D. Ifenthaler, D. Eseryel, & X. Ge (Eds.). *Language Learning & Technology*, *18*(3), 47–51. Retrieved from http://llt.msu.edu/issues/october2014/review3.pdf

SECTION II
Reactions to L2 E-Assessment during the COVID-19 Pandemic

7
RESPONDING TO THE PANDEMIC IN NEW ZEALAND

Opportunities and Challenges for Language Assessment in One Tertiary Institution

Martin East, Deborah Walker-Morrison, and Viviane Lelièvre-Lopes

THE UNIVERSITY OF AUCKLAND, AUCKLAND, NEW ZEALAND

7.1 Introduction

The COVID-19 pandemic has been recognised internationally as 'an unprecedented global crisis' (Han et al., 2020, p. 1525), and arguably the most disruptive event to have occurred on a global scale in many decades. It heralded unparalleled challenges, reverberations, and changes at all levels of society. In the education sector, initiatives that were already beginning to emerge pre-pandemic, such as moves to more blended and technologically mediated teaching, learning, and assessment, were vastly accelerated, but often without the appropriate training or infrastructure to ensure optimum course delivery. In this chapter, we present the case of changes to assessments of students' language proficiency made at the University of Auckland, Aotearoa-New Zealand. The chapter focuses on what the unstable and unpredictable scenario precipitated by COVID-19 meant for French as an additional language (L2) at the first year/*ab initio* level, that is, levels A1–A2 on the Common European Framework of Reference or CEFR (Council of Europe, 2001). With a specific focus on the productive skills of writing and speaking, we explore perceived challenges to the validity, reliability, and fairness of the assessments emerging from responses to the crisis, and consider some lessons learned from these experiences.

7.2 The New Zealand Context

As the pandemic unfolded in 2020, New Zealand was lauded internationally for its swift, positive, and successful response since the first case of the virus was confirmed in the country at the end of February that year (e.g., Han et al., 2020; Robert, 2020). In a lockdown strategy described as 'going hard and going early' (Hickey, 2020; Jamieson, 2020), the government implemented a so-called zero-COVID tolerance policy with a view to halting community transmission. A full month-long nationwide lockdown was instituted in late March, followed by a marginally less restrictive lockdown for a further two weeks. By early June, community transmission had been brought under control, minimal restrictions were in place, and life was almost as normal. Nonetheless, for Auckland (New Zealand's largest city), the challenges in the situation were exacerbated later in 2020 by sudden but shorter regional lockdowns when cases again emerged.

From a social (community) perspective, the New Zealand strategy at the time was, by and large, highly successful. However, the tertiary sector, including the University of Auckland, was substantially negatively impacted and confronted several challenges. First, the arrival of COVID-19 towards the start of the academic year 2020, and the subsequent sudden implementation of the first national lockdown, meant that all staff across the University were required to make abrupt, radical, and unanticipated changes to teaching (literally 3 weeks into our first 12-week semester). Initially, all teaching was moved online (with a one-week suspension of teaching in Week 4 to make the sudden transition), and remained online for the whole of Semester 1 (March to June 2020). Face-to-face classes did resume in Semester 2 (July to October) for a total of 7 out of the 12 weeks, when there were zero COVID cases in the community, but teaching was again disrupted by two short lockdowns (August–September and November), the second of which came in the middle of the final examination period.

Furthermore, border closures instituted from early in 2020 meant that many international students were unable to take up study places. Thus, in addition to periods of entirely online teaching and assessment, we were compelled to operate in a dual mode (face-to-face and online) in order primarily to meet the needs of international students stranded overseas. The University already had in place a robust online Learning Management System (LMS) – Canvas. All staff were additionally given access to paid Zoom accounts to ensure that teaching could continue online. Nevertheless, the vast majority of staff were unfamiliar with using Zoom for teaching purposes, and the online work (which was, after all, a response to an unanticipated crisis) took place in a largely hurried and variably supported way.

Brown et al. (2021) presented an overview of the preliminary findings of a student-focused study that investigated New Zealand tertiary students' perceptions of their online experiences during 2020. Valid survey responses ($n = 952$) were collected from all eight universities. Survey data were supplemented by interviews and focus groups, including both on- and off-shore students. Inevitably, both benefits and challenges for teaching and learning emerged. A short media release that summarised findings (Gedera et al., 2021) raised issues around assessments. With regard to the *L2 teaching* experience, at least at the University of Auckland, Wang and East (2020) documented what the lockdown circumstances meant for Mandarin language courses, framing the scenario as the development of an emergency curriculum.

The shift to technology-mediated courses raised many questions for assessment. Up to that time, a requirement for first year courses was that, overall, 50% of the assessment needed to be in supervised conditions. However, the pivot to online inevitably meant that, despite high-level technological infrastructure, many assessments became unsupervised. Problems inevitably emerged. Furthermore, assessment scenarios changed and developed throughout the year as the University was continually required to respond and adapt to the new learning environment and the uncertainties and inequities created by intermittent lockdowns. These changes impacted three crucial aspects of the assessment process: validity, reliability, and fairness. Before presenting the case in question, we briefly underscore the importance of these three concepts, with particular reference to assessing writing and speaking.

7.3 Validity and Reliability

Validity and reliability are two crucial dimensions likely to be significantly challenged by a sudden shift in delivery mode. That is, assessments designed to work in one medium (e.g., face-to-face, controlled [supervised/invigilated] conditions), and evaluated as valid and reliable in that context, may prove considerably less robust when delivered via a different medium and mode (e.g., online, unsupervised).

Let us apply these arguments to the skill of L2 writing. A traditional but nonetheless widespread assessment format is the so-called 'timed impromptu writing test' (Weigle, 2002, p. 59), whereby students have a set amount of time to complete, using pen and paper, a written response to a given prompt. The construct of interest here is 'writing performance' or 'the assessment *of* learning'. This represents 'a snapshot of test takers' writing proficiency at a particular point in time that aims to measure test takers' knowledge of key components of the writing construct such as vocabulary and grammar' (East, 2008, p. 170) where achievement is measured, usually in the form of a mark or series of marks. From this perspective, supervision contributes to the robustness and security of the test, hence dependability of the resultant scores.

If the traditional format for L2 writing assessment is moved into an unsupervised online environment, several problems emerge which threaten our ability to measure the writing performance construct. These include not being able to monitor the conditions in which the test takes place, or the extent to which test takers may have drawn on additional resources (such as automated translation tools) to complete the task. The evidence of writing proficiency, at least as defined above, is compromised, and the reliability of the evidence may be called into question. Of course, one solution may be to redefine the construct. That is, the writing proficiency construct might be more broadly defined as 'assessment *for* learning' (ARG, 2002a, 2002b), which represents 'an authentic reflection of writing in the "real world", including the strategies normally adopted to enhance the communicative effectiveness of the messages' (East, 2008, p. 170). Under such a construct definition, writing in one's own time, unsupervised, and with access to support resources, becomes perfectly valid. However, it requires a reinterpretation of what the evidence for proficiency (i.e., the writing sample produced by the test taker) actually tells us, and a re-envisioning of the construct we are aiming to measure. Even so, the accessibility of translation tools potentially distorts the evidence of both learning and proficiency provided by the writing sample.

7.4 Fairness

Validity and reliability are not the only issues that confront us as assessments are moved from one medium to another. There is also the issue of fairness. East (2008) suggested that one way of looking at fairness is to pose three questions:

> [D]id the test takers have the greatest opportunity to display in the test what they know and can do? Was there part of the test procedure that may have hindered this? What may be the consequences, for the test takers, of this?
>
> *(p. 26)*

Let us apply these arguments to the skill of L2 speaking. From a traditional perspective, the most common way of organising speaking assessments is 'to assess examinees one at a time, often in an interview format' (Luoma, 2004, p. 35). The single person interview has evolved over time by, for example, requiring testing in pairs or groups in recognition of a broader interactional competence construct whereby 'the examinees are asked to interact with each other, with the examiner observing rather than taking part in the interaction directly' (Luoma, 2004, p. 36) – see East (2016) for a New Zealand example. Nonetheless, the single interview test continues to be used, and can furthermore be used in different test conditions, such as in person, by phone or online, without necessarily compromising its authenticity. Indeed, speaking tests theoretically lend themselves well to online delivery.

With regard to fairness, several problems potentially emerge for speaking in the online environment. For example, there may be breakdowns in technology, including slow/unstable internet connection, microphone/speaker malfunctioning, or failure to record the speaking sample. Uneven access to quiet spaces and adequate technology – some students taking tests on their phone or iPad with others having access to large double screens – is another equity issue. In these cases, East's (2008) three questions become apposite. Finally, it is possible that some test takers may display support material on their own screens which is not visible to the examiner, with additional implications for validity and reliability.

7.5 Assessing Productive Language Proficiency: A New Zealand Case

In what follows, we present several assessment strategies designed to assess writing and speaking online in two *ab initio* courses in L2 French, taken consecutively in Semesters 1 and 2, 2020, at the University of Auckland. We explore the validity, reliability, and fairness of the assessments, as well as future opportunities and ongoing challenges presented for viable technology-mediated assessments in an online environment.

7.5.1 Semester 1, 2020

The first course, *Introductory French Language 1*, was directed by the third author of this chapter. The 12-week beginners course aims to help students reach basic (A1 level) proficiency in French in a variety of communicative situations relevant to France and the Francophone world. A balanced emphasis is placed on the four skill areas of reading, listening, speaking, and writing.

The course in 2020 had 169 enrolments. It was originally structured to comprise two 90-minute face-to-face, on campus class sessions per week, with class sizes ranging from 24 to 35. The course was delivered in a blended mode. That is, classes largely focused on oral and written production and were complemented by online multimedia material that introduced and practised language structures and vocabulary. Thus, the normal delivery pattern enabled emphasis on the productive skills (actual use of the language) during class time, with receptive skills and grammar input and practice already taking place online, and with several automatically marked formative online assessments (*devoirs* or homework activities) already built in.

As a consequence of the sudden lockdown, an announcement posted to students at the end of Week 3 (20th March) explained that 'we are transforming our course'. Although it was clearly recognised that the shift to fully online 'cannot presume to equate the experience of a traditional semester', it was made clear that the intention was 'to make it the best and most accessible possible'. It was further communicated to students that '[t]his is a stressful time for all of us, as things shift and information necessarily changes'. Students were assured that lecturers were 'doing our best to ensure that you are able to keep studying as effectively as possible, and we understand the need to stay flexible as the situation evolves' (Canvas course announcement, 20th March).

Attention was drawn to the materials that were already available online. Nevertheless, in a follow-up announcement in Week 5 that outlined the changes being made, it was stressed that a language class 'needs students to speak ... and interact with each other, to be the best (and most enjoyable) learning experience' (Canvas course announcement, 27th March). To facilitate this, the two 90-minute face-to-face lectures per week were modified as online 'learning packages' in two key ways. First, students were provided with two recorded and downloadable lectures of 60–70 minutes duration, with pauses for exercises. Thus, this input was made available asynchronously. Second, there would be two online and in real time tutorials per week with students' normal stream teacher. These would be delivered during the normal timetabled class time for participants' stream, but divided into two or three 20–25 minute slots (rather than one 50 minute slot). Students were subdivided into smaller groups (5–10 people), with different connection times, and distinct Zoom addresses, for the live Zoom session with their teacher. Students were instructed to go through the recordings before the online meeting, where the focus would be on interaction.

Furthermore, students were informed that assessments would need to be updated to reflect this new environment. A key driver here was to redesign the course for online delivery and assessment that would 'make all these aspects fair, accessible, and supportive of students' learning' (Canvas course announcement, 27th March). After considerable consultation with colleagues and students, several adjustments were made.

First was the removal of a classroom performance mark (focusing on oral skills and worth 10%) that would have been available to students in the face-to-face environment. It was considered that this was no longer fair, due essentially to inequitable access issues. Marks were redistributed. The online assessments that already existed, in the form of five homework exercises (*devoirs*), were weighted to be worth 20% of the final grade. Two further online tests, each worth 15%, focused on listening comprehension, dictation, reading comprehension, and grammar, as well as a small writing task. Speaking assessments (three very short video recordings to be uploaded to the LMS) represented 20%.

There was also a final 'examination', worth 30%, and delivered online. An oral component (15%) would be a one-on-one interaction with an examiner through Zoom. A written component (15%) would include reading comprehension, grammar, and writing. The writing task itself was highly structured, but designed to replicate an authentic scenario, with the prompt in English:

> You are leaving your house after lockdown has lifted, and you are meeting up with your old friends Claire and Andrew at a café. What would you say in these situations? Answer in French, in 1 to 3 phrases/sentences per question.

Questions to guide the responses required included greeting the friends, asking how they are, telling them how you are feeling, and describing living arrangements during lockdown (where you live, with whom, how difficult it is, etc.).

The final written examination replicated the format that had been used in previous iterations of the course, which had been entirely face-to-face, and students were directed to look at past papers as an indication of what might be required. Nonetheless, it represented a significant departure from regular practice in several respects.

First, standard practice had been for a purely written examination, worth 40% of the final grade, conducted during the University's formal examination period and taken as 'closed book' (i.e., timed examination conditions [2 hours] without access to any resources). In the new environment, the written component was reduced in weighting to 15% and was open book, and supplemented by the summative oral component (15%).

Second, due to the accommodations that the University insisted must be made for students working in this new fully online environment, all students were to be given a 24-hour window for the completion of any written assessed elements, without any imposed time limits within that window. Although it was *suggested* that students should spend up to 2 hours completing the written examination, in reality this was not controllable.

Third, students were asked to assent to an online Academic Honesty Declaration that they would complete the assessment 'in a fair, honest, responsible, and trustworthy manner'. This included declaring that the assessment was the students' own work, that no unauthorised help had been solicited, and that, for example, the writing tasks in the assessment had been completed independently, using only the tools and resources defined for use in the assessment. Again, control for the application of these conditions was impossible. In several respects, therefore, the ability to collect genuine evidence of (for example) writing proficiency (at least when the measurement of writing was conceptualised from a controlled and time-constrained perspective) was deemed to have been compromised.

The newly introduced oral component of the final examination (a one-on-one Zoom interview of approximately 7 minutes, with 10 minutes preparation time prior to the test) presented an opportunity to provide more scope for the collection of genuine evidence of proficiency than the writing component. The format was extensively practised in the online tutorials. Individual video meetings with the examiner included three tasks: monologue (2 minutes maximum) to be prepared during the 10 minutes in the Zoom waiting room (self-introduction and response to a set task, such as *talk about your family*); dialogue (2.5 minutes maximum) without preparation (questions from the examiner touching on different topics from the course, with answers expected to have some detail, not just yes/no); and document (2.5 minutes maximum) without preparation (reading a text of approximately 60–80 words out loud, and describing a document taken from the textbook, for example, an image of a scene, shared on screen by the examiner who would prompt with questions such as: qui est-ce? [who is it?]/Qu'est-ce que c'est? [what is it?]/Qu'est-ce qui se passe? [what's happening?]).

Due to the number of candidates being processed, time limits for each section had to be strictly adhered to, and candidates were advised not to be perturbed if they were cut off by the examiner. Candidates were instructed to log into Zoom, on whatever device they wished, 2 minutes prior to their scheduled time to troubleshoot any access issues. It was important for both audio and video to be used. Although there was no control over what candidates might do in the waiting room, and students were allowed to use support resources during this preparation time, there was control over who was in the waiting room at what time, and the real-time and time-constrained nature of the assessment, alongside the 'unseen' elements, created an environment in which potential for 'cheating' was limited.

Despite these more positive aspects of the oral assessment, several challenges in practice needed to be acknowledged.

First, it was apparent that not all students engaged with the live tutorials, and not all students had equal access to reliable computer equipment or mobile devices and high-speed broadband. Although a Canvas announcement communicated to students that they should 'please contact your teacher if Internet access is an issue for you during this lock-down: we do not want any student's learning compromised because of a broadband issue' (27th March), this was in reality a situation that was often out of the control of academic staff, although low-data alternative resources were offered where possible.

An allied concern was that real-time and time-constrained assessment could be compromised when unanticipated technological issues arose, such as internet outages, screens freezing, interrupted connections, and hardware challenges (e.g., sound or webcam not working). Although steps were taken to mitigate these (e.g., the University offered dedicated study spaces with stable connections that could be accessed by individuals), these cases raised issues for whether the assessment opportunity was actually creating space for best evidence of proficiency to be collected.

A third concern, although arguably more theoretical than actual, was that it was impossible to control for what students could access on their screens, which would not be visible to examiners. However, the time-limited context of the oral examination, alongside the examiner's ability to monitor students' performances and the accommodation to allow students to have notes beside them, meant that in practice students' use of 'unauthorised' resources was highly unlikely.

7.5.2 Semester 2, 2020

The second semester of the 2020 academic year began in July at a time when New Zealand had emerged from lockdown and, initially at least, on-campus courses could resume. The return to a level of normality was gladly received. However, although the on-campus taught classes (2 × 90 minutes) resumed as normal at the start of the semester, they were moved back online in Week 6, when Auckland was returned to lockdown due to cases of COVID-19 emerging in the community. Students subsequently returned to campus for the last four weeks of the semester.

The second course, *Introduction to French Language 2*, directed and co-taught by the second author, followed on directly from the first and utilised the same blended learning class structure, textbook and online *devoirs*. By the end of the second course, it was anticipated that students obtaining a pass grade would reach a level of competency in the four skills equating roughly to CEFR level A2. There were 51 participants.

For assessment purposes, 70% of the course grade was allocated to different types of coursework (including oral classwork, recorded speaking assignments that allowed resources for preparation and rehearsal, and written tests), and 30% was allocated to a final written examination. This represented a small adjustment to the weightings that had applied in 2019 (60% coursework and 40% final examination). One significant change was the decision to move gap-fill dictation and listening comprehension assessments from a controlled test environment to auto-marked online 'tests' (single attempt, restricted time but allowed use of resources). Of the two in-class writing tests originally scheduled, the first was cancelled due to lockdown and the grade weighting was transferred to the second which was held under normal supervised conditions.

For most of the course, and with the brief lockdown from Week 6 to Week 8 seemingly behind us, it was anticipated that the final examination would be taken as planned, in a controlled face-to-face environment. However, almost two weeks into the examination period, Auckland went into lockdown again and a snap decision was made by the University to pivot all remaining examinations online, together with a requirement that the examination should resemble, as far as possible, its original face-to-face form. Thus, although now fully online and unsupervised, the examination was still described as 'closed book', and the Academic Honesty Declaration was required and deemed to be fulfilled by those who completed the assessment. This time, a time limit was imposed. That is, the 24-hour completion window that had been applied in Semester 1 was removed, and students were required to take the online examination at the time at which the original face-to-face examination had been scheduled. (The University did, however, factor in an extra 15 minutes to allow for technical difficulties.)

The first section of the examination paper focused on writing (worth just over 10% of the final grade, which was half the weighting of previous years). Candidates were required to write between 180 and 200 words in French, on one of two unseen topics given in French.

In an attempt to replicate examination conditions as closely as possible, students were required to submit the assignment as a hand-written (and subsequently scanned) submission.

A practice activity was offered and it was transparently stated that submissions that were not hand-written (i.e., those that were electronically processed or typed) would not be graded. A Canvas announcement to students (18th November) made it clear that 'we are requiring handwritten essays because the Exam is Closed Book, which means NO external resources are allowed, including editing tools (Spelling & Grammar Check) available in Word'. To minimise the incidence of serious academic dishonesty, either via the use of automatic translation tools to produce their essay or by having it written by a third party, the following warning was added: 'You will not gain points for using structures and vocabulary that have not been presented during the course'.

Oral assessments were essentially the same as those that had been used in 2019. Since classes had been face-to-face for 9 out of 12 weeks, and since students had improved access to and familiarity with Zoom, it was possible to maintain the participation grade, albeit with relaxed minimum attendance requirements. This meant that a live Zoom-based summative oral examination was not required. Spoken proficiency was also assessed by two short video-recorded presentations (each worth 5%), with instructions about what to cover and opportunity to draw on support resources.

7.6 Discussion

The adjustments to assessments presented above raise crucial issues, not only for the shift to unsupervised and not fully controlled online assessments, but for assessments in general. The modes of assessment in play before the imposition of lockdowns tended towards a more traditional assessment *of* learning paradigm where controlling conditions for certain high-stakes assessments was deemed important, in terms of denying access to resources and/or requiring identity verification (ensuring that work was the student's own). The move to online assessment carried over that expectation. Thus, although some oral assessments included pre-recorded videos which allowed and encouraged use of resources, at least in preparation, this was counterbalanced (in part) by the oral examination (first course) and the in-class (i.e., in real time) performance mark (second course).

The implicit assumption of the more traditional assessment paradigm is that valid and reliable assessment relies on measuring students' unaided subject-matter acquisition and retention (Gipps & Stobart, 2003; Glaser, 1990). From this perspective, cases of students soliciting support (whether from peers or other resources) are deemed to be a serious and compromising matter. The reality facing academic staff was that full 'control' in the entirely online environment was all but impossible.

As expected, the prolonged move to online classes in Semester 1 and the emotional disruption caused by the pandemic negatively impacted students' learning. More importantly, it became clear that negative impacts were in fact exacerbated by the University's decision-making around the conditions of online assessments in Semester 1, which had an unfortunate spill-over effect into Semester 2. There was, for example, evidence, two weeks into the Semester 2 course, that students had not made the progress in the Semester 1 course that would have been anticipated in normal circumstances. This was despite the higher-than-normal final grades in Semester 1 – following the required shift to non-timed unsupervised assessments *and* a universal grade bump (e.g., A- to A) by increasing all students' overall percentage marks by 5%. As a consequence, course input for the second French course needed to be simplified and slowed down. Moreover, one student in the second course who had graduated from the first with a very high grade reported facing difficulties in keeping up with the demands of the second course and, despite the slowed pace, decided to withdraw. This student went so far as to attribute the high final assessment grade the student had received to the extended time period and to following a general trend of making extensive use of (forbidden) resources. Whatever this student may have relied on to get through the examination, it would seem that subject-matter acquisition and retention (i.e., learning) were markedly compromised.

The uncertain and unstable circumstances that surrounded Semester 2, 2020, continued to create significant challenges for all staff. Staff and students had genuinely begun Semester 2 with a sense of optimism that the worst may have been behind us and that tight border controls would keep the virus at bay, allowing members of the local community to get on with their lives relatively normally. This was not to be. Seen from an assessment perspective, the move back towards the status quo, as represented in summative controlled conditions examinations, was once more thrown into jeopardy. However, the stopgap solution – transferring written examinations pretty much 'as is' to the online environment – was at once both artificial and unrealistic.

7.7 Conclusion and Post-Pandemic Lessons Learned

At the time of writing this chapter, we in Auckland were once more faced with an ongoing lockdown that seriously disrupted the end of our academic year 2021, sending classes back online for 7 out of 12 weeks of Semester 2. Furthermore, borders remained closed throughout 2021, and even when on-campus classes were possible (as in Semester 1), students studying at a distance had to be catered for alongside on-campus students (who would also finish the academic year online). Nonetheless, as we reflected on our experiences during 2020, and as we anticipate a brighter future with the increasing roll-out of vaccines across the world and positive moves in 2022 to begin reopening our borders, several lessons were learned.

There is no 'one size fits all' when it comes to valid, reliable, and fair technology-mediated assessments. In the course of 2020, colleagues involved in the two courses had several conversations, facilitated by the second and third co-authors in their respective courses, around how to modify the assessments successfully to make them as meaningful as possible in this online environment. They devised a number of modifications that they perceived were manageable and reasonably effective. This included, for example, decreasing the weighting of the final examination in both semesters, and adding the extra oral component in Semester 1. The two lecturers differed in the approaches and modifications they made to assessments, driven in part by perceived differences in the two student cohorts. This exercise in personal and professional autonomy reflects a reality expressed by Bachman and Palmer (2010):

> In any [assessment] situation, there will be a number of alternatives, each with advantages and disadvantages. … If we assume that a single 'best' test exists, and we attempt either to use this test itself, or to use it as a model for developing a test of our own, we are likely to end up with a test that will be inappropriate for at least some of our test takers.
>
> (p. 6)

In light of no one size fitting all, it is important to continue reflecting on the purposes of assessment. East (2008) acknowledged the assessment dilemma emerging from apparent tensions between two assessment paradigms – the assessment *of* learning and assessment *for* learning, or – to use the expressions penned by Gipps and Murphy (1994) – assessment for 'managerial and accountability' purposes that relies on controlled conditions and timed tests versus assessment for 'professional and learning' purposes that draws on a range of assessment types, including those that set no time limits and allow for various kinds of support. In this context, East wrote:

> The big dilemma is that the two assessment paradigms are not mutually exclusive. We cannot say that either one is 'right' or 'wrong', 'better' or 'worse'. They are just different, and based on different assumptions about what we want to measure. As a result, there is tension between them and often an attempt to 'mix and match', with assessment *for* learning sometimes taking the dominant position in the arguments, and with the assessment *of* learning staking its claim when there is a feeling that its influence is being watered down.
>
> (p. 9)

The two courses under consideration in this chapter evidence the use of assessment opportunities that reflect a 'mix and match' approach. This was true even before COVID. That is, up to the events precipitated by the pandemic, the courses in question utilised a 'hybrid' assessment model that allowed for both formative and summative assessment opportunities, and this balance was considered important. Assessment practice was, however, also shaped and constrained by strong institutional requirements for a more traditional testing paradigm, namely the University's requirement that all first year courses include 50% of the total grade derived from assessments carried out under test conditions (such as a final examination). This reflected an established assessment *of* learning culture. The pandemic forced the institution to review this practice and accommodate greater flexibility. Thus, early in 2021, and in light of negative experiences with non-supervised online examinations, the decision was taken, at the departmental level, to opt many future L2 assessments out of the traditional final examination format. Instead, lecturers have been free to experiment with different assessment types (including smaller-scale, lower-stakes assessments in a variety of conditions). Seen from a perspective that encourages mixing and matching but that might now place greater emphasis on assessment *for* learning, this is arguably one positive, if unintended, consequence of the transition to online, technologically mediated assessments. Nevertheless, it has become clear that, in the absence of invigilation tools that are reliable, cost-effective and acceptable to students, any written assessment paradigm, whether *for* or *of* learning, is hard to implement in an online world. A tension still exists around ensuring adequate measurement of learning.

One finding emerging from the 2020 study into students' experiences with online learning in New Zealand (as reported by Gedera et al., 2021) was that many students struggled with the traditional examination format which required them to take a closed book examination at a particular set time, and expressed a preference for non-time-constrained open book assessments. Reflecting the managerial and accountability concerns of the more traditional assessment methods, the researchers commented that the latter approach 'might also help minimise problems with cheating and academic integrity in the online environment' (para. 20). That is, from an assessment *for* learning perspective, cheating and academic integrity no longer define the central concerns of assessment events.

One of the clear emerging benefits of attempts to overcome the obstacles for assessment created by the move to online in our context is that colleagues have become more formative in orientation, and more inventive in their attempts to overcome the obstacles. It must also be acknowledged that this was not easy. A huge amount of extra work was generated, and the process is not necessarily tenable in the long run. At this point, however, it seems that, despite questions that remain, the status quo has shifted somewhat away from the assessment *of* learning and more towards assessment *for* learning. Indeed, one area for potential exploration might be assessment *as* learning, an approach whereby students are encouraged to take responsibility for their own learning and become their own, or their peers', assessors, utilising formal and informal feedback and self-assessment to plot the next steps in their learning journeys. No doubt further lessons will emerge as we enter into a 'new normal' whereby blended learning and fully online course access by a range of students will define a new status quo.

References

ARG. (2002a). *Assessment for learning: 10 principles*. Retrieved from http://www.assessment-reform-group.org.uk

ARG. (2002b). *Testing, motivation and learning*. University of Cambridge, Faculty of Education.

Bachman, L. F., & Palmer, A. (2010). *Language assessment in practice: Developing language assessments and justifying their use in the real world*. Oxford University Press.

Brown, C., Datt, A., Forbes, D., Gedera, D., & Hartnett, M. (2021). *Report: University students' online learning experiences in COVID-times*. Retrieved from https://studentonlinelearningexperiences.wordpress.com/

Council of Europe. (2001). *Common European Framework of Reference for Languages*. Cambridge University Press.

East, M. (2008). *Dictionary use in foreign language writing exams: Impact and implications*. John Benjamins.

East, M. (2016). *Assessing foreign language students' spoken proficiency: Stakeholder perspectives on assessment innovation*. Springer.

Gedera, D., Datt, A., Brown, C., Forbes, D., & Hartnett, M. (2021). *Beyond Zoom, Teams and video lectures – What do university students really want from online learning?* Retrieved from https://theconversation.com/beyond-zoom-teams-and-video-lectures-what-do-university-students-really-want-from-online-learning-167705

Gipps, C., & Murphy, P. (1994). *A fair test? Assessment, achievement and equity*. Open University Press.

Gipps, C., & Stobart, G. (2003). Alternative assessment. In T. Kellaghan, D. L. Stufflebeam, & L. A. Wingate (Eds.), *International handbook of educational evaluation* (pp. 549–575). Kluwer Academic Publishers.

Glaser, R. (1990). Toward new models for assessment. *International Journal of Educational Research, 14*(5), 475–483.

Han, E., Tan, M., Turk, E., Sridhar, D., Leung, G., Shibuya, K., Asgari, N., Oh, J., García-Basteiro, A., Hanefeld, J., Cook, A., Hsu, L. Y., Teo, Y. Y., Heymann, D., Clark, H., McKee, M., & Legido-Quigley, H. (2020). Lessons learnt from easing COVID-19 restrictions: An analysis of countries and regions in Asia Pacific and Europe. *The Lancet – Health Policy, 396*(10261), 1525–1534.

Hickey, B. (2020). *We must go hard and we must go early*. Retrieved from https://www.newsroom.co.nz/we-must-go-hard-and-we-must-go-early

Jamieson, T. (2020). "Go hard, go early": Preliminary lessons from New Zealand's response to COVID-19. *American Review of Public Administration, 50*(6–7), 598–605.

Luoma, S. (2004). *Assessing speaking*. Cambridge University Press.

Robert, A. (2020). Lessons from New Zealand's COVID-19 outbreak response. *The Lancet – Comment, 5*(11), e569–e570.

Wang, D., & East, M. (2020). Constructing an Emergency Chinese Curriculum during the pandemic: A New Zealand experience. *International Journal of Chinese Language Teaching, 1*(1), 1–19. https://doi.org/10.46451/ijclt.2020.06.01

Weigle, S. C. (2002). *Assessing writing*. Cambridge University Press.

8
ONLINE REMOTE (AT-HOME) ASSESSMENT OF LANGUAGE MODULES DURING COVID-19

Changes, Challenges, and Students' Perceptions

Isabel Balteiro

UNIVERSIDAD DE ALICANTE, ALICANTE, SPAIN

8.1 Introduction

The COVID-19 pandemic has severely and unprecedentedly impacted all aspects of our lives, including education. As a way to mitigate the negative impact of the pandemic and the ensuing lockdowns, higher education institutions were forced to completely and abruptly switch to (online) remote teaching and assessment in a matter of days and, in most cases, without previous education or preparation. Although technology-enhanced learning, teaching, and assessment methods had already been largely used in teaching and learning, many universities in Spain continued teaching their courses in a traditional way, mainly due to their compulsory attendance policy, and limited online teaching to some lessons or modules in Masters' degrees. However, with the arrival of the COVID-19 pandemic and the lockdowns, universities, like any other educational institutions, were 'forced' to exclusively rely on online resources in order to reduce the negative impact of the conditions imposed by the isolation. Lecturers experienced an increase in their workload and had to adapt contents overnight as well as address other challenges imposed by remote teaching and assessment, such as adapting materials to online platforms, caring and 'controlling' all the students in virtual environments, etc. (see, for example, Kebritchi et al., 2017; Zhang et al., 2020). Students, on their side, were overwhelmed by new content, a different context or teaching environment, the inconveniences of learning at home, the lack of infrastructure, loss of interactivity and social interaction, and also the feeling of anxiety and concern for the assessment and/or evaluation methods. In some cases this situation led them to employ dishonest ways of passing examinations

DOI: 10.4324/9781003221463-10

with less effort. Thus, as we shall see, conducting and taking examinations remotely during COVID-19 has given rise to a wide array of challenges for all the stakeholders involved in remote evaluation methods due to lack of training in many aspects, e.g., infrastructure, problems of lack of academic integrity, etc.

8.2 Review of the Literature

Assessment was significantly and negatively affected due to lockdowns and subsequent cancellations of in-person events imposed by COVID-19. The lack of previous preparation in many higher education institutions turned evaluation into a demanding task and, consequently, administering examinations or tests remotely and, more importantly, in a fair and authentic way, became a major challenge. As García-Peñalvo et al. (2020, p. 1) have described,

> [...] having to face an online evaluation is something that the face-to-face universities, and most of the distance or online universities, had never faced from an institutional perspective. The teaching staff and students, therefore, have to give a response that integrates methodological and technological decisions, while ensuring equity, legal certainty and transparency for all actors, internal and external.

The literature in general has so far primarily focused on the teachers: the challenges they encountered for adapting content, material or tests, and also on their work overload, already in pre-COVID circumstances (e.g., Sangrá Morer, 2006). However, learners also need some attention, as they have also been negatively affected by this new and unexpected situation, which has generated stress on all the players in the educational field. Although at first sight students may have seemed to have been least affected – as they apparently simply shifted from traditional classrooms to their homes, where they could comfortably receive education through online learning – they bore the brunt of the shift to remote instruction. As Xie et al. (2019) put it, moving to online teaching 'has significantly changed the way in which learners engage and learn' in general, but also individually, due to their particular circumstances, settings, infrastructures, etc. Furthermore, even though present-day learners are usually referred to as 'digital natives' (Prensky, 2001) or also as the 'net' or 'digital' generations (Ali, 2018; Tapscott, 1998), recent events seem to prove that, as already pointed out in studies predating COVID-19, they are not technologically so skilful as expected (see, for example, Shava et al., 2016). Students show a high degree of familiarity and 'receptiveness' (Willms & Corbett, 2003) towards technological tools and related applications and games but only for leisure and enjoyment purposes, which does not extend to serious and educational situations, where a low degree of acceptance and much stress is shown or perceived.

Within the context of remote assessment, Kearns (2012), who focuses on pre-COVID times, and Capsim (2018), who analyses assessment during the pandemic, explore the design and implementation and the purposes of formative and summative assessments, as well as how they are used for diagnosis and how these, jointly with appropriate feedback support, promote learning and teaching, and measure students' progress in higher education. Guangul et al. (2020) review the challenges faced by higher education institutions during COVID-19 but also the options of remote assessment that were (and still are) available in order to avoid violation of academic integrity. They argue that remote assessment methods may be classified in two large types, namely remote proctored examinations (time-constrained ones) and open-ended questions assessment. However, what is certainly more important is that the type of assessment chosen should meet certain quality criteria (e.g., validity, reliability, clarity, and avoidance of concerns with technical problems) in order to ensure that the assessment objectives are fulfilled (see also Hsiao & Watering, 2020).

A rather different matter is how this pandemic may have psychologically impacted the two main players in the learning process: students and teachers. In general, the two factors that have apparently and mostly affected psychological well-being are the loss of habits and routines, and psychosocial stress (see Wang et al., 2020), though fear of the virus, lack of information, and social rejection towards people infected are also important (Brooks et al., 2020). In addition to pre-pandemic studies on students' beliefs and anxiety in online foreign language learning (see, for example, Martin & Alvarez Valdivia, 2017), other scholars, such as Bautista León and López Miranda (2020), Espinosa Ferro et al. (2020), Fidalgo et al. (2020), Hussein et al. (2020), or Mirahmadizadeh et al. (2020), analyse students' attitudes, perceptions, and emotions towards the sudden closure of schools and distance education during the COVID-19 pandemic. Studies report changes in attitudes or difficulties in concentrating but also an increase in negative emotional states such as stress, anxiety, and depression, which may be due to the changes in the educational context (see Balluerka et al., 2020; Ozamiz-Etxebarria et al., 2020; Piña-Ferrer, 2020). Some works such as Almuraqab (2020), Bao (2020), or Kapasia et al. (2020) examine the impact of COVID-19 on learning through online teaching, while others such as Wagner and Krylova (2021) address placement tests and evaluation. However, to our knowledge, no attention has been paid to the changes and challenges as well as to students' attitudes and perceptions towards the sudden migration to remote assessment in English language modules during COVID-19, which are actually the focus of this chapter.

8.3 The Study

8.3.1 Context

The University of Alicante, the setting of the present study, resorted to remote online continuous, formative, and final assessment (https://www.informacion.es/alicante/2020/04/04/universidad-alicante-asume-examenes-podran-4741615.html; last accessed 03/21/2022). Assessment was one of the most, if not the most, critical, controversial, and challenging issue that caused uncertainty and anxiety among lecturers and students for different reasons, as shown below.

The search for validity, reliability, clarity, and avoidance of technical problems were, without any doubt, the main objectives that most of the teachers had in mind as regards assessment (on this see Montejo Bernardo, 2020). However, some institutions did not always contribute to the achievement of these quality measures and to the maintenance of academic standards. That was the case of, among others, the University of Alicante, where academic integrity and preventing fraud or restraining cheating seemed not to be among the priorities of academic authorities at that moment. Instead, and apparently on the basis of an (in)appropriate interpretation of rules of privacy, lecturers at the University of Alicante were explicitly prevented from requiring students to have their cameras and microphones on during examinations, and thus there were no mechanisms of proctoring (see the Students' Council document, https://web.ua.es/es/consejo-estudiantes/documentos/covid-19/comunicados-camaras.pdf or news such as https://periodismo.ull.es/libertad-estudiantil-rechaza-el-uso-de-camaras-durante-los-examenes/; last accessed 03/21/2022). Hence, there was no control on who was sitting an examination, doing it or even submitting it. Furthermore, students (and teachers) had to face technical problems of several types: there were not only technical issues derived from individual difficulties with Internet access or failures in Internet connections, but also some lack of skills or know-how on the students' side. Thus, students unsuccessfully fought to solve technological malfunctions that teachers were also unable to solve remotely, as well as some technical incidents and failures with the University online platform itself, which made assessment procedures more complicated in certain occasions (cf. Iturbe-Ormaeche et al., 2020, p. 9).

8.3.2 Objectives and Methodology

8.3.2.1 Objectives

This study focuses on the strategies and changes that occurred during COVID-19 lockdown that affected aspects, competences and contents evaluated, criteria employed, types of tasks used in evaluation, etc., but mainly on its impact on students' attitudes and perceptions towards pandemic-conditioned assessment of English language modules.

8.3.2.2 Participants

Only 64 (out of approximately 350) students in the English Studies degree, from different courses (70.3% from the 3rd year and the rest from the 4th), completed the questionnaire. The age range was between 20 and 23; while 84.4% were women, 10.9% were men, 3.1% were non-binary, and 1.6% preferred not to say. The relatively low response percentage (around 18.3% of the students in the major) may be due to students' demotivation, work overload (on this see, Kochu et al., 2022), general and pandemic fatigue, and boredom of surveys, which they were repeatedly asked to complete, though voluntarily.

8.3.2.3 Instruments

Only one survey was used to attempt to obtain a wide and general sampling from learners majoring in English Studies: a web-based survey was conducted in order to explore the challenges and perceptions of remote assessment of English language modules delivered to English Studies undergraduates. The questionnaire was prepared using Google Forms and a link was sent to all the learners in English language courses of this major at the University of Alicante. The survey contained 40 items on the learners' experience, challenges, and perceptions of online remote examinations, with the main focus on (1) determining whether, in the students' opinion, all the basic language contents and skills had been evaluated or whether they had been altered or disregarded; (2) identifying the factors that caused alterations in examination tasks, contents, or skills evaluated; (3) identifying factors affecting the students' preference for remote tests (or not), compared to on-campus examinations; (4) identifying students' examination dishonest practices during remote examinations; and (5) identifying learners' perception, feelings, and attitudes towards the online remote assessment. The survey had been previously validated by ten experts, who considered it to have a 4.7 (in a scale of 0 to 5) of validity. Note also that the Cronbach's alpha test has been carried out and it has resulted in 0.67, which means that the score coefficient is approaching 0.7, the 'acceptable' score.

8.3.2.4 Procedure

The 40-item anonymous and voluntary survey was distributed and at the disposal of all the students enrolled in the English Studies degree via a link in the university's virtual platform. This directed them to the Google Forms survey so that the results were easily stored and saved. There was no time limitation for students to complete the questionnaire which was available for two weeks at mid-term.

8.4 Results and Discussion

8.4.1 Perceptions on the University as a Teaching Institution

One of the main hypotheses underlying this study is that COVID-19 has brought great changes in academic life which may have seriously and negatively affected students and, consequently, their perception of the university as an institution or as a leader of knowledge.

Students' answers corroborate our hypothesis: 22% (14) of the students reported that after the lockdown they give more importance to face-to-face situations and human contact at university; 17% (11) maintained that with the new situation they see university as an institution which leads them to demotivation, monotony, stress, anxiety, and even loneliness; 11% (7) describe their/our university as worse, while 4.7% (3) considered it better, in spite of the feeling of loneliness that they were experiencing. More negative perceptions were reported by other learners, who in 4.7% (3) of the cases related a negative perception of university systems due to lack of empathy on the lecturers' side, as these only seemed to be worried about avoiding students' dishonest practices in examinations. After the impact of COVID-19, students showed a quite pessimistic vision: while 4.7% (3 students) described this 'new' university as boring, 6.25% (4 students) felt that universities were not (and are not) prepared for such a great change, a change that made 4 of them feel disappointed and reconsider university as an option in life, whereas other 6.25% (4) of the learners mentioned that the changes were not so marked, and 4.7% (3) of the participants thought that their perceptions and feelings had not been altered. A negative view was also provided by one participant (1.56%), who considered that universities are not capable of quickly adapting to unexpected changes. However, more positive approaches were also reported: 3% (2) stated that they now perceive traditional university teaching as old-fashioned while online remote teaching was seen as innovative, learning effective, and comfortable, unlike other 3% (2) who believed that this new situation made university more demanding for students, insofar as there are objectives they cannot reach.

8.4.2 Changes in Teaching and Assessment in English Language Modules

In general, participants in our survey reported important changes in the teaching of University English language modules, where the transition from a face-to-face to an online system seemed to go parallel with a move from more practical tasks to more theoretical teaching, despite a reduction in content. Similarly, they also mention loss of oral practice, both regarding speaking (e.g., debates) and listening tasks. Furthermore, other differences include monotonous, chaotic, boring, and tiring online lessons. Among the positive changes, other students mentioned higher and increasing participation on their side, and a more dynamic and enjoyable environment, which has led to more or better learning, probably one of the reasons for better results in assessments.

Besides changes in teaching, students also experienced shifts in assessment methods and other evaluation elements. Thus, they described new examination formats in English language modules, with a preference for final multiple-choice questions rather than other types of tasks to evaluate vocabulary or grammar, for example. Apart from that, more importance was given to formative submissions of practical assignments such as essay writing, whose number was increased. In general, the assessment of writing tasks, as well as the teaching of the writing skill itself, did not seem to be affected by the abrupt change from a face-to-face education to an online remote one. On the contrary, students claimed that the knowledge of all the contents, competences, and skills either taught or acquired were assessed.

However, unlike in traditional on-campus examinations, 67% of the participants state that less attention was paid to the evaluation of oral skills, namely speaking and listening, which were difficult to assess online. Accordingly, when speaking skills were evaluated online, multimodal features were not taken into account, something that is usually considered as basic for communication purposes and also especially relevant in assessing communication skills. Still, some speaking tests were carried out through either group or individual presentations and reading texts aloud in Google Meet, but also with the submission of video recordings. Similarly, listening skills were evaluated through different activities via Moodle: submission of reports, comprehension questions, writing tasks and analyses of podcasts, audiobooks, films, debates, TEDTalks, etc. Although naturally fluent debates, dialogues, and conversations were disregarded, on the one hand, and asynchronous listening tasks for assessment purposes were more arduous than on-campus listening tests, on the other. Students in general claimed to be satisfied with both the way their oral skills were assessed and the results obtained. Still, there is a 17% of critical students (11) who consider that teachers were only concerned with simplifying their own duties, with no regard for the learners' work overload in asynchronous moments and, also that more emphasis should have been placed on practice during online synchronous lessons.

As explained below, the online remote examinations were conditioned by a number of factors: first, teachers' lack of trust in learners, that is, concerns regarding plagiarism and other dishonest practices (e.g., contacting other people for help); second, the reduction in time and length of the examination contents and, thirdly, the awareness of potential Internet connection problems.

8.4.3 *Time and Reliability as Exam-conditioning Factors*

Exam duration time was reported as one of the most important factors affecting examinations and students' negative feelings and perceptions. In fact, 72% (46) of the students agree on this, 23.4% (15) believed that time did not influence examination processes, and only 4.6% (3) could not decide. Students considered that they were given excessively tight time in order to prevent misconducts or dishonest practices and this caused them anxiety and discomfort. However, failures in examination results do not seem to be conditioned by the time factor, but mostly by either lack of knowledge of material or plagiarism. Directly related to the time factor is the confidence factor, which presents exactly the same results, that is, 72% of the learners include teachers' lack of confidence on students as one of the factors conditioning examination progress, as just explained. Time constraints and reliability factors have highly contributed to the way examinations took place, as well as the content assessed and the tasks incorporated.

Probably to a lesser extent, according to the data obtained in the survey, but still important, medium reliability was another important factor that conditioned the exam contents and, hence, teachers' evaluation of the knowledge and skills acquired by students. While 51.56% (33) of the learners believed that the online medium conditioned the contents, activities, and competences evaluated as well as the way they were assessed, 36% (23) thought that it had no impact, and 12.5% (8) replied that they do not know and, hence, could not say.

8.4.4 Dishonest Practices during Online Remote English Language Examinations

Examination dishonesty seemed to be one of the major challenges for teachers to overcome, imposed by online remote testing. This was a general and common concern on the lecturers' side which was clearly expounded not only in online Faculty meetings during the lockdown but also in other publications (see Rodríguez & Esteban, 2020). When asked, over 67% (43) of the students reported no acts of dishonesty, while 33% (21), that is, one third of the students, admitted that they had used human, material, or technological help. Basically, they checked, used, or copied from lesson notes, Google, and/or academic articles; sought assistance from other people, friends or family either in person or by phone calls, WhatsApp, or even videoconferencing (including Skype). In spite of this, only around 11% (7) of the students believed that the high percentage of people passing examinations and also obtaining good grades could be due to dishonest practices, while the rest either could not find a reason or simply stated that they had more time to revise due to lockdown (20; 31.25%) and only 11% (7) considered that the examinations were probably easier than on-campus ones. This latter idea apparently conflicts with answers to the question of whether the 'lockdown' examinations were easier than usual, as 76.5% (49) participants believed that online remote English language tests were not easier than on-campus ones, and 12.5% (8) did not know, whereas only those 11% (7) felt that they were easier.

8.4.5 Students' Preference for Remote English Language Examinations

Unlike what we expected, given the good results obtained by students in online remote examinations (see also https://web.ua.es/es/actualidad-universitaria/2021/mayo2021/24-31/los-alumnos-de-la-ua-mejoraron-sus-calificaciones-un-20-durante-el-semestre-covid.html; last accessed 03/21/2022), the majority of respondents (39; 61%) preferred traditional on-campus examinations, while around one fourth of the students (16; 25%) preferred the online remote (at-home) option (cf. Saleh et al., 2022). For 14% (9) of the learners, their preference depended on the type of tests, examination tasks, and/or the contents and skills tested (multiple choice, open questions, oral test, listening comprehension, etc.).

8.4.6 Students' Attitudes and Feelings Before, During, and After Sitting Remote (At-Home) Testing

More than half of the respondents (41; 64%) reported that they felt either nervous or very nervous and almost 5% (3) felt anxious and stressed out *before* remote at-home examinations, while only around 19% (12) stated they felt calm or fine. More positive feelings were found in only 3% (2) of the students, who felt happy or confident. Interestingly enough, around 8% of the students (5) disclosed that they felt 'indifferent' or 'as usual'. Figures were quite similar when their feelings *during* the examinations are considered: 51.6% (33) claimed to be 'nervous' or 'very nervous', 14% (9) stated that they felt anxious and stressed out, and almost 8% (5) of them felt 'overwhelmed'. However, percentages change quite radically *after* the examination had finished: only 7.8% (5) of students said they felt nervous, while the highest percentage, one fourth of the students (16; 25%), reported that they felt relieved after ending the online remote examinations. To this, a 12.5% (8) of the students who declared a feeling of calmness should be added.

In line with the negative feelings describing what learners experienced just before, while or after taking online remote examinations taken from home, 34.4% (22) of the students expressed their negative attitude towards having online remote (at-home) tests in English language modules. However, more than half of the learners (34; 53%) related positive attitudes towards this remote evaluation of English language modules, such as 'very good', 'positive', 'participative', 'active', 'hard-working', 'highly motivated', 'highly involved', or 'tenacious'. While 7.8% (5) of learners showed indifference or lack of feeling and impartiality, 4.7% (3) of them claimed to have maintained the same attitude as that they had previous to the pandemic.

A high percentage of participants 81.25% (52) reported that they felt more anxiety in online remote examinations, mainly due to their fears of Internet connection failures during the test or at the moment of submitting it, and also uncomfortable for having family, pets, etc. at home while taking the tests. Unlike these, the rest of the students claimed they felt better in online at-home tests precisely because they were in a comfortable and familiar location.

8.4.7 Challenges Faced by Students in Online Remote English Language Module Examinations

Students reported a wide variety of challenges encountered when facing tests in English language modules during the lockdown period. Among others, the most common were: maintaining attention and lack of concentration in online remote tests; being able to submit papers, activities or tests within either the estimated time in synchronous tasks and/or within the deadline in asynchronous ones; maintaining the speed and/or a stable Internet connection; time management; being able to study from notes; talking or making an oral presentation to the teacher and all the students through the screen; overcoming the anxiety caused by online and remote oral examinations (14 students, 22% reported this); understanding teacher's instructions; passing tests; switching the camera on; using Moodle effectively and efficiently; being able to concentrate in order to read questions, think of the answers and/or choose the correct answer in tests; or even completing a well-written task.

8.5 Lessons Learned from the COVID-19 Crisis

Once this pandemic ends, and especially considering potential similar scenarios in the future, educational institutions should reconsider the experience gained during the COVID-19 crisis in order to make adjustments in the entire teaching-learning and assessment processes, and probably redesign module and programs using online remote technology. As St-Onge et al. (2021) put it, COVID-19 is 'the tipping point for integrating e-assessment in higher education practices'. In general, technology should be prepared in case of need, but also seen as a means to improve and facilitate teaching quality and maintain academic standards, in addition to some other benefits which are not within the scope of this chapter, such as socio-economic benefits (by making higher institutions more comprehensive and accessible to all, combatting inequality by providing education but also Internet access and devices), or being more environment-friendly with fewer people moving from home daily and hence using polluting means of transport, etc. Apart from that, at an institutional level, the pandemic has taught us that universities should carefully schedule online examinations in order to avoid the coincidence of many groups simultaneously using the online platforms or virtual classrooms and thus avoid failures or collapse such as those reported by subjects in our survey, but also prepare contingency procedures in order to address potential problems that may be more or less foreseeable.

As to online (at-home) assessment, the aforementioned results seem to indicate that an increase in continuous, formative, and diverse assessment tasks may be useful so that the weight of the final grade does not fall only on the final examinations, where avoiding dishonesty or misconduct may be a greater challenge. Lecturers should explore new ways of overcoming these problems as well as others that may arise while attempting to solve the initial ones. For example, in our study, students reported lack of time in completing their online remote examinations; such time restrictions appeared to be a measure adopted by language teachers to minimise the risks and prevent students from using other human, technological, or material (re)sources. Teachers should instead prepare different types of examinations which may not prevent from the use of materials and where the time limit fits the test conditions. More importantly, it would be highly advisable that institutions incorporate a varied range of e-proctoring solutions in order to contribute to academic honesty and rigour.

However, continuous formative tasks are not exempt of problems either, as learners may have asked other people to prepare their assignments, which in the case of English language modules could include essays, listening comprehension reports, etc. This could be balanced by requiring students to orally (or in a recorded video) explain their work. Furthermore, students' speaking skills may be assessed either by submitting videos or in synchronous oral presentations using videoconference tools such as Google Meet, Zoom, etc.

In addition to these, the greatest challenges are probably making students more self-confident and, hence, less anxious, worried, and nervous, and also contributing to teachers' trust of and sympathy with students, and, most of all, generating mutual understanding and a good communicative environment between teachers and learners.

8.6 Conclusions

The main findings of the study showed a general positive attitude towards online remote teaching on the learners' side, despite negative perceptions of the changes in the institution, as well as negative and stressful feelings such as anxiety or demotivation towards at-home online language tests due to a wide range of reasons. However, in line with the latter, there seems to be a preference for non-online testing by students with higher grades and higher skills in the foreign language and those who do not cheat, as attested in the data obtained for the present study.

In general, an urgent need appears to emerge to primarily improve and increase the range of (synchronous and asynchronous) assessment methods, tasks, and a better/higher combination of all of these, on the one hand. On the other, according to students' opinions and also considering our own experience and observation, lecturers seemed to be concerned about measures, such as e-proctoring, to prevent examination dishonesty, maintain academic integrity, and quality standards, and to be able to confirm the work has really been done by the student. All these means may also contribute to ameliorating and enriching students' perceptions of higher education institutions, whose transitions from face-to-face to online systems apparently do not always convince the learners. Unproctored assessment (and fear and suspicions about cheating) has led lecturers to embrace decisions such as an excessive limitation of time to complete examination so that students had no time to check other sources. This decision, however, makes students anxious and critical, although they sometimes admit human, technological, and material cheating.

Assessment is probably one of the most complex aspects of online education. In fact, even online or long/remote-distance universities (e.g., UNED in Spain) tend to conduct face-to-face examinations. This difficulty, together with the lack of institutional and academic experience and the abrupt and urgent changes, has increased the challenges of implementing the most appropriate solutions. In spite of this, unprepared lecturers have attempted to reproduce face-to-face assessment tasks and methods as well as including the same contents, competences, and skills, in the new online formats, either for their own convenience or to avoid disruptive situations for students. This might have been the best solution at a given moment, as technologies served as facilitators and there was no time for major changes. However, universities and higher institutions in general should educate their lecturers on how to use online environments, teaching, and assessment being their primary goals.

Although the Google Forms questionnaire has proven a valuable tool for obtaining data from students involved in English language online and remote assessment processes, the low number of participants limits the validity of this preliminary study, where gender and age have revealed themselves as non-significant elements, although female participants were comparatively over-represented. Further research with a larger population and at an institutional level is called for in order to make these findings more reliable or valid.

To conclude, we could learn from this experience that all the players involved in education should invest in different measures (time and/or money on connections, materials, teachers, and students' training) but also be academically and emotionally more empathic and generous. Moreover, they all should be allowed time to reflect, make decisions, adaptations, and reformulation when necessary, paying attention to challenges such as examination conduction, authenticity, reliability, and technological problems that affect students' perceptions of educational institutions.

References

Ali, W. (2018). Influence of evolving technology in emerging online lives of the digital native university students. *Asia Pacific Journal of Contemporary Education and Communication Technology*, 4(2), 141–155.

Almuraqab, N. (2020). Shall universities at the UAE continue distance learning after the COVID-19 pandemic? Revealing students' perspective. *International Journal of Advanced Research in Engineering and Technology*, 11(5), 226–233.

Balluerka, N., Gómez, J., Hidalgo, M. D., Gorostiaga, A., Espada, J. P., Padilla, J. L., & Santed, M. (2020). *Las consecuencias psicológicas de la COVID-19 y el confinamiento*. Servicio de Publicaciones de la Universidad del País Vasco.

Bao, W. (2020). COVID-19 and online teaching in higher education: A case study of Peking University. *Human Behavior and Emerging Technologies*, 2(2), 113–115.

Bautista León, A., & López Miranda, G. A. (2020). El género importa: Efectos esperados sobre la educación superior entre las mujeres mexicanas en tiempos de la pandemia por COVID-19. *Revista de Administración Pública*, 152(LV,2), 109–128.

Brooks, S. K., Webster, R. K., Smith, L. E., Woodland, L., Wessely, S., Greenberg, N., & Rubin, G. J. (2020). The psychological impact of quarantine and how to reduce it: Rapid review of the evidence. *Lancet, 395*(10227), 912–920.

Capsim. (2018). *The five levels of assessment in higher education.* Retrieved from https://www.capsim.com/blog/the-five-levels-of-assessment-in-higher-education/

Espinosa Ferro, Y., Mesa Trujillo, D., Díaz Castro, Y., Caraballo García, L., & Mesa Landín, M. (2020). Estudio del impacto psicológico de la COVID-19 en estudiantes de Ciencias Médicas, Los Palacios. *Revista Cubana de Salud Pública, 26*, 1–17.

Fidalgo, P., Thormann, J., Kulyk, O., & Lencastre, J. A. (2020). Students' perceptions on distance education: A multinational study. *International Journal of Educational Technology in Higher Education, 17*, 1–18.

García-Peñalvo, F. J., Corell, A., Abella-García, V., & Grande, M. (2020). Online assessment in higher education in the time of COVID-19. *Education in the Knowledge, 12*, 1–26.

Guangul, F. M., Suhail, A. H., Khalit, M. I., & Khidhir, B. A. (2020). Challenges of remote assessment in higher education in the context of COVID-19: A case study of Middle East College. *Educational Assessment, Evaluation and Accountability, 32*, 519–535.

Hsiao, Y. P., & Watering, G. A. (2020). *Guide for choosing a suitable method for remote assessment considerations and options.* University of Twente.

Hussein, E., Daoud, S., Alrabaiah, H., & Badawi, R. (2020). Exploring undergraduate students' attitudes towards emergency online learning during COVID-19: A case from the UAE. *Children and Youth Services Review, 119*, 105699.

Iturbe-Ormaeche, I., Albarrán, P., Collado, M. D., & Pérez, L. (2020). *Efecto del COVID-19 en los resultados académicos de los estudiantes de las universidades públicas valencianas.* Universidad de Alicante.

Kapasia, N., Paul, P., Roy, A., Saha, J., Zaveri, A., Mallick, R., Barman, B., Das, P., & Chouhan, P. (2020). Impact of lockdown on learning status of undergraduate and postgraduate students during COVID-19 pandemic in West Bengal, India. *Children and Youth Services Review, 116*, 105194.

Kearns, L. R. (2012). Student assessment in online learning: Challenges and effective practices. *Journal of Online Learning and Teaching, 8*(3), 198–208.

Kebritchi, M., Lipschuetz, A., & Santiague, L. (2017). Issues and challenges for teaching successful online courses in higher education: A literature review. *Journal of Educational Technology Systems, 46*(1), 4–29.

Kochu, K., Beena, T., & Sony, M. (2022). Student workload assessment for online learning: An empirical analysis during Covid-19. *Cogent Engineering, 9*, 2010509.

Martin, S., & Alvarez Valdivia, I. M. (2017). Students' feedback beliefs and anxiety in online foreign language oral tasks. *International Journal of Educational Technology in Higher Education, 14*(18), 1–15.

Mirahmadizadeh, A., Ranjbar, J., Shahriarirad, R., Erfani, E., Ghaem, H., Jafari, K., & Rahimi, T. (2020). Evaluation of students' attitude and emotions towards the sudden closure of schools during the COVID-19 pandemic: A cross-sectional study. *BMC Psychology, 8*(134), 1–7.

Montejo Bernardo, J. M. (2020). Exámenes no presenciales en época del COVID-19 y el temor al engaño. Un estudio de caso en la Universidad de Oviedo. *MAGISTER, 32*(1), 101–110.

Ozamiz-Etxebarria, N., Dosil-Santamaria, M., Picaza-Gorrochategui, M., & Idoiaga-Mondragon, N. (2020). Niveles de estrés, ansiedad y depresión en la primera fase del brote del COVID-19 en una muestra recogida en el norte de España. *Cadernos de Saúde Pública, 36*(4), 1–10.

Piña-Ferrer, L. (2020). El COVID 19: Impacto psicológico en los seres humanos. *Revista Arbitrada Interdisciplinaria de Ciencias de la Salud Salud y Vida, 4*(7), 188–199.

Prensky, M. (2001). Digital Natives, Digital Immigrants, part 1. *On the Horizon, 9*(5), 1–6.

Rodríguez, E., & Esteban, O. (2020). Los decanos de la Universidad de Oviedo, preocupados antes la "proeza" de hacer fiables los exámenes online. *El Comercio. (Ed. Digital)*.

Saleh, M. N., Salem, T. A. R., Alamro, A. S., & Wadi, M. M. (2022). Web-based and paper-based examinations: Lessons learnt during the COVID-19 pandemic lockdown. *Journal of Taibah University Medical Sciences, 17*(1), 128–136.

Sangrá Morer, A. (2006). Educación a distancia, educación presencial y usos de la tecnología: Una tríada para el progreso educativo. *Edutec. Revista Electrónica de Tecnología Educativa, 15*(2), 1–8.

Shava, H., Chinyamurindi, W., & Somdyala, A. (2016). An investigation into the usage of mobile phones among technical and vocational educational and training students in South Africa. *South African Journal of Information Management, 18*(1), 1–8.

St-Onge, C., Ouellet, K., Lakhal, S., Dubé, T., & Marceau, M. (2021). COVID-19 as the tipping point for integrating e-assessment in higher education practices. *British Journal of Educational Technology, 53*(2), 349–366.

Tapscott, D. (1998). *Growing up digital: The rise of the net generation.* McGraw-Hill.

Wagner, E., & Krylova, A. (2021). Temple University's ITA placement test in times of COVID-19. *Language Assessment Quarterly, 18*(1), 12–16.

Wang, C., Pan, R., Wan, X., Tan, Y., Xu, L., Ho, C. S., & Ho, R. C. (2020). Immediate psychological responses and associated factors during the initial stage of the 2019 Coronavirus disease (COVID-19) epidemic among the general population in China. *International Journal of Environmental Research and Public Health, 17*(5), 1729.

Willms, J. D., & Corbett, B. A. (2003). Summer. Tech and teens: Access and use. *Canadian Social Trends, 11*(008), 15–20.

Xie, K., Heddy, B., & Vongkulluksn, V. (2019). Examining engagement in context using experience-sampling method with mobile technology. *Contemporary Educational Psychology, 59*, 101788.

Zhang, W., Wang, Y., Yang, L., & Wang, C. (2020). Suspending classes without stopping learning: China's education emergency management policy in the COVID-19 outbreak. *Journal of Risk and Financial Management, 13*, 1–6.

9
ASSESSING UNIVERSITY STUDENTS' WRITING DEVELOPMENT AND PERFORMANCE DURING REMOTE INSTRUCTION

Bahiyyih Hardacre

CALIFORNIA STATE UNIVERSITY, LOS ANGELES, CA, UNITED STATES

9.1 Introduction

One of the most elusive challenges of language assessment is being able to measure the complete repertoire of a language-learner's competence in their second language (L2). Teachers must deal with the fact that all an assessment tool can do is elicit a very specific type of performance from a test-taker based on what they were asked to do in a given task. This fact applies to the assessment of the four language skills, including writing. For this reason, L2 writing instructors often aggregate different types of writing tasks in the design of their formal and informal L2 writing assessments in order to give their students multiple chances to showcase their micro and macro writing sub-skills.

Furthermore, the writing tests that language teachers create need to be useful for accurately assessing their students' writing skills. According to Bachman and Palmer (1996), a test's usefulness is measured by qualities such as reliability, construct validity, authenticity, interactiveness, practicality, and their washback effect and impact should be considered. For example, teachers must choose not only writing task(s) that would elicit the desired performance from their students, but they also should manipulate tests parameters such as timing and complexity of writing tasks so that they can provide relevant information about L2 learners' progress and achievement.

In English as a Second Language (ESL) writing courses at the college and university level, L2 writing assessments are usually timed and are taken during class time. For example, in the United States in particular, ESL writing programs in colleges require that students produce two to three essays per term, and these essays are written during class. Most teachers who work in this type of educational setting believe that students must be closely monitored while

DOI: 10.4324/9781003221463-11

writing these essays so that they produce more accurate samples of their ability to write academically. Therefore, a lot of effort is put into the prevention of cheating and academic dishonesty. These graded essays are perceived as high-stakes due to their direct impact on students' final grades, and therefore, their ability to pass the ESL writing pre-requisite courses and enrol in English courses, which are the ones that ultimately count towards their degrees. So even though peer feedback and the use of support materials such as dictionaries, translators, textbooks, readings, and students' notes have been shown to support language development in the long run, their use is not allowed in college-level graded essays because the latter are seen as measurements of students' L2 progress (if done mid-term) and achievement (if done at the end of a term).

With the forced shift to remote instruction due to the start of the COVID-19 pandemic in April 2020, challenges abounded. Students and instructors alike had their lives turned upside down, and many lost family members, lost their jobs or had to take on additional work shifts, and/or had increased childcare responsibilities. In the United States, teachers were asked to switch to remote videoconferencing tools such as Zoom or Microsoft Teams and to use online learning management systems such as Moodle, Blackboard, and Canvas, with very little training or support provided by their employers. What is worse, it was taken for granted that all instructors had access to a desk and a computer with reliable internet at home, which was not necessarily true. In addition to these personal and instructional challenges, instructors were asked to make accommodations for their students, such as allowing them to take quizzes, midterms, and final tests at home, or giving students additional time to complete assignments. So classroom assessments went from in-class to at-home, from paper-based to computer-based, from not allowing the use of outside resources to allowing them, from being limited to class time to having flexible and having negotiable deadlines (Bashir et al., 2021; Biwer et al., 2021).

This chapter describes how three L2 writing instructors at a public university in southern California adjusted their instruction and assessment instruments during the pandemic, it evaluates students' overall achievement of student learning outcomes (SLOs) through rubrics and graded writing assessments, and it describes students' self-reported progress on the course.

9.2 The Need to Develop Writing Skills for Higher Education and Professional Careers

Attaining writing skills in standard and/or academic English has become a ubiquitous necessity in most professional spaces. Various work sectors have increasingly required the ability to transfer knowledge into a usable, meaningful, and shareable written form (Bazerman et al., 2017). Therefore, students' success during and beyond college depends heavily on their ability to write and communicate well (Roksa & Arum, 2012). Therefore, college and university students are often expected to take required English composition courses (Strickland, 2011) or other writing-intensive courses designed to introduce and guide disciplinary knowledge production, such as science writing, business writing, and academic writing in the social sciences and the humanities. In addition, both undergraduate and graduate students are expected to develop proficiency in writing standards within their disciplines (Zawacki & Rogers, 2012) and to develop disciplinary rhetorical fluency (Shanahan & Shanahan, 2012).

Writing is intrinsically connected to students' development of academic language, critical thinking, and knowledge in diverse content areas (Graham et al., 2020; Sawyer et al., 2017). Nevertheless, despite its importance for college and career success, writing is one of the most challenging skills to develop because it involves multiple processes related to cognitive and affective factors and is shaped by the rhetorical situations in which it takes place (Bazerman et al., 2017). Given the importance and complexity of writing, undergraduate and graduate students' writing development requires ample writing practice, opportunities to engage in various writing tasks, and continued support at the curricular and instructional level. Students' writing development is closely tied to their exposure to and experiences of writing opportunities, practices, and community resources and support (Graham, 2018).

9.3 Assessing Students' Writing Skills during Remote Instruction

L2 writing assessment typically engages the collection of different types of writing tasks that represent samples of students' written language performance (Bachman & Dambock, 2018). It is important to consider both the time-based snapshots of learning which are addressed by ongoing incremental measurements of formative assessments, and culminating end-of-term measurement of the entire term through summative assessments (Brown, 2013).

In remote educational settings, where the students and instructor meet remotely via a video-conferencing application, implementing writing assessments becomes more challenging than in a traditional face-to-face class. This is partly because the instructor is not immediately available to students to clarify instructions if there is a need, or to proctor in-class tests to maintain academic integrity. When exam supervision is not an option, other means of monitoring student behaviour and performance must be utilised. Current technology has made it possible for an instructor to conduct quizzes, papers, and projects online and still maintain academic integrity, but it is still important to collect evidence of the performance being assessed through different types of tasks to strengthen assessment reliability of the online testing instruments (Airasian & Russell, 2007).

As many teachers had to move from physical to virtual classrooms, there was an urgent need to adopt testing approaches that promoted deep student engagement. Writing assignments comprise an alternative that can be facilitated online by making use of tasks that ask students to write about complex ideas through an iterative process of writing, feedback, and revision (Kuh, 2008; Reynolds et al., 2020). With this purpose in mind, Malecki (2014) proposes assessing students' writing skills by (i) requiring the student to determine where an error has been made in a presented item and offer a correction for that error and (ii) utilising either holistic or analytic rubrics to evaluate the quality of students' responses to a prompt. Adding to this list of suggestions, McCallum and Coombe (2021) recommend giving students multiple opportunities to handwrite and type up assignment tasks, to involve students in the assessment process, and to turn peer feedback into a learning opportunity that complements teacher feedback. Finally, Reynolds et al. (2020) add that implementing certain steps into the design of writing tasks can benefit an online or remote writing assessment, such as choosing relevant and meaningful topics, providing detailed guidelines, offering high-quality feedback, and designing assignments that promote metacognition, which makes use of students' ability to predict how well they will do on a task. Some of the most effective writing assignments involve metacognitive processes such as planning what to write, monitoring the development of the narrative, and evaluating the clarity of one's own writing (Bransford et al., 2000).

Instructors should also make an effort to reduce incentives for academic dishonesty, which comprises the chief challenge to assessing students' writing skills remotely or online. A study conducted by Al-Bargi (2022) reports teachers' perceptions on cheating on online writing assessments, explaining that teachers 'were doubtful whether the submitted online written work reflected their students' true proficiency' (p. 14). The same teachers also reported being doubtful that a remote unproctored writing assessment could be as authentic as an onsite assessment, and they agreed that it was difficult to verify the authenticity of online writing tasks if they were done remotely. These teacher perceptions of the disadvantages of conducting writing assessments remotely have been reported in other studies as well (see Alghamdi et al., 2016; Olt, 2002; Sileo & Sileo, 2008). To reduce the likelihood of cheating and plagiarism, Reynolds et al. (2020) recommend creating knowledge-transforming assignments which require students to offer an evaluation, suggest applications, or defend a position because these types of questions are less amenable to copy-and-paste answers and cheating.

9.4 Methodology

The guiding question of this study was, 'Did the sudden transition to remote instruction imposed by the COVID-19 pandemic lockdown affect students' writing development and performance in a L2 writing course?' This study is qualitative in nature and utilises a case study design with the aim of conducting an in-depth, detailed examination of a particular case within a real-world context (Crowe et al., 2011).

9.4.1 Setting

The setting in this report is a public university in southern California. Located at the intersection of the largest Latina/o and Asian communities in the nation, this university is one of the most culturally diverse four-year institutions in the United States. This university also welcomes a good number of international students, especially in its graduate programs.

9.4.2 Participants

Students who typically enrol in this course are: (i) English as first and second language students enrolled in teaching credential programs who are preparing to pass state-mandated exams; (ii) English as first and second language graduate students who are working on their theses and need help with their academic writing skills; and (iii) ESL undergraduate students who may or may not be international students. Many of these students come from local high schools and undergraduate programs that do not offer a strong academic writing curriculum, and most of them are multilingual writers.

A total of 23 students participated in this study. When asked about their ethnicity, twelve students described themselves as Latino(a), ten as Asian, and one declined to answer. Eighteen students were working towards their master's degree, three were in a credential program, one was in a bachelor's degree, and one was in a certificate program. Six students reported being international students and having been living in the country for varying lengths of time.

9.4.3 Course

The course is an upper-division academic writing class consisting mostly of students enrolled in programs in this university's College of Education. The title of this course is 'Improving Academic Literacy.' The main purpose of this course is to help students develop their academic literacy with emphasis on academic writing conventions and critical thinking skills. With the switch from onsite to remote instruction, the three instructors teaching this course decided on a number of adjustments to ensure assessment fairness and reliability while still helping all students be successful in meeting the SLOs.

9.4.3.1 Adjustments Made to the Mode of Instruction

This course went from being offered onsite, once a week, meeting for the duration of 3 hours and requiring 2 hours of remote work (that included assignments such as academic language homework and readings), to being offered remotely, once a week, with 2 hours of synchronous meetings and 3–5 hours of weekly asynchronous remote work. This institution had suggested that teachers reduce the total hours of weekly synchronous meetings and compensate with asynchronous work to be mindful or students' challenges with internet bandwidth and computer access. This institution adopted the Zoom software program developed by Zoom Video Communications for video-conferencing, to facilitate remote and synchronous meetings. The institution already had a partnership with Canvas, an online learning management software system developed by Instructure, for the upload and download of class materials and assignments, and the posting of homework and weekly discussions of assigned readings.

9.4.3.2 Adjustments Made to the Assessment of Students' Writing

The first and most obvious change was not a decision made by the instructors, but by the reality of the pandemic lockdown, which required that all in-class graded writing assignments were to be done remotely. This meant moving the course assessments away from a controlled and proctored environment to one over which the instructors had no control. Instructors had to acknowledge the strong possibility that students would have access to internet-based resources that could potentially help them improve their writing performance. If that were to be the case, then that possibility had to be embraced. That meant changing the approach to the writing assignments from a proctored and product-based to a more collaborative and process-based approach. In process writing, students have the chance to think about what they are going to write, produce drafts, revise, edit, and give and receive feedback on their work before coming up with the final version of the text (Kadmiry, 2021). That was the first significant change made that would affect students' performance on the writing assessments. A number of other adjustments had to be made to implement this change.

The second adjustment agreed upon by the course instructors was that students would be allowed to use outside resources such as dictionaries, thesaurus, Google searches, the textbook, and class notes while doing the graded assignments. Being fully aware that there was a strong possibility that these resources would be utilised by students working from home, the instructors made them officially permissible to increase test fairness. However, they told students that all writing assignments had to represent their own original work, and that the instructors would check for plagiarism using Turnitin, an internet-based plagiarism detection service. Another service that Turnitin provides, and one which the instructors decided to make use of, is that of immediate proofreading and feedback on basic grammar, punctuation, conciseness, etc., which was also advantageous due to the fact that the university's Writing Center was also shut down during the pandemic. In order to use these Turnitin features, students were to submit their work before the deadline, and by doing so, they would be able to download the 'similarity' report and the 'automated grammar checker' report.

The third adjustment incorporated by the course instructors was a change in grading. For example, teachers are aware of the problem that even before the move to remote teaching brought about by the COVID-19 pandemic, that there had been a concerning number of American college students paying others to write essays for them (Wexler, 2019). This type of '[c]heating is nothing new, but the internet has made the practice easier and more widespread' (Wexler, 2019, para. 2). What often leads students to cheat in this manner is making an assignment worth a lot of points and not giving students the chance to revise their work after receiving feedback from a peer and/or from the instructor. For this reason, the instructors decided to only grade a writing assignment after students had received feedback from their peers and from the instructor, and after they had had the opportunity to revise and resubmit their work.

The fourth adjustment was to adopt Google Docs for the peer feedback activities. This decision was made because Google Docs is a free resource that affords instant remote collaboration by providing immediate updates of edits and useful copy-editing tools. In addition, for these peer feedback activities to go smoothly, very specific guiding questions and instructions were created and shared, allowing the students to work more independently from the instructor. Students are typically more engaged with peer feedback if they are given clear guidelines and are asked to work within pre-established criteria (Simmons, 2003). These peer feedback sessions were conducted during the weekly synchronous class meetings. To make sure students were on task while they worked on the feedback on their peers' drafts, they were individually assigned to Zoom breakout rooms where they were asked to permanently share their screens so that the instructors could see their progress and provide support when they entered the breakout room. The other important purpose of assigning students to their own individual breakout rooms was to afford them privacy in case they had questions for the instructors, which was common. Finally, an additional step worth mentioning is that the individualised Google Doc links were created by the instructors and shared with their students so that the instructors would have the ability to monitor students' progress simply by clicking on those links.

The fifth adjustment made that affected the course writing assignments was two-pronged: providing instructor feedback on submitted assessments within a week of when they were due, and adding a mandatory (i.e., graded) virtual student-teacher one-on-one meeting to discuss this feedback. For this meeting, students were required to have read the instructor's feedback before the meeting and bring at least three questions or revisions based on the feedback.

The sixth and final adjustment involved the grading rubrics and assignment guidelines. Analytical grading rubrics had already been created for this course's original assignments, but they focused exclusively on the writing assignment's final product, the academic conventions, and expectations for each one of them. The three assignments described in this chapter – an academic paragraph, an academic essay, and a critique of a peer-reviewed article – were also the original graded assignments. Nevertheless, each rubric was revised to reflect the inclusion of the SLOs as part of the assessment objectives of those rubrics and assignments. The remaining grading criteria were kept. Handouts with detailed guidelines and instructions for the three assignments were refined to remove ambiguity and improve clarity. These guidelines and rubrics were shared with students ahead of time.

9.4.4 Data Collected

The first set of data collected for this study were the final drafts of the writing assessments that students submitted through Canvas. The second set of data were the course's SLOs. These SLOs were to be used as the specific assessment objectives for the writing assignments. The third set of data collected for this study were the students' answers to a student survey conducted at the end of the term. The fourth set of data gathered for this study were students' grade average at the end of the semester taught remotely, and from the previous two instances when the course was taught face-to-face before the pandemic. Finally, the instructors' perspectives on the evaluation of students' work and on their answers to open-ended questions on the survey can also be considered part of the qualitative information available in this study. The decision of conducting a survey was made to allow students' answers to be kept anonymous; interviews were not conducted because there were no volunteers. This researcher understands that the lack of volunteers to interview might have been caused by the fact that students had been burdened with Zoom over-usage at school and at work during that time.

9.4.4.1 Graded Writing Assessments

To evaluate students' achievement of assessment objectives, instructors examined the final drafts of the following graded writing assessments (see Table 9.1).

TABLE 9.1 Graded Writing Assessments

Graded writing assessments	Assignment
Writing Assignment #1	An Academic Paragraph
Writing Assignment #2	An Academic Essay
Writing Assignment #3	A Critique of a Published Peer-reviewed Article in the Student's Field.

Students made the necessary revisions to their first drafts after they had received feedback from their peers and from their instructors. Grades were only assigned after the final drafts were submitted, using assignment-specific rubrics that took into account the course's SLOs.

9.4.4.2 Student Learning Outcomes

One way to assess students' development and achievement was to consider the SLOs as part of the assessment objectives of the graded assignments. This course contains nine SLOs (see Table 9.2). To achieve the task of assessing students' written work through meeting the course's SLOs, a student performance assessment feature on Canvas called *Outcomes* was used. *Outcomes* allows faculty to track students' progress as measured by course assessment goals, and in this case, it was used to determine if students had met each of the SLOs after the three assessments were graded. To determine if a student had met a specific SLO, the final drafts of the graded writing assignments submitted on Canvas were examined.

TABLE 9.2 Student Learning Outcomes

SLO number	SLO description
1	Gain rhetorical consciousness awareness about academic discourse to accurately present the analytical skills expected in your chosen discipline: The cycle of analysis, awareness, acquisition, and achievement of academic writing leads to self-assessment and confidence in academic writing.
2	Apply academic writing skills in a variety of genres (e.g., literature reviews, syntheses and summaries, case studies, critiques, reading responses, abstracts, research papers, etc.); part-genres (e.g., problem-process-solutions, methods, discussion sections); planning, drafting, and revising actual assignments given in the credential and MA degree programs.
3	Improve sentence and discourse-level grammar.
4	Improve punctuation and mechanics.
5	Expand use of strategies to build academic vocabulary and awareness of academic register.
6	Expand critical thinking skills such as making inferences, arguments, and counter arguments.
7	Develop proofing skills through peer editing and focused tasks.
8	Apply student learning outcomes (1–7) above to in-class writing assignments and student's own writing assignments from a selected credential or MA course.
9	Use appropriately the style sheet of the American Psychological Association style in academic writing assignments, including in-text citations, proper attribution of sources through paraphrase and quotations (to avoid plagiarism), and reference lists.

TABLE 9.3 Sample Questions from the Student Survey

Survey areas	Sample questions
Importance of Academic Writing Skills for Students' Educational Goals	'How important are academic writing skills to your current educational goals?'
Self-Assessment of Academic Writing Skills Development	'How would you evaluate your academic writing skills before taking this course?' 'How would you evaluate your proficiency in academic writing after having taken this course?'
Students' Experience with the Academic Writing Assessments	'How would you describe your experience with the academic writing assessments we used this semester?'
Remote Versus In-class Writing	'How did you feel about being allowed to work on your essays and other assignments remotely and not in-class?'

9.4.4.3 Student Survey

At the end of the semester, students were asked to take a survey. This survey was created on Qualtrics, which is a cloud-based platform for creating and distributing web-based surveys. Survey-takers can access it on any internet-connected device, including tablets and cellphones. Some questions on this survey were about students' experience with academic writing, some were about their perception of academic writing conventions, some were about their own progress in this course in a remote format, and some were about the assessment tasks in this course (see Table 9.3). Roughly half the questions on the survey were open-ended, and the other half were close-ended. The closed-ended questions are reported in this study in percentage distribution. The open-ended questions were loaded onto NVivo in order to look for themes within students' answers. NVivo is a qualitative data analysis computer software package produced by QSR International that helps qualitative researchers organise, analyse, and find insights in qualitative data. Table 9.3 displays some examples of questions asked in the survey.

9.5 Findings

9.5.1 Measuring Students' Achievement of the Student Learning Outcomes

Canvas *Outcomes* was used to assess students' achievement of the SLOs. The instructors used students' final drafts of each of the three main writing assignments (see Table 9.1) to verify that they had met each SLO. The SLO evaluation decisions that the instructors were to select from 'Meets SLO' or 'Does not Meet SLO' (see Table 9.4).

TABLE 9.4 Assessment of Student Learning Outcomes (SLOs)

SLOs	Writing assignment(s) evaluated	Number of students who met the SLO (n = 23)	Number of students who did not meet the SLO (n = 23)
1	#3	23	0
2	#2, 3	23	0
3	#1, 2, 3	23	0
4	#1, 2, 3	23	0
5	#2, 3	23	0
6	#2, 3	23	0
7	#1, 2, 3	23	0
8	#3	23	0
9	#1, 2, 3	23	0

Likely due to the nature of the writing process adopted, which allowed for the use of additional resources, Turnitin reports, multiple sources of feedback and multiple rounds of revisions of students' work, all students were able to meet the nine SLOs for this course. This was a surprising result. From previous experience teaching this course, the instructors had always had students who had not been able to meet all the SLOs by the end of the term.

9.5.2 Responses to Student Survey

Below is a summary of students' answers to some of the questions asked in the student survey that relate to writing assessment. The responses are grouped by the topic areas that they address.

9.5.2.1 Importance of Academic Writing Skills for Students' Educational Goals

Student investment in a course and their performance in its assessments are closely related to their awareness of their immediate need for those skills. Therefore, the survey asked students the question, '*How important are academic writing skills to your current educational goals?*', to which 54% of the students reported being 'extremely important,' and 46% of the students said it was 'very important.' This clearly shows that the students enrolled in that class agreed that developing academic writing skills were important in the pursuit of their degrees and credentials.

9.5.2.2 Self-Assessment of Academic Writing Skills Development

To examine what students thought of their own progress after having taken this course, they were asked to rate their own academic writing skills development. Two questions were asked: '*How would you evaluate your academic writing skills before taking this course?*' to which 43% of the students chose 'above average,' 41% chose 'average,' and 16% chose 'below average;' and *'How would you evaluate your proficiency in academic writing after having taken this course?'* to which 69% of the students chose 'above average,' 23% chose 'average,' and 8% chose 'below average.' These numbers show a clear increase in confidence in their own academic writing skills, a progress that can be correlated with their final performance on the graded assignments and final grades. Nevertheless, there were a few students who expressed lack of confidence in their academic writing skills and reported believing their skills were below average.

9.5.2.3 Students' Experience with the Writing Assessments

Students who see the value in improving their academic writing skills may also have a positive attitude about the writing assessments being done remotely provided that they are getting sufficient feedback from their instructors and peers, and that they have access to the resources they need. When asked the open-ended question, *'How would you describe your experience with the academic writing assessments we used this semester?'* students reported the following (see Table 9.5).

9.5.2.4 Remote versus In-class Writing

With the move to remote instruction, all essays and assignments that were to be done in-class were now being done remotely from each student's computer, tablet, or phone. In preparation for that, the assignments had been modified to discourage cheating and plagiarism. When asked, *'How did you feel about being allowed to work on your essays and other assignments remotely and not in-class?'*, 92% of the students reported believing it had a positive impact on their performance, while 8% reported feeling like the assignments were not helpful in allowing them to improve their academic writing skills significantly. An open-ended follow-up question asked students to elaborate on their answers. Students who had reported a positive impact on their learning also mentioned what they perceived as advantages, such as having more time to work on assignments, being less anxious about it, having more opportunities for feedback and revisions. Students who had reported not thinking that their academic writing skills had improved much, elaborated that the graded writing assignments were not directly applicable to their programs. Given that this class has students from different programs, it is indeed possible that those assignments did not match the usual writing assignments required in their programs.

9.5.2.5 Students' Grade Averages

For the purpose of quantifying, albeit on a qualitative and small scale, the overall improvement of students' performance on the graded assessments, the

TABLE 9.5 Students' Experience with the Academic Writing Assessments

Themes	Quotes from student survey
Enjoyed writing and were willing to improve their skills	'I personally enjoy writing and so I feel open to the writing process.' 'I am willing to learn more and practice more writing skill, I really enjoy writing, and writing is really important for my future career. I hope I can do better.'
Learned to like academic writing this semester	'I have grown to enjoy academic writing because of adequate instruction in my EDUC 4000 Course. I believe I would still have a terrible relationship with my academic writing if I did not enroll in this class.' 'At first, I felt like it's board, and I did not want to do it, but I became interested in it now and realized how important it is in my field.' 'It can be a negative feeling but overall I've found it enjoyable.'
Learned something new this semester	'I feel a little intimidated, but this course was helpful to me. I have taken academic writing courses before, but most the emphasis was placed on APA rather than talking about flow or other writing considerations.' 'It's definitely a love-hate relationship I don't always enjoy writing it but in the end, I'm always glad that I did because I learn something new or I understand something better.'
Willing to learn and improve their writing	'I am very willing to learn more academic writing, because I hope my writing can be liked by readers one day.'
Lack of confidence in their writing skills	'I enjoy learning and researching academic writing in my field, however I do not feel that I can confidently say my writing is academic writing. I prefer to read it rather than write it because my field is constantly evolving.' 'I do not feel very confident with my academic writing, but I think I did well.'

average of the final scores of all students were obtained (see Table 9.6). It is possible to see a significant grade average increase in the students' performance in the Spring 2021, compared to Spring 2019 and Spring 2018. When the assessments were conducted in-class and proctored by the instructors, the average ranged was around a B grade (keeping in mind that this is an average, and the actual grade distribution contained some As and Cs), whereas in Spring 2021 the class average was an A.

TABLE 9.6 Class Total Average Grades per Term for Three Different Semesters

	Spring 2021 (Remote)	Spring 2020 (Onsite/Remote)	Spring 2019 (Onsite)	Spring 2018 (Onsite)
Average Grades (Out of 100 Points)	94.4	Course not offered	87.6	88.1

9.6 Discussion

The question that guided this study was, 'Did the sudden transition to remote instruction imposed by the COVID-19 pandemic lockdown affect students' writing performance in a L2 writing course?' To answer this question, first we need to consider that students' writing performance was measured in a slightly different way from what it had been in previous pre-pandemic semesters.

However, it is important to note that the guidelines and expectations for the level of quality of the graded assignments in this course did not change from previous semesters, and that the assignments themselves were not made easier by any means. The three graded assignments were unchanged from previous semesters. Even though the grading rubrics were expanded to accommodate the inclusion of language from the SLOs, the descriptors of the original grading criteria were not removed. Therefore, the fact that students did better during a semester in which the class was taught remotely due to the COVID-19 pandemic was not due to a change in the actual assessments; it is more likely that the use of technology and internet-based services were positive affordances that overturned a potentially problematic scenario of assessing students' writing development outside the physical classroom environment.

Students' high final grades and their meeting the course SLO requirements was paired with their overall positive responses to the student survey, painting a generally encouraging picture of the changes made to the approach adopted to grading and to the drafting process. Preventing cheating and plagiarism that can occur during unsupervised performance was the chief motivator driving those course adjustments, but the course instructors gained an appreciation for the value of allowing students to work through their challenges by revising their work multiple times after collecting feedback from others and using the technological resources available to them. Therefore, such adaptations had a positive (though indirect) effect on students' writing performance in the course.

9.7 Post-Pandemic Lessons and Conclusion

This chapter described a few adjustments made to a university academic writing course for multilingual students and its assessments during the COVID-19 pandemic era's remote instruction. This chapter also evaluated these students' overall achievement of SLOs through graded writing assessments, and it described students' self-reported progress on the course.

In line with published literature on effective online writing assessment (Al-Bargi, 2022), the course instructors allowed the use of internet-based linguistic resources, created detailed guidelines and rubrics for all writing assignments to be distributed early to all students, created several opportunities for collaborative peer feedback on Google Docs, provided quick turnaround of instructor feedback, allowed the submission of multiple revisions of drafts before a final draft was submitted for a grade, and used Turnitin for assignment submission and to grant students access to Turnitin's similarity report and its grammar checker report, all of which were likely to have decreased the incentive for academic dishonesty and plagiarism.

It was found that the digital technology described above improved students' ability to meet the course's SLOs, significantly improved the class average grades on those assignments compared with previous semesters, and students reported that access to those had a positive impact on their performance and on their learning. Instructors were asked to be mindful of the limitations and challenges that probably afflicted many of our students, namely availability of computers at home, access to the internet, or even to Wi-Fi with sufficient bandwidth to attend class on Zoom or carry out activities such as the peer feedback on Google Docs during synchronous meetings. For this reason, it is important to allow students to perform this work asynchronously if needed.

Online writing assessment is not a new practice, and safeguards can be used to prevent academic dishonesty. The challenge is to make the switch from one mode to another (i.e., onsite to online) when the assessments are part of a course that had been designed to be delivered face-to-face, with face-to-face proctored writing assessments. While the use of internet-based technology might be seen as a potential solution when a pandemic overwhelms not only a country but the entire world, teachers need to be mindful of the reasons why students chose an educational setting with a physical campus that offers face-to-face instruction, and whether they have access to those technological resources.

References

Airasian, P. W., & Russell, M. K. (2007). *Classroom assessment: Concepts and application* (6th ed.). McGraw-Hill.

Al-Bargi, A. (2022). Exploring online writing assessment amid Covid-19: Challenges and opportunities from teachers' perspectives. *Arab World English Journal (AWEJ) 2nd Special Issue on Covid 19 Challenges, 2*, 3–21. https://doi.org/10.24093/awej/covid2.1

Alghamdi, E. A., Rajab, H., & Rashid, S. (2016). Unmonitored students self-created WhatsApp groups in distance learning environments: A collaborative learning tool or cheating technique. *International Journal of Research Studies in Educational Technology, 5*(2), 71–82.

Bachman, L., & Dambock, B. (2018). *Language assessment for classroom teachers*. Oxford University Press.

Bachman, L., & Palmer, A. (1996). *Language testing in practice: Designing and developing useful language tests*. Oxford University Press.

Bashir, A., Bashir, S., Rana, K., Lambert, P., & Vernallis, A. (2021). Post-COVID-19 adaptations: The shifts towards online learning, hybrid course delivery and the implications for biosciences courses in the higher education setting. *Frontiers in Education, 6*. https://doi.org/10.3389/feduc.2021.711619

Bazerman, C., Applebee, A., Berninger, V., Brandt, D., Graham, S., Matsuda, P., Murphy, S., Wells Rowe, D., & Schleppegrell, M. (2017). Taking the long view of writing development. *Research in the Teaching of English, 51*(3), 351–360.

Biwer, F., Wiradhany, W., oude Egbrink, M., Hospers, H., Wasenitz, S., Jansen, W., & de Bruin, A. (2021). Changes and adaptations: How university students self-regulate their online learning during the COVID-19 pandemic. *Frontiers in Psychology, 12*. https://doi.org/10.3389/fpsyg.2021.642593

Bransford, J. D., Brown, A. L., & Cocking, R. R. (2000). *How people learn: Brain, mind, experience, and school*. National Academies Press.

Brown, J. D. (Ed.). (2013). *New ways of classroom assessment*. Teachers of English to Speakers of Other Languages.

Crowe, S., Cresswell, K., Robertson, A., Huby, G., Avery, A., & Sheikh, A. (2011). The case study approach. *BMC Medical Research Methodology, 11*, 100. https://doi.org/10.1186/1471-2288-11-100

Graham, S. (2018). A revised writer(s)-within-community model of writing. *Educational Psychologist, 53*(4), 258–279. doi: 10.1080/00461520.2018.1481406

Graham, S., Kiuhara, S. A., & MacKay, M. (2020). The effects of writing on learning in science, social studies, and mathematics: A meta-analysis. *Review of Educational Research, 90*(2), 179–226. https://doi.org/10.3102/0034654320914744

Kadmiry, M. (2021). The comparison between the process-oriented approach and the product-oriented approach in teaching writing: The case of Moroccan EFL students in preparatory classes for the grandes ecoles. *Arab World English Journal, 12*(1), 198–214. https://doi.org/10.24093/awej/vol12no1.14

Kuh, G. D. (2008). *High-impact educational practices: What they are, who has access to them, and why they matter*. Association of American Colleges and Universities.

Malecki, C. K. (2014). Best practices in written language assessment and intervention. In P. L. Harrison, & A. Thomas (Eds.), *Best practices in school psychology: Data-based and collaborative decision making* (pp. 187–202). National Association of School Psychologists.

McCallum, L., & Coombe, C. (2021). Examining the cycle of assessing writing in MENA contexts: Trends, challenges, and best practice. *European Journal of Applied Linguistics and TEFL, 10*(1), 79–99.

Olt, M. R. (2002). Ethics and distance education: Strategies for minimizing academic dishonesty in online assessment. *Online Journal of Distance Learning Administration, 5*(3), 1–7.

Reynolds, J., Cai, V., Choi, J., Faller, S., Hu, M., Kozhumam, A., Schwartman, J., & Vohra, A. (2020). Teaching during a pandemic: Using high-impact writing assignments to balance rigor, engagement, flexibility, and workload. *Ecology and Evolution, 10*, 12573–12580. https://doi.org/10.1002/ece3.6776

Roksa, J., & Arum, R. (2012). Life after college: The challenging transitions of the *Academically Adrift* cohort, change. *The Magazine of Higher Learning, 44*(4), 8–14. doi: 10.1080/00091383.2012.691857

Sawyer, J., Obeid, R., Bublitz, D., Schwartz, A., Brooks, P., & Richmond, A. (2017). Which forms of active learning are most effective: Cooperative learning, writing-to-learn, multimedia instruction, or some combination? *Scholarship of Teaching and Learning in Psychology, 3*(4), 257–271. https://doi.org/10.1037/stl0000095

Shanahan, T., & Shanahan, C. (2012). What is disciplinary literacy and why does it matter? *Top Language Disorders, 32*(1), 7–18.

Sileo, J. M., & Sileo, T. W. (2008). Academic dishonesty and online classes: A rural education perspective. *Rural Special Education Quarterly, 27*(1–2), 55–60.

Simmons, J. (2003). Responders are taught, not born. *Journal of Adolescent and Adult Literacy, 46*(8), 684–693.

Strickland, D. (2011). *The managerial unconscious: In the history of composition studies.* Southern Illinois University.

Wexler, N. (2019, September 14). Paying others to write college essays involves more cheating that meets the eye. *Forbes.* https://www.forbes.com/sites/nataliewexler/2019/09/14/paying-others-to-write-college-essays-involves-more-cheating-than-meets-the-eye/?sh=50c383107662

Zawacki, T., & Rogers, P. (2012). *Writing across the curriculum: A critical sourcebook.* Macmillan Learning.

10
FAIRNESS IN REMOTE ENGLISH PLACEMENT TESTING AT IOWA STATE UNIVERSITY DURING THE COVID-19 PANDEMIC

Reza Neiriz, Shireen Baghestani, Ananda Astrini Muhammad, and Jim Ranalli

DEPARTMENT OF ENGLISH, IOWA STATE UNIVERSITY, AMES, IA, UNITED STATES

10.1 Introduction

In the face of limitations imposed by the COVID-19 pandemic, many local or 'in-house' testing programs (Dimova et al., 2020) implemented modifications to continue operation while accommodating the safety of the examinees. For instance, Brigham Young University-Hawaii's placement test battery underwent a major shift from on-campus test delivery to a virtual platform delivery (Green & Lung, 2021). Similarly, the Community English Language Program at Teachers College, Columbia University, adapted their placement exam so that the test previously administered in a computer lab became a test delivered fully online (Purpura et al., 2021). While these two institutions chose to adapt their placement exams, for Temple University, the pandemic provided the opportunity to develop a new test to assess international teaching assistants' oral communication abilities (Wagner & Krylova, 2021) that better met their present needs.

Similar to the tests mentioned above, the English Placement Test (EPT) at Iowa State University was also modified in response to the pandemic. The EPT is required for incoming (matriculated) undergraduate and graduate students who have met the minimum English requirement for admission to the university (e.g., TOEFL iBT score of 71 for undergraduates) but who do not meet the EPT exemption criteria (e.g., TOEFL iBT score of 100 or more). The purpose of the test is to identify those who need additional instruction in using the language for academic purposes. The test comprises two sub-tests: writing and oral communication. In the writing test, students read and integrate information from source texts, and in the speaking test, they listen

DOI: 10.4324/9781003221463-12

to another speaker before formulating an appropriate response. The detailed description of both components will be presented in their respective sections.

In this chapter, we discuss our response as administrators of the EPT to the COVID-19 pandemic – in particular, the technological and administrative modifications we had to make to continue testing in the face of this unprecedented global health emergency. We also go beyond the description of these modifications and discuss the implications that these changes had from a test fairness perspective. In doing so, we draw upon Kunnan's (2004, 2008) Test Fairness Framework. This framework was proposed as an alternative to test evaluation frameworks that, according to Kunnan, have focused primarily on validity and reliability to the exclusion of other important considerations, such as the ethicality of tests and testing practices. In Kunnan's framework, fairness is the ultimate goal of any test or testing program.

Kunnan's framework is based on the two principles of *justice* and *beneficence* (Kunnan, 2004), where *justice* entails that 'A test ought to have comparable construct validity in terms of its test-score interpretation for all test takers' and 'ought not to be biased against any test-taker groups' (p. 33), while *beneficence* refers to the extent to which a test 'bring[s] about good in the society' (p. 33). The framework consists of five components or test qualities necessary for upholding these principles: validity, absence of bias, access, administration, and social consequences. Each quality is further broken down into subcomponents (validity, for example, comprises content representativeness and relevance, construct or theory-based validity, criterion-related validity, and reliability[1]). While each of the elements of the framework are relevant to a discussion of the EPT, our goal in this chapter is to examine the comparability of the original and modified test forms rather than to evaluate the test as a whole. As a result, we focus more on the aspects of Kunnan's framework pertaining to justice than to beneficence, though we acknowledge the importance of both. With this in mind, we have organised our discussion around those aspects of the test most affected by the move from in-person to remote administration: construct representation, test security, and testing conditions. As we discuss each topic, we draw upon relevant issues highlighted in Kunnan's Test Fairness Framework as well as in other literature.

The first theme, construct representation, is discussed in terms of test design (the test tasks), including their modality (e.g., face-to-face vs. video conferencing) as well as timing, topic, and audience. As will be shown, changes to construct representation were much more pronounced in the oral communication component, which required changes to both the modality and audience (conversation partner). The two other themes, test security and testing conditions, are shown to be two sides of the same coin. Remote administration necessitates changes in testing conditions as well as security measures, and the security measures themselves further influence testing conditions.

In addition to sharing the challenges we faced and the ways we addressed these, we highlight notable tensions within considerations of fairness that have raised questions that, as of yet, we have been unable to answer, and which will require further evaluation and research.

10.2 EPT Writing

The EPT writing test (EPT-W) is designed to measure English academic writing ability, defined as the ability to 'summarize, synthesize, and evaluate information presented from different sources and to state and support [one's] arguments with sufficient details and examples in standard English' (English Placement Test, n.d.). The test consists of two writing tasks based on two short readings (250–300 words each) expressing opposing viewpoints. The first writing task is a 100–120-word summary of both viewpoints, and the second is a 300–350-word essay in which test-takers present their position on the issue. The test is 50 minutes, which includes time to read both passages and respond to each task.

Each task is scored by 2–3 raters based on content (development and task completion), organisation (cohesion and logical structure), grammar and vocabulary (accuracy and complexity/range), and writing conventions (spelling, punctuation, and source attribution). Placement decisions are based on scores which have been adjusted for rater severity using many-facet Rasch analysis. Students who score in the low, middle, or high range are required to take two, one, or no English as a second language (ESL) writing course, respectively.

The EPT-W has been delivered online through Canvas, the University's learning management system (LMS), since the Spring of 2018. Canvas provides a test interface that can be configured to display test instructions, reading passages, and text boxes for students to type their responses. Canvas saves responses in real time to a server to prevent data loss and shows a timer to the examinees. Test responses stored on the server can be downloaded by test administrators. The test interface also offers security features such as password protection and integration with LockDown Browser, an internet browser that blocks students from accessing other websites and opening other programs on the computer.

Prior to the pandemic, the EPT-W was delivered in-person through the university testing centre, with dedicated computers and trained exam proctors. In a typical in-person administration, students check in to the testing centre and have their identities verified before being allowed to enter the testing room. They must place any personal belongings in a plastic bag before being escorted to an open computer. They also receive blank paper and a pencil for note-taking. Once seated, the proctors instruct them to open the test interface. The test is password-protected to ensure that only students in the testing room can access it. During the test, proctors monitor the session to deter cheating and to assist students with technological issues or questions about the test. These procedures help minimise cheating and ensure a relatively uniform and stress-free examination experience.

10.2.1 COVID-19 Modifications

In the Summer of 2020, with most of the university closed due to COVID-19, it became necessary to administer the EPT-W remotely. However, since the test was already designed to be delivered online, none of the task characteristics had to be changed. Therefore, we adopted the same rating scale and scoring procedures that were used for the in-person test. We did, however, have to administer the test at a different time of day, as most students would be taking it in their home countries spanning multiple time zones. Selecting a suitable time meant considering where most of our prospective students were from (namely, China and India) and choosing a time that was not too early or too late in any time zone.

Beyond the testing time, an important concern was test security – implementing measures to both deter and detect cheating. We decided to adopt Respondus Monitor for this purpose, a remote-proctoring tool available to us through the University. Respondus Monitor works in conjunction with Canvas and LockDown Browser to video record test-takers during the exam. It can also facilitate security checks, such as requiring students to provide a 360-degree view of the room in which they are taking the test. The video footage is made available in Canvas for test administrators to review following the test. This means that test administrators do not have access to the live webcam feed of examinee computers, and all the footage is recorded into a secure server for post-administration review. Respondus Monitor also uses automation to flag suspicious activity (such as a test-taker moving out of frame) to help test administrators review the videos more efficiently.

To ensure the software would work during the test and students would be taking the test under the required conditions, we created a 'system check' that had to be completed prior to the test date. The system check involved the test-taker downloading and installing LockDown Browser and Respondus Monitor on the computer they intended to use for the test, and then running those programs to take a simple practice test in Canvas. The required conditions included having a stable internet connection, being alone in the testing room, remaining within the frame of the camera at all times, and not wearing headphones or covering one's face. In addition, students had to conduct an 'environment check' in which they panned their webcam 360 degrees around the room. An EPT administrator reviewed the footage of each system check and informed test-takers of any unmet requirements that could result in disqualification of their scores. To make the system check feedback process manageable, we created a checklist using Microsoft Forms to record system check reports systematically and generate automated feedback emails through Mail Merge to be sent to examinees.

During the actual test, at least two EPT administrators were available by phone and email to address technical or administrative issues. We also added a 30-minute grace period for students who were unable to start the test on time because of technical problems. The most common of such problems were LockDown Browser not opening or Respondus Monitor being unable to detect a test-taker's face. Students who were still unable to start the exam after 30 minutes were required to reschedule for a later test date. In some cases, students emailed us after the test to report technical problems and ask to retake it. We dealt with such requests case-by-case, reviewing the video footage to determine if there was sufficient evidence to warrant retesting.

10.2.2 Test Fairness Considerations

10.2.2.1 Construct Representation

Because our COVID-19 modifications did not require changes to the test tasks, rubric, or scoring procedures, we believe the in-person and remotely proctored versions measured the same construct described above. In line with this determination, we have continued to develop test forms based on our original test specifications. To clarify, our claim is not that the EPT-W perfectly represents the construct of academic writing ability but rather that the move to remote administration did not seem to warrant changes in score interpretation based on construct representation.

Nevertheless, remote administration created a tension related to another aspect of construct representation: authenticity, or the correspondence between test tasks and the real-world abilities a test is designed to measure (Bachman & Palmer, 1996). One criticism of timed writing tasks such as the EPT-W is that they fail to reflect the actual conditions under which students perform academic writing tasks. Normally, students write assignments on their personal computers in locations other than classrooms and testing centres. Since the scores of the EPT-W are meant to be generalised to this situation, the fact that students could take the test from home on their personal computers suggests authenticity was enhanced by this change. On the other hand, the reliability of the scores might be affected by non-uniform testing conditions. While test-taking in a familiar setting could reduce some sources of construct-irrelevant variance, such as the requirement to use unfamiliar equipment (Gallagher et al., 2021; Scully-Allison et al., 2019; van Ittersum, 2008), it may also introduce or increase distracting factors normally controlled for in testing rooms.

10.2.2.2 Test Security

In Kunnan's Test Fairness Framework (2004, 2008), test security is an aspect of test administration – the data gathering stage of the testing process in which test-takers produce performance samples meant to represent their abilities. Test security helps ensure that this data is truly a reflection of the ability defined through the operationalisation of the test construct. In the EPT-W, the operational construct stipulates that test-takers are not allowed to use external resources for language or content support, or get help from other people. Violations of these parameters therefore corrupt or invalidate their performance sample.

While we had at our disposal two fairly robust remote-proctoring tools (LockDown Browser and Respondus Monitor), maintaining test security remained challenging for several reasons. First, the time required to review the video recordings from Respondus Monitor was considerable given the large number of test-takers and our small staff. Reviewing every recording was not feasible, so we decided to focus on those test-takers who had scored high enough to exempt themselves from both ESL writing courses and those whose recordings had been flagged for review by the software. While this procedure enhanced practicality, it also meant cheating that resulted in higher-level ESL course placement or which had somehow fooled the software was more likely to go undetected.

Furthermore, we had to rely on test-takers' webcams to monitor the testing process, which greatly restricted our observations. After students recorded their 360-degree environment checks, they were supposed to keep their faces in the camera frame for the rest of the test. This meant their hands, computer screens, and anything else beside or in front of them was out of frame. Test-takers so inclined could have surreptitiously used unauthorised resources that would have been unavailable to them during the in-person test. It would even have been possible to hide a second computer nearby, allowing one to access applications blocked by LockDown Browser on the other computer. On the positive side, knowing that test administrators could see their faces throughout the test likely deterred cheating. In addition, we could still use indirect cues, such as posture or gaze, to detect suspicious activity. While it would be difficult to make a conclusive determination on such cues alone, they could add to the evidence in cases where there were other indications of cheating.

Finally, we found it necessary to relax some security measures for ethical reasons. We did not require students to present a photo ID on camera as part of Respondus Monitor's pre-test security routine out of concern that confidential information, such as a passport number, could be compromised. Instead, we decided to confirm test-takers' identities later using university records in cases where we suspected the test-taker was not who they said they were. In addition, the 30-minute grace period could have been used by some to view the prompts and share them with others who started the test later. This risk could have been mitigated by administering different test forms to different test-takers, as was done for the at-home version of the TOEFL iBT (Papageorgiou & Manna, 2021). However, we viewed the risk of this as low and mitigated by post-exam measures; namely, making note of students who started the test late, reviewing video footage, and administering diagnostic tests at the beginning of the writing courses to confirm students' placements (which admittedly was not applicable to students who passed the EPT-W).

Having administered the EPT-W remotely for several semesters now, we have found no evidence of students scoring substantially higher compared to in-person administrations. That is, the proportion of students scoring in the upper, middle, and higher ranges has remained stable across both types of testing conditions. For this reason, we consider our test-security measures to be sufficiently stringent. This could change, however, as test-takers become more familiar with remote testing and its vulnerabilities, so we will need to continuously monitor this issue and update our practices accordingly.

10.2.2.3 Testing Conditions

Testing conditions that influence fairness include one's physical surroundings – specifically, 'appropriate conditions for test administration such as optimum light, temperature and facilities' (Kunnan, 2008, p. 238). Students take the in-person EPT-W, administered on-campus in a computer lab, in such uniform conditions. With remote administration however, we have little control over physical surroundings beyond what can be specified in our system-check feedback, and due to time zone differences, students can be taking the test early in the morning, in the middle of the day, or late in the evening. We have observed great variation in individual testing environments; in one case, the sounds of traffic and livestock were audible from an open window behind the test-taker. And yet, as noted by Fielding (2016), individuals will view the effects of remote delivery differently depending on their life conditions, experiences, and preferences. Whereas some perceive background noise as distracting, others may find it conducive to writing.

Testing conditions influencing fairness also include access to, and familiarity with, equipment (Kunnan, 2008). As noted above, the remote version of the EPT-W requires test-takers to use three technologies – Canvas, LockDown Browser, and Respondus Monitor – most if not all of which are likely to be unfamiliar. Test-takers must provide a computer on which to install the software, a webcam if the computer does not already have one, and a broadband internet connection. These requirements could impose burdens of time, energy, and finances. Some examinees' lack of access to reliable technology means they are more likely to need help during the test, but our capacity to provide such help remotely is limited. On the other hand, they are likely to feel more comfortable typing on their own computer than on an unfamiliar keyboard, which can affect writing productivity (Gallagher et al., 2021; Scully-Allison et al., 2019; van Ittersum, 2008).

In addition, some aspects of remote proctoring itself lead to variation in testing conditions. Test-takers must allow themselves to be video recorded, knowing this recording will be reviewed later by an unknown person or persons. Anxiety about being surveilled – whether due to privacy concerns, the need to maintain a certain physical posture to remain in the webcam frame, or other such issues – may affect one's writing performance (Gallagher et al., 2021; Hoover et al., 2018). Moreover, having to conform to an observer's expectations can also lead to self-policing (Foucault, 1995), which may increase both self-consciousness and cognitive load. Conversely, some students may perform better with remote proctoring if they are prone to being distracted by the coming and going of proctors or the sounds and movements of other test-takers. This has implications for fairness at both individual and group levels. At an individual level, some test-takers may not mind sitting in one position throughout the test or sharing footage of themselves and the personal spaces in which they take the test, and thus they have an advantage over those who do. At a group level, students who take the in-person EPT-W do not experience these varying conditions as either advantages or disadvantages.

Finally, we note that the remotely proctored EPT-W is unable to accommodate test-takers with disabilities, in part because the university requires disabilities to be documented in-person by student accessibility services as part of the accommodations process. Accommodations such as longer testing times, assisted reading, and assisted writing, are facilitated through on-campus resources.

With our pre-exam system check, we tried to maintain some control over variation in testing conditions but could do nothing about test-takers' perceptions of variation in testing conditions as advantages, hindrances, or both. Thus, our picture of how remote administration of the EPT-W affects fairness of testing conditions remains incomplete and requires further scrutiny and evaluation.

10.3 EPT Oral Communication

The oral communication (OC) part of the EPT is designed to measure the ability of students to successfully participate in oral communication in campus and student-life situations. The construct of the EPT-OC has four components: (1) interactional competence, (2) appropriate use of phonology, (3) appropriate and accurate use of lexicogrammar, and (4) fluency (Ockey & Li, 2015). The first of these, interactional competence (IC), was the component most affected by our COVID-19 modifications. Ockey and Li (2015) define IC as 'an individual's underlying ability to actively structure appropriate speech in response to incoming stimuli ... in real time' (p. 5). This definition contrasts with views of IC as co-constructed and evolving through the mutual contributions of interlocutors, which are challenging to operationalise psychometrically with the aim of assigning individual scores.

In the pre-pandemic version of the EPT-OC, the four components of the construct were operationalised through three tasks. In the first task, an individual interview, two students were paired with two raters. Each student-rater pair sat together in opposite corners of the testing room. The student was asked three questions related to campus-life situations based on the context set by a still image. Following the interview task, the students were seated in the middle of the room for the second and third tasks. Raters remained in their seats to let students focus on communicating with each other. In the second task, the students first listened to an audio recording of two speakers, male and female, arguing for two opposing views on a topic. After playing each recording, raters tasked one of the students with summarising the audio content in a minute. In the third and final task, the student pair had four minutes to defend the position of the speaker whose argument they summarised in the second task in a paired discussion. This latter task was designed to facilitate maximal elicitation of IC, in contrast to the first two tasks, which allowed only limited interaction with the examiner. Since extended speech samples were elicited in all three tasks, the other aspects of the construct (lexicogrammar, pronunciation, and fluency) were considered to be well covered.

Students' performances were rated on the spot using a scale based on the four components of the construct (https://apling.engl.iastate.edu/wp-content/uploads/sites/221/2020/09/EPT-OC-Scale.pdf). The first task was rated by one rater and the second and third by both raters. The raw scores were then converted to fair scores through a many-facet Rasch model.

10.3.1 COVID-19 Modifications

Modifying the EPT-OC in response to COVID-19 was in some ways more challenging than the EPT-W. University policies mandating indoor mask use, social distancing, and reduced room capacity greatly affected face-to-face, natural oral communication, which is a focal aspect of the test. In addition, the implementation of these pandemic policies gave us little time to modify the test for the August 2020 administration.

To keep the construct of the test and test tasks as intact as possible, we decided first to try administering the test outdoors. We set up exam spaces in open areas around a campus building and kept all other aspects of the test the same. This obviated the need to train raters in new testing procedures, but it also meant the test took place in a noisy and distracting outdoor environment that presented test security risks. In addition, it would not have been a feasible option for the following administration in January 2021 because of the cold winter weather.

For the following spring semester and subsequent administrations while pandemic precautions remained in effect, we decided to use live video conferencing to deliver the EPT-OC. The platform selected was WebEx, which was recommended as the most stable and secure software by the University's IT department. The format developed for the video-conferencing administration (henceforth VCA) involved two examiners giving the test to individual examinees on two continuous video-conferencing feeds. These feeds were provided via laptops in different rooms in the exam building. An examinee was shown into the first room containing one laptop to find an examiner waiting on Webex to administer the first task to them. When the first task was done, an assistant ushered the examinee to a different room containing another laptop to have the second part of the test administered by a different rater on Webex. All the procedures were explained to examinees, and assistants made sure they found their exam rooms to ensure minimal anxiety and distraction caused by mid-test changes of settings.

In contrast to the outdoor administration in August 2020, the VCA involved considerable modifications to procedures, logistics, and rater training. While the first task remained unchanged, we removed examinee pairings for the second and third tasks, instead having the raters act as the interlocutor in order to reduce the number of connections to each WebEx exam session and thus the chances of things going wrong. If problems did occur, only one examinee would be affected, and this individual could more easily be retested. Finally, both the raters and the examinee laptops were on campus to avoid connection issues by using the university's reliable Wi-Fi network.

10.3.2 Test Fairness Considerations

10.3.2.1 Construct Representation

The outdoor version of the test did not require any changes to the original tasks, thus allowing the same operationalisation of the EPT-OC construct in terms of task content and construct. Instead, a major source of concern was variance in distractors, mainly caused by ambient noise. Although ambient noise may be part of the target language situation, lending support to the criterion-related validity of the score interpretation, it could be distracting for test-takers as well as raters variably, impacting performance and introducing construct-irrelevant variance (Ockey et al., 2021). Thus, one aspect of validity – that is, reliability – could have been affected by the outdoor administration.

By contrast, the VCA entailed more potential changes to construct representation by virtue of switching the audience for the retelling task from a peer examinee to an examiner. Since the first two tasks are limited in eliciting two-way interaction even in the original form, this was seen to have only a marginal effect on the construct representation of these two tasks (that is, the only difference was the audience, and the IC component of the construct measures the ability to respond appropriately regardless of audience). The major change involved the third task, which also affected construct representation in terms of IC. Rather than defending one recorded speaker's position in a discussion with another examinee, individual examinees had to argue both for and against the topic, which largely nullified two-way oral interaction. In other words, even though the capacity to elicit IC as defined by the construct was marginally affected in the third task, the nature of interaction was different, meaning that the construct representation of the face-to-face and VCA modes were not completely comparable.

In short, the VCA affected the operationalisation of the EPT-OC construct in terms of the nature of the IC elicited, although video-mediated oral communication tasks have the potential to better elicit IC than other remote administration alternatives, such as spoken dialogue systems (Ockey & Neiriz, 2021). Simply put, the interpretation of the scores from the two modes of administration might differ slightly in terms of the quality of IC ability they reflect. However, the implications of this for test fairness require further research. One question to consider is how construct modification differentially impacts test-takers. Another question is to what extent the IC elicited in the VCA administration represents the criterion situation compared to the face-to-face administration. Despite this difference in the operationalisation of the IC construct between the pre- and during pandemic administrations, the IC component remained in our rubric due to its importance in the Oral Communication course taken by students who do not pass the test. In this course, students receive their adjusted EPT-OC scores, and they and their instructors are encouraged to use that information to determine which aspects of oral communication to focus on improving.

10.3.2.2 Test Security

During the outdoor administration, maintaining the security of the test prompts was daunting, as they would have been easy for anyone nearby to hear. Thus, some examinees could have known about them beforehand, gaining an unfair advantage. One solution would have been to set a perimeter around the testing spaces, but this would be resource-intensive and impractical. Another strategy would have been to use different test forms across administrations (Weir & Wu, 2006). However, this would require the development of a large number of items which, again, was impractical given our capacities. As noted earlier, such unfair advantage can skew the score interpretation towards ability to perform prepared, rather than spontaneous, speech. Moreover, the test scores can be biased towards the group who had unfair access to test prompts.

The VCA, however, offered more control in terms of security. We prohibited examinees from touching the video-conferencing computers and kept the video feeds running continuously so the raters could see what the test-takers were doing in the exam rooms at all times. This likely deterred students from taking pictures or recording the session with the goal of sharing the prompts with others. The better security control allowed us to retain the test items used in the administration for future administrations. It must be noted that test-takers could still memorise the prompts and share them with others, but this can also happen in a face-to-face administration, and hence, the VCA can be said to be invariant to this security threat compared to the face-to-face mode.

10.3.2.3 Testing Conditions

While neither the outdoor administration nor the VCA required modifications to the test items, other aspects of the testing conditions obviously differed. In the original version, the picture that raters show to test-takers was clearly visible. In the VCA, for instance, the clarity of the picture held up to the camera by the rater was affected by screen glare and picture contrast, which some examinees said made it difficult to comprehend. Using an image description task to elicit spoken performance requires that the pictures used 'must be clear and unambiguous' (O'Sullivan, 2008, p. 11) which is difficult in the VCA context as we did not allow raters to screen share the picture as it required several steps of audio and video setup on WebEx for each test administration making it impractical.

In contrast to the EPT-W, fairness in terms of access was not seen to be affected by either the outdoor or VCA versions of the EPT-OC. In both cases, all equipment and testing locations were provided by the university, ensuring no differences in costs to examinees and no examinees being disadvantaged by unfamiliar technology. Test-takers simply had to sit in front of a computer and respond to the test tasks. This also ensured uniform testing conditions. Finally, in both versions, we made sure that the two-way communication aspect remained as intact as possible. Retaining this was seen as important for supporting good instructional and test preparation practices and discouraging excessive focus on monologic tasks that are not representative of the target language situation. This can be considered a positive washback effect, one which Kunnan (2008) regards as an important social consequence in his framework.

10.4 Conclusion and Post-Pandemic Lessons

Test adaptation is a common practice in the field of education in general and in language testing in particular. The main goal is to address the measurement needs of test administrators without having to develop a test from scratch. Whether the goal is to change the language of the test (e.g., Güven & Topbaş,

2014; Stansfield, 2003) or to respond to the limitations of the original administration (Green & Lung, 2021; Ockey et al., 2021; Purpura et al., 2021), two major challenges are to keep the construct unaltered and to avoid bias. Test adaptation projects do not follow a straight path and can be influenced both by testing considerations and contextual factors. Hence, learning how test adaptation has been undertaken in diverse contexts with different needs and priorities and how these changes affect testing considerations can support development of a knowledge base useful in times of emergency.

Looking back, it is clear that the experience of responding to the COVID-19 pandemic provided us with valuable insights into our existing assessment practices, priorities, and assumptions. The modifications we made allowed us to continue meeting the language assessment needs of our stakeholders but not without raising fairness concerns related to construct representation, test security, and test conditions. The more we thought through the implications of our changes, the clearer it became that fairness issues often worked in more than one direction; some modifications benefitted some students and disadvantaged others, and in ways that were not necessarily straightforward, depending on test-takers' individual situations.

The move to online, remote testing formats for both the EPT-W and EPT-OC showed us that it is indeed possible to administer the EPT remotely. Although, as this chapter has shown, there are disadvantages to remote testing, there are also many advantages, particularly for test-takers. For instance, the fact that students did not have to be on campus for the EPT-W meant that we were able to offer an 'early bird' administration six weeks before the start of the semester. This allowed ample time for students to receive their test results and modify their class schedule if supplemental English courses were required. In contrast, those taking the test in-person must take it the week before classes begin, leaving them little time to modify their schedule and possibly delaying their enrolment in English classes to a later semester. Such delays in completing English coursework run counter to the purpose of the EPT, which is to identify and support students with language support needs as early in their academic careers as possible.

Another valuable lesson was that technical failure is a reality of any remote administration, and measures must be in place to identify and address them proactively. We also learned that maintaining test security is less of a challenge if an examiner is involved in the administration process. For instance, it was easier to ensure test security in EPT-OC, as an examiner was constantly communicating with the examinee through a live feed. If resources are available, a similar live proctoring procedure can be implemented for EPT-W with a few proctors checking on the examinees through webcam a few times randomly throughout the test. Finally, shifting to remote administration is easier if it does not require changing the test format in a significant way. For instance, the original format of the speaking test involved face-to-face test-taker/examiner and test-taker/test-taker interactions. In the VCA format, we lost the authenticity of not only face-to-face interactions, but of student-to-student interaction, both of which constituted a fundamental part of the test's target domain.

The need to consider principles of assessment while prioritising health and safety was a thought-provoking challenge that stretched our capacities for resourcefulness and innovation. It also posed new and interesting questions such as, to what extent, and in what ways, might some test-takers try to circumvent our security measures, and how do the stakes of our tests affect consideration of such efforts? How do the apparatuses and processes of remote testing influence test-takers' stress levels, and how should this be factored into evaluation? Questions such as these seem very relevant given that, as a result of this pandemic, demand for remotely administered language testing is likely to not only continue but grow. And thus, such questions will continue to challenge our testing program and others like it.

Note

1 In this framework, validity is ostensibly defined in terms of score meaning only, instead of score meaning and use (Messick, 1989). In addition, validity and social consequences are treated as separate entities, unlike other models which view social consequences as part of validity (Messick, 1989).

References

Bachman, L. F., & Palmer, A. S. (1996). *Language testing in practice: Designing and developing useful language tests*. Oxford University Press.

Dimova, S., Yan, X., & Ginther, A. (2020). *Local language testing: Design, implementation, and development*. Routledge. https://doi.org/10.4324/9780429492242

English Placement Test. (n.d.). Retrieved October 25, 2021, from https://apling.engl.iastate.edu/english-placement-test/

Fielding, H. (2016). "Any time, any place": The myth of universal access and the semiprivate space of online education. *Computers and Composition*, *40*, 103–114. https://doi.org/10.1016/j.compcom.2016.03.002

Foucault, M. (1995). *Discipline and punish: The birth of the prison* (A. Sheridan, Trans; 2nd ed.). Vintage Books (Original work published 1975).

Gallagher, P. B., Meister, P., & Russell, D. R. (2021). Phenomenology of writing with unfamiliar tools in a semi-public environment: A case study. *Computers and Composition*, *62*, Article 1026688. https://doi.org/10.1016/j.compcom.2021.102668

Green, B. A., & Lung, Y. S. M. (2021). English language placement testing at BYU-Hawaii in the time of COVID-19. *Language Assessment Quarterly*, *18*(1), 6–11. https://doi.org/10.1080/15434303.2020.1863966

Güven, S., & Topbaş, S. (2014). Adaptation of the test of early language development-(TELD-3) into Turkish: Reliability and validity study. *International Journal of Early Childhood Special Education*, *6*(2), 151–176. http://www.int-jecse.net/abstract.php?id=90

Hoover, K. C., Crampton, J. W., Smith, H., & Berbesque, J. C. (2018). An empirical study of surveillance anxiety. *SocArXiv*. https://doi.org/10.31235/osf.io/yx6nk

Kunnan, A. J. (2004). Test fairness. In M. Milanovic, & C. Weir (Eds.), *European language testing in a global context* (pp. 27–48). Cambridge University Press.

Kunnan, A. J. (2008). Towards a model of test evaluation: Using the Test Fairness and Wider Context Frameworks. In L. Taylor, & C. Weir (Eds.), *Multilingualism and assessment: Achieving transparency, assuring quality, sustaining diversity* (pp. 229–251). Cambridge University Press.

Messick, S. (1989). Validity. In R. L. Linn (Ed.), *Educational measurement* (3rd ed., pp. 13–103). Macmillan.

O'Sullivan, B. (2008). *Notes on assessing speaking.* Retrieved November 17, 2021, from http://lrc.cornell.edu/events/past/2008-2009/papers08/osull1.pdf

Ockey, G., & Li, Z. (2015). New and not so new methods for assessing oral communication. *Language Value, 7*(1), 1–21. https://doi.org/10.6035/LanguageV.2015.7.2

Ockey, G. J., Muhammad, A. A., Prasetyo, A. H., Elnegahy, S., Kochem, T., Neiriz, R., Kim, H., & Beck, J. (2021). Iowa State University's English placement test of oral communication in times of COVID-19. *Language Assessment Quarterly, 18*(1), 26–35. https://doi.org/10.1080/15434303.2020.1862122

Ockey, G. J., & Neiriz, R. (2021). Evaluating technology-mediated second language oral communication assessment delivery models. *Assessment in Education: Principles, Policy & Practice, 28*(4), 350–368. https://doi.org/10.1080/0969594X.2021.1976106

Papageorgiou, S., & Manna, V. F. (2021). Maintaining access to a large-scale test of academic language proficiency during the pandemic: The launch of TOEFL iBT Home Edition. *Language Assessment Quarterly, 18*(1), 36–41. https://doi.org/10.1080/15434303.2020.1864376

Purpura, J. E., Davoodifard, M., & Voss, E. (2021). Conversion to remote proctoring of the Community English Language Program Online Placement Exam at Teachers College, Columbia University. *Language Assessment Quarterly, 18*(1), 42–50. https://doi.org/10.1080/15434303.2020.1867145

Scully-Allison, C. F., Parekh, H., Harris, F. C., & Dascalu, S. M. (2019). *Analysis of user experience and performance at initial exposure to novel keyboard input methods.* University of Nevada Reno. https://www.cse.unr.edu/~cscully/pubs/sca_conf_1.pdf

Stansfield, C. W. (2003). Test translation and adaptation in public education in the USA. *Language Testing, 20*(2), 189–207. https://doi.org/10.1191/0265532203lt252oa

van Ittersum, D. (2008). Computing attachments: Engelbarts' controversial writing technology. *Computers and Composition, 25*(2), 143–164. https://doi.org/10.1016/j.compcom.2007.12.001

Wagner, E., & Krylova, A. (2021). Temple University's ITA placement test in times of COVID-19. *Language Assessment Quarterly, 18*(1), 12–16. https://doi.org/10.1080/15434303.2020.1862849

Weir, C. J., & Wu, J. R. (2006). Establishing test form and individual task comparability: A case study of a semi-direct speaking test. *Language Testing, 23*(2), 167–197. https://doi.org/10.1191%2F0265532206lt326oa

11
INTEGRATION OF DATA-DRIVEN LEARNING AND ASSESSMENT THROUGH A MULTIMODAL CORPUS OF LEARNING OBJECTS AT THE TIME OF THE COVID-19 PANDEMIC

María Luisa Carrió-Pastor
UNIVERSITAT POLITÈCNICA DE VALÈNCIA, VALENCIA, SPAIN

11.1 Introduction

The main aim of this chapter is to present the patterns of the outcomes obtained in a project based on the compilation of a multimodal corpus of digital learning objects for English as a foreign language assessment purposes grounded on data-driven learning (DDL from now on). Digital learning objects are recordings of presentations for up to 10 minutes in which speakers focus on explaining a topic. In this study, Spanish students recorded examples of DDL in English to be shown to their peers. This project was initially designed and implemented for the lockdown period due to the COVID-19 pandemic in Spain (March to June 2020). Its main aim was to produce a repository of offline activities for assessing learners' oral skills. The study had the following objectives:

a. To create a repository of digital objects in English on DDL.
b. To propose a grid for the assessment of digital learning objects.
c. To provide guidelines for the use of multimodal assessment as a holistic way to motivate English learners in times of pandemic.

Obviously, the COVID-19 pandemic forced the reformulation of materials and assessment practices in English language teaching. On the one hand, during lockdown, all the activities and assessments had to be carried out remotely and, on the other hand, after lockdown, learners and teachers could not work in a physically close collaborative way, and thus some activities and assessment practices had to be reformulated.

DOI: 10.4324/9781003221463-13

The project was carried out at the Universitat Politècnica de València (Spain) and, for this experiment, 30 Spanish learners with an intermediate English level, that is, a B2 level following the Common European Framework of Reference for Languages (Council of Europe, 2001, 2020) were selected. These students were enrolled on an English for specific purposes subject, as part of their undergraduate engineering degree.

In the following section, previous studies on DDL and assessment of multimodality and digital objects are reviewed. Then, the materials and methods are described and the results section presents the data and examples compiled from the analysis. Finally, conclusions are drawn.

11.2 Data-Driven Learning

DDL is an approach that emerged from corpus linguistics. Large collections of electronic texts are compiled with many applications, including their use to illustrate real examples of grammatical rules and language descriptions. It is an approach that has been studied by several researchers. For example, Boulton and Vyatkina (2021) reflected on the new directions of DDL after 30 years of applying this approach in foreign language learning. They highlighted the lack of a theoretical-ideological base and the need to apply this approach in non-university contexts to improve the types of learner interaction with technology.

There are three aspects of DDL that should be emphasised. The first is the role of learners, as they are generally guided by teachers, but in DDL they work in an autonomous way. Learners access the corpus, study the use of words inductively, and look for the meaning of words, identifying the patterns to be learnt in a foreign language (Johns, 1991). As Gavioli (2001) explained, learners act as researchers; the instructors train them to investigate and identify language patterns.

The second aspect is the capacity to find answers to learning questions posed by learners (Boulton, 2017; Boulton & Cobb, 2017). Corpus tools are used by learners to study and analyse words and linguistic patterns autonomously. This approach could be used for self-study, as it is learner-centred and motivates self-discovery of a foreign language.

The third one is the use of real language to acquire a foreign language (Boulton, 2010, 2017). Learners pragmatically acquire a foreign language, being aware of the context and the specific use of some expressions. The process is inductive and a bottom-up procedure.

I would like to highlight some studies that pose several questions to be considered by DDL researchers. On the one hand, a key aspect is the difference between corpus-based and corpus-driven DDL. In general, these different approaches are applied to linguistic variation (Biber, 2009), but I consider they should also be taken into account in DDL. The main difference between these two approaches is that corpus-based DDL focuses on the grammatical and lexical features of corpora and learners acquire them through the identification of their functions, whereas corpus-driven DDL is more intuitive and language features are acquired through observation, in an inductive manner (Huang, 2014).

It is also important to identify the two teaching strategies that use DDL (Boulton, 2010). One is hands-on DDL, which is when learners search directly with a corpus tool or web. Learners are autonomous and acquire a foreign language guided by corpora (Chambers, 2007). The other one is hands-off DDL (Chambers, 2007), which is based on the use of corpora during class time. The teacher is the one who uses the corpora, selects the data to be used depending on the students' language proficiency level and prepares materials.

The effectiveness of DDL may be assessed from three different perspectives:

a. The evaluation of attitude (What do students think about DDL?), as showed by Yoon and Hirvela (2004).
b. Different practices (How do teachers use DDL?), illustrated by the studies by Carrió-Pastor (2020), Le Bruyn and Paquot (2021), and Pérez-Paredes and Mark (2021), who investigated how learner corpora and second language acquisition have come significantly closer in recent years.
c. Effectiveness (Can learners be more proficient with DDL?), analysed by Viatkina (2016). Similarly, Karpenko-Seccombe (2021) proposed DDL as a language-learner-as-detective approach as well as concordance-based corpus analysis for second language writers of English to improve foreign language proficiency.

Most of the studies that analyse the impact of DDL on foreign language learners identify a positive effect (Charles, 2014), but some others (Gilquin & Granger, 2010) explain that difficulties should also be considered, for example, the time invested in looking for the corpus and the language proficiency needed to identify corpora and their implications.

Quantitative studies are frequently used to analyse whether DDL is effective in increasing foreign language proficiency. Stevens' (1991) analysis can be considered the first to use quantitative studies to teach vocabulary, by applying exercises based on concordances. Likewise, Cobb (1997, 1999) presented quantitative studies and designed the software Compleat Lexical Tutor (https://www.lextutor.ca/), which presents an interactive interface that helps students to find concordances of words in English, French, German, and Spanish. Similarly, Allan (2009) provided an argument for using graded corpora in DDL; a small corpus does not seem to be a disadvantage and the fact that it is not a real corpus seems to help students as 'moving through levels of learner corpora would allow them to deepen knowledge gradually' (Allan, 2009, p. 30).

More recently, DDL research has focused on different aspects apart from vocabulary and grammar (Charles, 2012), that is, language comprehension and production (Frankenberg-García, 2014), reading speed (Hadley & Charles, 2017), pragmatic routines (Bardovi-Harlig et al., 2017), and aspects of the rhetoric of genres (Cotos et al., 2017).

The importance of mobile learning and the integration of DDL (Pérez-Paredes et al., 2019) should also be noted. In this regard, DDL is associated with the use of tools, and learners therefore need extensive training to fully understand its possibilities as a learning approach and to use DDL tools effectively (Carrió-Pastor, 2016). Moreover, Boulton and Vyatkina (2021) examined empirical research on DDL over 30 years. Their analysis is relevant in the sense that they not only reflected on the different empirical research conducted but also identified future research directions of these studies. Several aspects that can be improved in DDL research are identified: statistical analysis, types of learner interaction with technology, and lack of any theoretical-ideological base.

11.3 Using Multimodality and Digital Objects for Assessment

The second relevant topic of this chapter is assessment. Assessment typically deals with evaluating the written and oral skills of learners (Aull, 2015) and it is not an easy task for teachers (Rea-Dickins, 2007). Here, this chapter deals with the assessment of digital objects, so multimodality becomes crucial for this study as it includes visual communication, oral and written language, and gesture (Kress, 2010; Kress & van Leeuwen, 2001). Multimodality shows learners the multiple aspects implied in communicating in a foreign language, that is, languages are multimodal, as can be observed in our daily communication (Carrió-Pastor, 2014). Hence, multimodality is a must when teaching a foreign language (Yeo & Nielsen, 2020). This was also a key issue during the COVID-19 pandemic as students should be aware of the multimodal nature of language as a way to communicate while keeping a safe distance.

Regarding teaching with a multimodal perspective, many researchers have focused on the implications of multimodal learning models (Yeo & Nielsen, 2020), the design of learning activities (Jiang & Luk, 2016), or the study of multimodal instruction to support student learning (Coccetta, 2018). Yet, not many studies have focused on the assessment of multimodality (Adsanathan, 2012; Chang, 2019) and none of them concentrates on the assessment of digital objects based on DDL from a multimodal perspective.

In this vein, multimodal assessment poses some challenges for teachers such as what should be assessed (multimodal aspects, content, disciplinary understanding, etc.) and what criteria are to be followed to do so. Clear goals, criteria, and expected standards are features to be explained to foreign language learners before multimodal assessment (Chang, 2019). In addition, students should be active in the feedback process, collaborating with teachers in the assessment process. To assess the multimodal activities that were recorded, some aspects could be considered, such as the composition of the presentation, structure and discourse, language, and the design of the digital object.

Multimodal assessment benefits foreign language acquisition (Jewitt, 2003) as it keeps learners on-task, can be creative, assesses authentic material and eliminates repetitive assessment tasks. Additionally, teachers should guide learners, engaging them in composing their assessment criteria, which may be discussed during class time or 'out-of-school' (Van Leeuwen, 2015). Teachers may encourage students to submit a comment on each other's work collaboratively, thereby autonomously offering feedback.

11.4 Materials and Methods

11.4.1 Participants and Materials

The participants were 30 Spanish students enrolled in an optional English subject offered in an undergraduate engineering degree at the Universitat Politècnica de València (UPV) in the academic years 2019–2020 and 2020–2021. Their ages ranged from 20 to 29 years old and 80% were males. Only students with a B2 or intermediate level of English proficiency were selected to avoid inconsistencies in the recording of the learning objects and their assessment. Students worked individually on the design and delivery of the oral presentation but collaboratively in Microsoft Teams for the assessment and discussion of the learning objects.

One part of the materials of this study was composed of a corpus of 30 learning objects that were recorded by these students. A learning object is a 10-minute recording in which the presenter explains a concept with the help of a written presentation. In this chapter, the decision was made to compile learning objects recorded by students explaining an activity based on DDL. It was considered that during the COVID-19 pandemic, learners needed new activities that helped them to be creative.

In this regard, as technology has been vital for Spanish universities during times of pandemic due to governmental restrictions, before recording the digital learning objects for the global assessment of the English subject taught at the UPV, the advantages and disadvantages of the use of technology were considered after reading some previous research (Riasati et al., 2012; Warschauer & Meskill, 2000). In this vein, the different functions of the proposal by Laurillard (2002) to be used in foreign language teaching were considered:

a. Narrative: lectures, e-books, audio, and video.
b. Interactive: web, blogs, and social networks.

c. Adaptive: simulations and tutorials.
d. Communicative: text, audio, video conferencing, and discussion.
e. Productive: intranet.

Here, the activity proposed for assessment was narrative and adaptive, as students recorded a video of a tutorial to do DDL exercises. It was also communicative as the digital learning objects were assessed, shown, and discussed in Microsoft Teams.

The second part of the materials under study was the grid for the multimodal assessment of the digital learning objects in times of pandemic. It was initially designed by the three teachers of the English subject and later discussed with students, who suggested not including some aspects to be evaluated in the different sections, as they made the grid too long. Besides, the assessment of digital objects suggested by several researchers was taken into account to design this proposal for multimodal assessment (Adsanathan, 2012; Chang, 2019; Kleinfeld & Braziller, 2015; Weeks, 2018). Table 11.1 shows the grid designed in a collaborative way (by teachers and students) for the multimodal assessment of digital learning objects:

11.4.2 Methods

As the COVID-19 pandemic restricted the possibilities of collaborative work with physical contact, narrative and communicative technology were used to

TABLE 11.1 Grid for the Assessment of Learning Objects

Multimodal assessment of learning objects	*Mark*
(A) Communication	
The learner makes an arguable claim; effective communication	0–5
The learner appeals to a specific audience using visual and textual rhetorical appeals	0–5
Language use, intonation, and clarity	0–5
(B) Multimodality	
The claim is supported by spatial design, such as typography, colour, graphics, layout, etc.	0–5
The presentation is primarily visual rather than linguistic or alphabetic	0–5
The visual argument appeals to a specific audience	0–5
The description of design principles to create a visual argument	0–5
Links between text, images, and gestures	0–5
(C) Specific activity	
Explanation of the steps of the DDL activity	0–5
Discussion of how DDL benefits English learning with text and images	0–5
Comments	
Areas of strength	
Areas to be developed	

record learning objects made by students explaining DDL activities to their partners, adopting a multimodal perspective. This was adopted during the academic year 2019–2020, as in Spain it was decided to teach the subjects virtually due to the COVID-19 pandemic, and during the academic year 2020–2021 physical distancing of one and a half metres had to be maintained between desks or between individual students. Additionally, teachers had to avoid close face-to-face contact with students. This situation forced teachers to reformulate some activities and their assessment that had been designed before the pandemic. In this case, an on-site activity in which learners worked in pairs to present data-driven activities had to be redesigned in the form of an online activity. The presentations were part of the regular curriculum of the subject and the objectives were to assess the gestural, oral, and written patterns of presentations on DDL.

Thus, at the pre-implementation phase, all the students were informed about the implications of the task. The importance of DDL was taught by the three teachers and several examples of tools and corpora were shown. After that, it was explained that learners should record a presentation of about 10 minutes, that is, a learning object, explaining how DDL can improve English language proficiency. They could use their mobile phones or computers to record their proposal. The main aim of the task was to assess the oral proficiency of students in times of pandemic, but it was also designed to put into practice the advantages of using DDL for teaching a foreign language.

Teachers trained learners to integrate multimodal sources into the slides of their presentations. To that end, model presentations of multimodal sources and presentations (see Table 11.2) were explained and discussed in virtual classroom instruction (via Microsoft Teams).

Learners were taught how to prepare attractive and engaging presentations that can effectively draw the audience's attention to the message. Examples include the colours of the slides, using music or recordings, bold letters, animation effects, gestures by the presenters, visual design, and so on. The most popular corpora selected were: Corpus of Contemporary American English, British National Corpus, Lextutor, and Linguee but most learners preferred to select their own corpus from newspapers, political speech, or social media. Regarding the tools for DDL, most learners preferred Sketch Engine, AntConc, AntFileSplitter, and AntMover.

After being instructed on how to perform the digital learning objects, teachers and learners held meetings in Microsoft Teams to discuss the different aspects to be included in the multimodal assessment grid, which was uploaded to the teaching platform '*Poliforma-T*'. For example, students proposed to merge some of the sections to be evaluated as, in the initial proposal, teachers suggested that 'Language use, intonation, clarity' should be evaluated with individual marks and not just one mark for all of them. After discussing the advantages and disadvantages, it was considered that if they were assessed

TABLE 11.2 Theory-driven design rubric for assessing multimodal texts (Hung et al., 2013, pp. 402–403).

Design elements	Evaluation questions
Linguistic design	• Was the linguistic content comprehensible without major grammatical errors? • Was the linguistic content structured in a logical and organized manner? • How did the linguistic design represented in the multimodal text enable or limit the author's communication of meaning?
Visual design	• Did the author adopt a visual theme? • Did the author carefully design the use of color and typology to reflect the selected visual theme? • If chosen to use, did the author make meaningful use of available visual elements, such as graphics, to construct meaning in a cohesive manner? • How did the visual design represented in the multimodal text enable or limit the author's communication of meaning?
Gestural design	• Did the author make use of any animated elements or special effects to design dynamic sequencing of the content? • If chosen to use, was the animation used purposefully and meaningfully to complement or supplement the other design modes for meaning construction in a cohesive manner? • How did the gestural design represented in the multimodal text enable or limit the author's communication of meaning?
Auditory design	• Did the author make use of any auditory elements, such as music, sound effect or narration? • If chosen to use, were the auditory elements used purposefully and meaningfully to complement or supplement the other design modes for meaning construction in a cohesive manner? • How did the auditory design represented in the multimodal text enable or limit the author's communication of meaning?
Spatial design	• Did the author adopt a specific layout to structure design elements? • If chosen to use, did the author make use of text alignment and margins as design elements to complement or supplement the other design modes for meaning construction in a cohesive manner? • How did the spatial design represented in the multimodal text enable or limit the author's communication of meaning?

separately, the overall weight was excessive for the global mark. Hence, these three aspects were evaluated with a single mark. Further aspects discussed are detailed in Section 11.5.

Once students were aware of the way they were going to be assessed, the presentations were recorded. All the learning objects were then uploaded to a repository in *Poliforma-T* that was part of a corpus compiled as samples to improve the oral performance of English learners.

After that, students and teachers worked collaboratively in Microsoft Teams to watch (in meetings), assess (using the multimodal assessment grid), and give feedback (using the chat feature and the grid) on the learning objects. After watching the digital learning objects, students had to participate actively, explaining the process and the way they proceeded as well as the difficulties encountered. If students asked teachers to do so, some of the presentations could be repeated.

Hence, following a multimodal approach, in 'Communication', the keywords, language, and rhetorical strategies were assessed, while the visual arguments, gestures, intonation, and other multimodal aspects were evaluated in 'Multimodality' and the organisational patterns and the importance of DDL were tagged and analysed in 'Specific Activity'. Additionally, the assessor could take some notes regarding aspects to be improved. The main intention was to assess the oral performance of learners but an additional aim was to use this corpus as input for future groups of students. The learners were informed that the total point grades on this task would be decided by the recording of the learning object with the assessment grid (50%), the DDL activity presented (20%), and the pre- and post-discussion in Microsoft Teams with a statement reflecting on the learning object (30%), following the general evaluation rules of the subject.

Finally, guidelines were proposed for the use of multimodal assessment as a holistic procedure to motivate English learners in times of pandemic.

11.5 Results and Discussion

This section is divided into the different objectives set out in the introduction of the chapter.

11.5.1 To Create a Repository of Digital Learning Objects on DDL

Thirty digital learning objects that explain the way DDL can improve English proficiency were recorded by the students and uploaded to the teaching platform *Poliforma-T*, in which the contents, tests, and activities of the subject were shown. One of the purposes of the activity was to create a repository to teach DDL in a multimodal way, that is, following hands-on DDL (Boulton, 2017). Thus, learners had to choose a corpus and a tool and prepare the activity based on DDL. In the presentation, students had to convince readers of the benefits of their proposals, explaining how to find the corpus, how to use the tool, and the different possibilities of using DDL.

As explained in Section 11.4.2, to obtain the desired goals and ensure students did the task correctly, teachers explained the assessment grid and the different aspects to be thought about before recording the presentation. The first aspect was that learners had to be aware of the main characteristics of a multimodal presentation, its benefits and constraints. Furthermore, learners had to decide which was the best multimodal presentation taking into account their goals. Also, the technical aspects of multimodal presentations had to be considered. Additionally, learners had to be aware of the marking criteria of multimodal presentations (that is, the multimodal assessment grid).

Once the activity had finished, teachers and students commented on it. Learners felt proud of the final product of the activity. In the different meetings in Microsoft Teams, all the learners were excited to describe the way they created the DDL activity and how they recorded the presentation. The experience was extremely positive given the participation of learners in the oral feedback and considering the special circumstances caused by the COVID-19 pandemic. All the learners involved in the activity carefully prepared the content of the DDL activity, recorded the presentations several times and justified every step they took for the activity.

11.5.2 To Propose a Grid for the Assessment of Learning Objects

The second objective was to prepare a rubric for assessing a multimodal activity. In the preparation of the grid, different stages were followed, which are shown below. Both the rubric and the steps were explained to learners before the activity was carried out.

11.5.2.1 Preparation of the Activity

The grid (see Table 11.1) based on the studies by Adsanathan (2012), Chang (2019), Kleinfeld and Braziller (2015), and Weeks (2018) was designed collaboratively (by teachers and students) as a rubric for assessing learning objects. In this case, due to COVID-19 restrictions, the grid was first designed by teachers and discussed in Microsoft Teams meetings with learners, as explained above. Learners should know the concepts to be assessed to be able to prepare for the activity adequately.

11.5.2.2 Identification of the Outcomes to Be Assessed

The outcomes of the activity to be assessed had to be identified. They were discussed with students and it was agreed that improving communication in a foreign language, taking advantage of DDL, and enhancing the digital skills of learners were the crucial aspects to be improved and assessed. Hence, it was considered whether learners working independently could select a range of long texts for DDL. This meant that learners had to critically analyse and use language structures of texts and vocabulary. Additionally, learners were expected to investigate and evaluate the linguistic relationships that had to be identified in corpora. Moreover, learners needed to evaluate specific texts and tools and choose the most appropriate ones.

In the assessment grid, the following aspects were initially considered by teachers, taking into account previous studies by Adsanathan (2012), Chang (2019), Kleinfeld and Braziller (2015), and Weeks (2018):

1. Argumentation: to compose a presentation that showed an insightful understanding of DDL.
2. Language use: to use, explain, and communicate with adequate language, which could be specific or general depending on the DDL activity.
3. Links between text, images, and gesture: to draw links among texts, pictures, data-driven activities, gestures, videos, recordings, etc.
4. Effective communication: to be able to communicate effectively to teachers and other learners.

Once all these aspects had been discussed with students, the assessment rubric was designed and uploaded in *Poliforma-T*.

11.5.2.3 The Assessment Grid

Following the recommendation by Chang (2019, p. 16), 'The assessment rubric encompasses general aspects of oral presentation skills not limited to the aspect of multimodality, to ensure the assessment validity', different categories and subcategories were proposed (Communication, Multimodality and Specific activity).

During the meetings in Microsoft Teams, the first draft of the assessment grid was shown to the students, who suggested merging some of the sections (see Section 11.4.2). Learners also proposed incorporating two additional sections: areas of strength and areas to be developed. It should be highlighted that more points were included in the multimodality section, as students also wished to stress the importance of this component in the presentations of digital objects. The final version of the multimodal assessment grid can be seen in Table 11.1. The assessment grid was validated, as the three teachers previously used this final version with a group composed of ten students. The three teachers assessed the same students and contrasted their assessments, discussing possible incongruences and validating the need to include the different categories and sections.

11.5.3 Guidelines for Multimodal Assessment

The last objective of the study was to suggest guidelines for multimodal assessment. The guidelines were drawn up by the three teachers involved in the project after assessing, first, 10 students and then the 30 students addressed in this chapter. Even when, in the academic year 2020–2021, learners were taught in the classroom, as personal distance had to be maintained, teachers also used the digital learning objects repository. After that, it was considered positive to design some guidelines for multimodal assessment in a formative way. The steps included in these guidelines were as follows:

11.5.3.1 Pre-implementation: Instructions to Learners

Lectures on multimodal presentations and assessment are delivered. It should be explained to learners that the recording of a multimodal presentation is a combination of two or more communication modes, for example, images, gestures, texts, etc. A multimodal presentation includes at least one mode other than reading and writing, such as listening, speaking, viewing, and representing. Learners should prepare the presentation adequately. All the modes to be included in a multimodal presentation should be considered. Additionally, the content to be explained (in this case, a DDL activity) should be prepared in a PowerPoint or Prezi presentation and explained step by step. Learners should be aware that they have to dedicate a fair amount of time to preparing their multimodal presentations. Regarding assessment, they are instructed to practise with peers in Microsoft Teams. Additionally, they are told to follow these steps:

- Research the content to be included.
- Produce the multimodal presentation.
- Write the script.
- Rehearse it.

Thus, learners are trained and assessed on how to represent ideas and the strategies that they employ. The assessment rubric is designed and discussed with learners to obtain feedback and adjust it to learners' interests. Learners should know the assessment criteria in advance.

11.5.3.2 Implementation: Multimodal Digital Objects and Their Assessment

During the recording of multimodal digital objects, most learners feel anxious as they are assessed. While presenting, students have to take into account the following aspects: language, pronunciation, gestures, using rhetorical strategies, especially engagement, and the specific topic to be explained. Learners also have to be aware of the time limit and should demonstrate aptitude across various modes. Teachers should be sure that learners have the necessary skills to use technology and explain a concept, thereby allowing them to communicate successfully. Learners should see and be aware of the aspects of the assessment grid, paying attention to pacing, clarity of speech, tone and volume, eye contact, and gestures. If teachers decide to discuss the recordings in a group activity, it should be explained clearly to students whether this is part of the assessment or not.

11.5.3.3 Post-implementation: A Reflection Statement

To finish the assessment of multimodal presentations, a reflection statement, in which learners discuss the process of recording and participating in the assessment, should be required. Learners explain to their peers the way they proceeded throughout the whole process. The reflection statement also offers learners an opportunity to think about what they would change if they could do it again. This self-reflection activity exercises critical and creative thinking, personal responsibility, useful failure, adaptability, etc. To guide learners in self-reflection, some brainstorming ideas are provided in Microsoft Teams. These outlines address the structure of the reflection statement, grammar and sentence structure, spelling errors, literary devices to convey meaning, connections among ideas, communication of ideas with insightful visual aids, effective control of voice, and body language.

11.6 Conclusions

The outcomes of this project are twofold. On the one hand, students worked collaboratively on the assessment of multimodal learning objects with teachers in Microsoft Teams and, on the other, a repository of multimodal learning objects that provided guidelines for the production and assessment of oral skills was compiled. These outcomes were devised to assess oral skills when face-to-face classes were not possible or a safe distance should be maintained due to the COVID-19 pandemic, but they can also be used in online classes or for self-study.

DDL was the content to be developed by English learners for recording presentations on activities based on corpus studies, thus creating a repository of digital learning objects and teaching them to look for self-study material. Teachers instructed learners on the preparation of multimodal presentations and discussed multimodal assessment as a holistic way to improve their oral skills during lockdown. Learners discussed the adaptation of the multimodal assessment grid collaboratively with teachers online. Finally, after carrying out this project for two academic years, guidelines were proposed for the use of multimodal assessment as a holistic way to motivate English learners in times of pandemic, highlighting the importance of reflection.

To conclude, during class time the teachers observed that the 30 English learners showed strong positive attitudes towards multimodal assessment. They appreciated teachers' expertise and experience, acting as researchers, as Gavioli (2001), Boulton and Cobb (2017), and Karpenko-Seccombe (2021) proposed, that is, using DDL as a language-learner-as-detective approach. Hence, the findings of this study shed light on promoting the multimodal assessment of academic presentations by incorporating DDL and digital learning objects. Learners were engaged in DDL, and struggled with preparing activities for their peers, incorporated new concepts of oral presentations in their training and acknowledged the importance of assessment. Additionally, learners worked collaboratively with teachers during the assessment sessions to develop their knowledge of evaluation practices.

Regarding post-pandemic lessons, the product resulting from the project carried out over two academic years was the proposal for the multimodal assessment of digital learning objects. All these materials were used in the following academic years to guide learners in the preparation and self-assessment of their multimodal learning objects. In this chapter, assessment is the key aspect to be taken into account to help learners understand the implications of the activity and to be aware of the characteristics of communication.

In future studies, the results of multimodal assessment will be compared with traditional assessment, and more learning objects will be incorporated into the repository to show teachers that even in periods of lockdown, learners can be motivated and participate actively in their training and assessment process.

References

Adsanathan, C. (2012). Integrating assessment and instruction: Using student-generated grading criteria to evaluate multimodal digital projects. *Computers and Composition, 29*, 152–174.

Allan, R. (2009). Can a graded reader corpus provide 'authentic' input? *ELT Journal, 63*(1), 23–32.

Aull, L. (2015). Connecting writing and language in assessment: Examining style, tone, and argument in the U.S. Common Core standards and in exemplary student writing. *Assessing Writing, 24*, 59–73.

Bardovi-Harlig, K., Mossman, S., & Su, Y. (2017). The effect of corpus-based instruction on pragmatic routines. *Language Learning & Technology, 21*(3), 76–103.

Biber, D. (2009). Corpus-based and corpus-driven analyses of language variation and use. In B. Heine, & H. Narrog (Eds.), *The Oxford handbook of linguistics analysis* (pp. 1–34). Oxford University Press.

Boulton, A. (2010). Data-driven learning: Taking the computer out of the equation. *Language Learning, 60*(3), 534–572.

Boulton, A. (2017). Research timeline: Corpora in language teaching and learning. *Language Teaching, 50*(4), 483–506.

Boulton, A., & Cobb, T. (2017). Corpus use in language learning: A meta-analysis. *Language Learning, 67*(2), 348–393.

Boulton, A., & Vyatkina, N. (2021). Thirty years of data-driven learning: Taking stock and charting new directions over time. *Language Learning & Technology, 25*(3), 66–89.

Carrió-Pastor, M. L. (2014). Estudio contrastivo de la variación de términos e imágenes en el discurso multimodal. In C. Vargas (Ed.), *TIC, trabajo colaborativo e interacción en Terminología y Traducción* (pp. 556–564). Comares.

Carrió-Pastor, M. L. (Ed.). (2016). *Technology implementation in second language teaching and translation studies. New tools, new approaches*. Springer.

Carrió-Pastor, M. L. (Ed.). (2020). *Corpus analysis in different genres. Academic discourse and learner corpora*. Routledge.

Chambers, A. (2007). Popularising corpus consultation by language learners and teachers. In E. Hidalgo, L. Quereda, & J. Santana (Eds.), *Corpora in the foreign language classroom* (pp. 3–16). Rodopi.

Chang, Y. (2019). Assessment for learning to integrate multimodality with academic presentations in a multilingual MBA classroom. *Multimedia-Assisted Language Learning, 22*(1), 9–40.

Charles, M. (2012). Proper vocabulary and juicy collocations: EAP students evaluate do-it-yourself corpus building. *English for Specific Purposes, 31*(2), 93–102.

Charles, M. (2014). Getting the corpus habit: EAP students' long-term use of personal corpora. *English for Specific Purposes, 35*(1), 30–40.

Cobb, T. (1997). Is there any measurable learning from hands-on concordancing? *System, 25*(3), 301–315.

Cobb, T. (1999). Breadth and depth of lexical acquisition with hands-on concordancing. *Computer Assisted Language Learning, 12*(4), 345–360.

Coccetta, F. (2018). Developing university students' multimodal communicative competence: Field research into multimodal text studies in English. *System, 77*, 19–27. https://doi.org/10.1016/j.system.2018.01.004

Cotos, E., Link, S., & Huffman, S. (2017). Effects of technology on genre learning. *Language Learning & Technology, 21*(3), 104–130.

Council of Europe. (2001). *The common European framework of reference for languages.* Council of Europe Publishing.

Council of Europe. (2020). *The common European framework of reference for languages: Learning, teaching, assessment. Companion Volume.* Council of Europe Publishing.

Frankenberg-García, A. (2014). The use of corpus examples for language comprehension and production. *ReCALL, 26*(Special Issue 2), 128–146.

Gavioli, L. (2001). The learner as researcher: Introducing corpus concordancing in the classroom. In G. Aston (Ed.), *Learning with corpora* (pp. 109–137). Athelstan.

Gilquin, G., & Granger, S. (2010). How can DDL be used in language teaching. In A. O'Keeffe, & M. McCarthy (Eds.), *The Routledge handbook of corpus linguistics* (pp. 359–370). Routledge.

Hadley, G., & Charles, M. (2017). Enhancing extensive reading with data-driven learning. *Language Learning & Technology, 21*(3), 131–152.

Huang, Z. (2014). The effects of paper-based DDL on the acquisition of lexicogrammatical patterns in L2 writing. *ReCALL, 26*, 163–183.

Hung, H., Chiu, Y., & Yeh, H. (2013). Multimodal assessment of and for learning: A theory-driven design rubric. *British Journal of Educational Technology, 44*(3), 400–409.

Jewitt, C. (2003). Re-thinking assessment: Multimodality, literacy and computer-mediated learning. *Assessment in Education: Principles, Policy & Practice, 10*, 83–102.

Jiang, L., & Luk, J. (2016). Multimodal composing as a learning activity in English classrooms: Inquiring into the sources of its motivational capacity. *System, 59*, 1–11. https://doi.org/10.1016/j.system.2016.04.001

Johns, T. (1991). Should you be persuaded-two samples of data-driven learning materials. *ELR Journal, 4*, 1–16.

Karpenko-Seccombe, T. (2021). *Academic writing with corpora: A resource book for data-driven learning.* Routledge.

Kleinfeld, E., & Braziller, A. (2015). Evaluating multimodal assignments. *Digital rhetoric collaborative.* https://www.digitalrhetoriccollaborative.org/2015/09/17/evaluating-multimodal-assignments/

Kress, G. (2010). *Multimodality. A semiotic approach to contemporary communication.* Routledge.

Kress, G., & van Leeuwen, T. (2001). *Multimodal discourse*. Bloomsbury Academic.
Laurillard, D. (2002). *Rethinking university teaching: A conversational framework for the effective use of learning technologies*. Routledge.
Le Bruyn, B., & Paquot, M. (Eds.). (2021). *Learner corpus research meets second language acquisition*. Cambridge University Press.
Pérez-Paredes, P., & Mark, G. (Eds.). (2021). *Beyond concordance lines. Corpora in language education*. John Benjamins.
Pérez-Paredes, P., Ordoñana Guillamón, C., Van de Vyver, J., Meurice, A., Aguado Jiménez, P., Conole, G., & Sánchez Hernández, P. (2019). Mobile data-driven language learning: Affordances and learners' perception. *System, 84*, 145–159.
Rea-Dickins, P. (2007). Classroom-based assessment: Possibilities and pitfalls. In J. Cummins, & C. Davison (Eds.), *International handbook of English language teaching* (pp. 505–520). Springer.
Riasati, M. J., Allahyar, N., & Tan, K.-E. (2012). Technology in language education: Benefits and barriers. *Journal of Education and Practice, 3*(5), 25–31.
Stevens, V. (1991). Concordance-based vocabulary exercises: A viable alternative to gap-fillers. *English Language Research Journal, 4*, 47–63.
Van Leeuwen, T. (2015). Multimodality. In D. Tannen, H. Hamilton, & D. Schiffrin (Eds.), *The Handbook of Discourse Analysis* (pp. 447–465). John Wiley & Sons.
Viatkina, N. (2016). Data-driven learning of collocations: Learner performance, proficiency, and perceptions. *Language Learning & Technology, 20*(3), 159–179.
Warschauer, M., & Meskill, C. (2000). Technology and second language teaching. In J. Rosenthal (Ed.), *Handbook of undergraduate second language education* (pp. 303–318). Lawrence Erlbaum.
Weeks, R. (2018). *Multimodal assessment – What, why and how?* The University of Sydney. https://educationalinnovation.sydney.edu.au/teaching@sydney/multimodal-assessment-what-why-and-how/
Yeo, J., & Nielsen, W. (2020). Multimodal science teaching and learning. *Learning, Research and Practice, 6*(1), 1–4. https://doi.org/10.1080/23735082.2020.1752043
Yoon, H., & Hirvela, A. (2004). ESL student attitudes toward corpus use in L2. *Journal of Second Language Writing, 13*(4), 257–283.

SECTION III
Managing L2 Assessment at the Time of the Crisis: The Way Forward

12

TEST USEFULNESS OF E-PORTFOLIOS

An Alternative Approach during and Beyond the Pandemic

Ricky Lam

HONG KONG BAPTIST UNIVERSITY, KOWLOON TONG, HONG KONG

12.1 Background

E-Portfolios are broadly defined as digital containers, which document learners' efforts, growth, and achievements over time. They are the natural successors of paper-based portfolios when the Internet and e-Learning became popular around the turn of the century. In first and second language education research, e-Portfolios are adopted as an auxiliary component alongside the mainstream didactic instruction. Despite being widely recognised, e-Portfolios, when used for summative assessment in language classrooms, remain underexplored, both before and during the COVID-19 pandemic. At this unprecedented time, research evidence has shown that student learning has been seriously affected, including incessant suspension of face-to-face classes, postponement of school-based assessments, distraught social and mental well-being of students, and a sudden shift to home-based learning without sufficient preparation (Chiu et al., 2021). These phenomena create huge, if not harmful, impacts on student learning. Likewise, recent language teaching studies demonstrate that teachers may not necessarily adjust well to remote teaching due to their belief systems, levels of computer literacy, and professional training in online pedagogy (Cheung, 2021). Because of these reasons, Reich (2021) has claimed that only a minority of students could thrive; and educational technology, at times, could not facilitate student learning as promised.

Although e-Portfolios are reportedly beneficial to student language learning, such as enhanced motivation and improved writing skills, more evidence is certainly needed to prove its usefulness when e-Portfolios are applied as a dependable assessment tool for online learning (Aygün & Aydin, 2016). There are some initial studies reporting how e-Portfolios could be utilised as an

DOI: 10.4324/9781003221463-15

assessment tool during the pandemic (cf. Lam, 2021a). However, its full potential as an alternative to complement or substitute in-person evaluation of students' integrated language skills remains to be seen, because, thus far, there have been no studies to examine the test usefulness of e-Portfolios during and beyond the pandemic. To this end, this chapter aims to fill this much-needed gap in language assessment research. Subsequent to this opening section, the chapter unpacks the theoretical rationale for alternative assessment relating to e-Portfolios. Then, it describes the notion of test usefulness in terms of four major test qualities, namely validity, reliability, washback, and practicality which are most relevant to language teachers' lives. The chapter goes on to evaluate a contextualised e-Portfolio program with the four test qualities. After that, the post-pandemic lessons learnt from the aforementioned program evaluation are discussed. The chapter ends with implications suggesting future directions if e-Portfolios are accepted as an up-and-coming alternative in language assessment.

12.2 Rationale for Alternative Assessment

In the 1990s, theorists began to criticise the traditional discrete-point assessment and multiple-choice tests, because they were not able to evaluate students' language ability authentically, for instance, communicative competence. While these discrete-point tests were somewhat easy to administer and score, they were unable to make a fair, accurate judgment of students' language learning per se, i.e., developmental progress. Since then, assessment scholars have advocated alternative assessment, which generally refers to continuous assessment or performance assessment that involves students in completing real-life tasks, such as project works, peer assessment tasks, and reflective journals over time (Brown & Hudson, 1998). As opposed to a prevailing testing culture at that time, the direct nature of alternative assessment dovetails with the quintessence of an assessment culture, which supports using classroom-based assessment to improve language teaching and learning, for example, assessment for learning (Allal, 2020). High-stakes standardised testing encapsulated in the testing culture tends to demotivate learning and limit teaching contents, whereas alternative assessment epitomised in the assessment culture enhances both learners' autonomy and teachers' language assessment literacy (Lam, 2019a). More importantly, alternative assessments allow 'a more valid interpretation of information, e.g., test scores and qualitative feedback than that obtained from more traditional standardised tests' (Hamayan, 1995, p. 215). Regardless of the learning-oriented potential of alternative assessment, Fox (2008) summarised that there were always ongoing barriers when teachers attempted an alternative assessment approach at the classroom level, including preparation time, costs, assessment expertise, restriction of prescriptive school-based curriculum, and influence of a larger exam-driven culture.

Among many assessment methods, digital portfolios can be considered one of the most pre-eminent forms of alternative assessment in language assessment. It is because the attributes of e-Portfolios fit in well with those of alternative assessment. For instance, alternative assessment is low-stakes and low-impact as compared to high-stakes testing, which usually creates negative impacts on student learning. Alternative assessment permits multiple attempts and numerous opportunities to revise before final summative evaluation (i.e., delayed scoring in e-Portfolio assessment). It is also student-centred, process-oriented, as well as data-driven, denoting that throughout the ongoing assessment process, students and teachers will create a wealth of multimodal evidence to inform effective language teaching and learning (Yancey, 2019). The unique element of multiple referencing warrants an ethical and equitable assessment approach as exemplified in e-Portfolio compilation processes. Besides those features, alternative assessment is culturally sensitive, accommodating students' learning needs from diverse ethnic and linguistic backgrounds (Cummins & Davesne, 2009). In addition, it promotes deep learning, acquisition of higher-order thinking skills, problem-solving skills, learner independence, and metacognitive capacity in second language classroom settings (Lam, 2021b). As mentioned by Brown and Hudson (1998), the alternative assessment approach has three pedagogical advantages, including strengthening of student learning, teacher empowerment, and improvement of assessment procedures, which remain highly relevant to the 21st century's language assessment landscape. Although alternative assessment such as e-Portfolios appears to have countless educational merits, their test usefulness has not been systematically reviewed and investigated. The next two sections discuss the idea of test usefulness, and then evaluate a Hong Kong-based e-Portfolio program in terms of four test qualities respectively.

12.3 Notion of Test Usefulness and Key Test Qualities

Bachman and Palmer (1996) theorised the notion of test usefulness in their seminal work. They proposed that if a test was to be useful, it should fulfil six test qualities, including 'reliability, construct validity, authenticity, interactiveness, impact (washback) and practicality' (p. 18). These six test qualities are regarded as one entity, because they operate in compliance with three principles coherently. They entail: Principle 1: we can only maximise *the overall test usefulness* not individual test qualities; Principle 2: we can only evaluate *the combined effect* on the overall usefulness of a test; and Principle 3: we can only determine the degree of test usefulness and the appropriate balance among different qualities for each unique assessment situation (Bachman & Palmer, 1996). These principles emphasise any given test should take test purposes, intended test takers, and target language use (TLU) into consideration. The TLU tasks are defined as authentic and communicative tasks students can apply outside of the test. Although these theorists have argued for the totality and combined effect of the overall usefulness of a test, there is always a trade-off between one quality and the other. For instance, a classroom-based e-Portfolio assessment is likely to be valid in terms of simulation of real-life tasks, but may not deem reliable as its scoring methods remain complex and inconsistent (Lam, 2021a).

To align with the scope of this chapter, I have chosen four major test qualities for discussion and evaluation, namely validity, reliability, washback, and practicality. The reasons for choosing these four test qualities are threefold. First, they are much more pertinent to frontline teachers' lives and works than the other two qualities. For example, if teachers do not plan ahead the purpose of their e-Portfolio assessment programs explicitly, they may not achieve desirable intended learning outcomes. Similarly, if teachers do not seriously consider any intended and unintended impacts of their e-Portfolio assessment programs on instruction, they may work less efficiently and are unable to facilitate students' language learning as planned. Second, like what Bachman and Palmer (1996) have stated previously, these four test qualities are inter-related conceptually and likely to influence one another pedagogically. The purpose of a test or the interpretation and use of test scores (validity) will closely link to the consistency of grading (reliability). Then, the test purpose and scoring accuracy are likely to exert impacts (washback) on teachers and students, and the purpose, consistency, and consequence of the test will ultimately influence the extent to which the test could be administered properly in terms of time, expertise, and financial resources (practicality). Third, owing to the theme of the chapter and space limitation, I simply have room to discuss the four test qualities in greater detail. In the following paragraphs, I delineate each test quality (validity, reliability, washback, and practicality) one after another.

Validity means what a test intends to measure. There are many types of validity, such as content, criterion, face, as well as consequential validity. In this chapter, we solely discuss *construct validity*. It is defined as the degree to which we interpret a test score as a parameter of the language skill(s) or construct(s) we plan to measure (Shepard, 2016). Hughes (2003, p. 26) argued that 'construct validity has been increasingly used to refer to the general, overarching notion of validity'. To enhance construct validity, Hughes proposed teachers to adopt direct testing of language abilities, for instance, using paper-based or digital portfolios to evaluate students' composing skills directly rather than using multiple-choice testing. By so doing, teachers can accurately measure students' writing skills over time and utilise those assessment data to fine-tune their writing instruction for effective teaching and learning. In addition, construct validity warrants a content alignment of TLU tasks (e.g., collaborative project works, e-Portfolios on writing) and test tasks within any given contextualised testing situations. In other words, this alignment is likely to evaluate students' specific language abilities more purposefully, accurately, and authentically. The quality of construct validity may promote test fairness and ethics as every test taker is treated impartially in theory despite their cultural and linguistic diversity (Newton & Baird, 2016).

Reliability is broadly defined as the consistency of scoring. There are three types of consistency, namely (a) across time (test-retest reliability); (b) across items (internal consistency of test items/tasks); and (c) across markers (inter-rater reliability; Brown & Abeywickrama, 2018). In educational assessment scholarship, there have been ongoing debates about the dichotomy between validity and reliability. Prior to the 1990s, scholars tended to prefer reliability to validity, because maintenance of a high to acceptable level of inter-rater reliability was indispensable, particularly in those state-wide direct writing assessments and large-scale portfolio assessments which needed to warrant test fairness (Linn et al., 1991). After the 1990s, there was a conceptual change, in which theorists started refocusing on the significance of validity over reliability although they advocated re-examining the construct of reliability from a hermeneutic approach to assessment. In other words, classroom teachers could score learners' works dependably, since they were much more familiar with the learners' educational contexts and able to monitor the assessment tasks over time as exemplified in e-Portfolio assessment (Chapelle, 1999; Shepard, 2006). As White (1994) challenged the supremacy of reliability in writing assessment, he pointed out that the dichotomy between validity and reliability was not legitimate. In support of White's opinions, Moss (1994) claimed that reliability was only considered one key aspect of construct validity rather than a prerequisite to validity. In a similar vein, Yancey (1999) proposed that the reliability of e-Portfolios relied not on statistical consistency but on consensus built upon communal reading, interpretations, and negotiations of portfolio tasks.

Washback is one major facet of impact. It occurs at the micro level, influencing individuals like students and teachers, whereas impact exists at the macro level, affecting society and education systems (Taylor, 2005). In this chapter, we merely focus on the former concept. What draws this notion and construct validity together is that 'the effects of testing on teaching and learning have been associated with test validity' (i.e., consequential validity; Cheng, 2008, p. 350). Messick (1996) redefined the notion of construct validity 'by placing washback within the consequential aspect of construct validity' (p. 242). In other words, washback could be regarded as one significant aspect of construct validity. This test quality can also be classified into both positive and negative. Nonetheless, Alderson and Wall (1993) regarded the term as neutral, since failure to create positive washback of a test was caused by lots of issues, say society, educational policies, and schools (Hamp-Lyons, 1997). Cheng (2008) concurred that it was an intricate test quality, stating that simply changing the syllabi and procedures of a test might not necessarily result in obvious changes in language instruction. Based upon her review of language assessment research, she found that 'language tests had a noticeable consequence on curriculum more than on pedagogy' (Cheng, 2008, p. 351). As Messick (1996) argued, researchers should not measure washback alone, because there are numerous confounding variables that determine the effects of a test on teaching and learning.

Practicality refers to pragmatic issues when a test is administered, such as time, costs, and efficiency (Crusan, 2010). Unlike validity, reliability, and washback, practicality does not involve any interpretation and use of test scores. In fact, practicality is about resources and ease of test implementation. Bachman and Palmer (1996) defined practicality as 'the relationship between (a) the resources that will be required in the design, development, and use of the test and (b) the resources that will be available for these activities' (p. 36). They explained that if (b)/(a) < 1, the test was impractical; whereas if (b)/(a) ≥ 1, the test was practical. Taking individual oral exams as an example, their practicality is relatively low although the exams have high construct validity in their scoring, positive washback on speaking instruction, and high authenticity by connecting test tasks with specific TLU domains. Large-scale portfolio assessment of writing is another case in point. Pittsburgh and Vermont's state-wide portfolio programs (1990–1995) introduced in the U.S. were said to be impractical due to exorbitant administrative costs and low inter-rater reliability as compared to the conventional impromptu essay testing (Lam, 2017). Bachman and Palmer (1996) outlined that there were three types of resources, i.e., human (test writers, scorers), material (space, equipment), and time to determine whether a test was practical or not. In the following section, I will evaluate a local e-Portfolio assessment program with the above four test qualities.

12.4 Evaluation of e-Portfolios with Test Usefulness

To contextualise the evaluation of test usefulness, I introduce the e-Portfolio assessment program created by Manson (a pseudonym). Manson is a Hong Kong English teacher with two-year work experience, serving in one middle-range government-funded secondary school. He teaches both junior and senior secondary-level students. When he set up his e-Portfolio program during the third class suspension back in early December 2020, he targeted a class of 14 eleventh-graders with English proficiency ranging from average to slightly below average, equivalent to the highest end of B2 level in the Common European Framework of Reference. At that time, Manson designed a school-based teaching package, and delivered an elective module called 'Learning English through Workplace Communication', one of the three mandatory electives to be taught in the three-year senior secondary curriculum (i.e., Grades 10–12). The language focus was to learn how to write a school magazine article on whether Hong Kong graduates should look for job opportunities in other Asian cities. The genre of writing was an argumentative essay, which would be tested in the standardised school-leaving exam – the Hong Kong Diploma of Secondary Education Exam.

In this elective, Manson attempted the process writing approach, requiring students to write in drafts for each paragraph they composed. He further integrated the 'PASCOLT' elements (i.e., **p**urpose, **a**udience, **s**tyle, **c**ontent, **o**rganization, **l**anguage, and **t**ext-type) into his writing instruction. Manson explained that he replicated these instructional elements based upon the process-genre approach introduced by Hyland (2016). From a diagnostic pre-writing test, these 14 eleventh-graders obtained 4.3 marks out of 7 in content and 3.7 marks out of 7 in language. These scores reflected that the students were in urgent need of well-constructed sentence structures in order to improve their academic writing. During the course of the elective, all in-person classes were suspended from December 2020 until March 2021 due to the fourth wave of the COVID-19 pandemic. Hence, Manson's school immediately switched to remote teaching by using Google Classroom and Zoom. Building on this infrastructure, Manson developed his e-Portfolio program by requiring students to perform self- and peer-assessments on their drafts before uploading them for marks and qualitative comments. Besides regular lessons, Manson arranged additional online tutorials to debrief students about the strengths and weaknesses of their writings with collective feedback. Furthermore, he gave students individual written feedback in the scanned PDF files uploaded on Google Classroom.

Manson's e-Portfolio program emphasised three features. First, Manson provided students with multiple opportunities to improve writing. The process-oriented approach could enhance motivation and self-efficacy. After all, Manson's students were not top-scorers, and were still struggling with how to write accurately and fluently for the public exam. Second, Manson utilised Google Classroom as a peer learning site to display students' drafts during the pre-writing (brainstorming) and while-writing stages (drafting). Additionally, to promote collaborative writing in the post-writing stage (revising), Manson created a Google Docs, in which students could edit and rewrite their rebuttals during online class time by either consulting Manson or referring to exemplars composed by former graduates. Third, Manson was able to monitor students' writing progress more frequently on virtual classes than via in-person classes, as the e-Portfolio tool was highly accessible and synchronised. Due to the dynamic nature of Google Classroom and Google Docs, Manson managed to encourage peer assessment skills and a community of practice throughout the program. Now, I turn to evaluating four test qualities relating to Manson's e-Portfolio program.

His program has high to moderate construct validity due to the following reasons. First, Manson adopted a direct assessment of writing by inviting students to submit written drafts in process, say in about two to three weeks' time. In real contexts, students composed their works in an extended timeframe rather than under a timed condition, like in the public exam. Second, Manson provided students with tentative scores and qualitative feedback in stages, and interpreted those scores for both diagnostic and formative purposes. He used the early comments appearing in students' first drafts as his own pedagogical input for altering writing instruction in the subsequent online lectures. The acts of blending learning and assessment pedagogically promote construct validity, because those scores and feedback are likely to help improve students' writings eventually. Third, the e-Portfolio assessment tasks corresponded to authentic TLU domains, namely peer learning and collaborative writing skills. On Google Classroom, students were required to read, share, edit, and comment on each other's works publicly. Online peer assessment exercises aligned with the TLUs as suggested on Manson's teaching agendas, i.e., peer interactions and communicative competence. Concerning collaborative writing skills, the Google Docs task facilitated a community of practice by involving all students in composing and editing teammates' rebuttals during online lectures. The connection between assessment tasks and TLU tasks improves overall validity as well as authenticity of Manson's e-Portfolio program.

Reliability remains a thorny issue in alternative assessment. When we gauge Manson's e-Portfolio program from a hermeneutic perspective to assessment, it has high to moderate reliability due to the following two reasons. First, Manson could monitor students' writing progress regularly within a period of four months and was able to triangulate students' initial, interim, and final drafts on Google Classroom synchronously. Such formative assessment practices were conducive to high consistency of scoring in terms of (a) across time (e.g., observations throughout remote teaching) and (b) across tasks (e.g., timely feedback provision on e-Portfolio tasks). Second, since Manson graded students' writings by himself, he was supposed to understand their learning needs, academic aptitudes, and levels of participation the best. With this in mind, Manson's scoring was likely to be dependable. Nonetheless, when we evaluate Manson's e-Portfolio program from a psychometric perspective to assessment, it may have low reliability due to the fact that e-Portfolio scoring is always complex, challenging, and subjective, especially when Manson did not involve double marking. Although Manson's e-Portfolio program could not achieve high reliability in a psychometric sense, scholars have suggested that the notion of reliability need a renewed interpretation, namely dependability or trustworthiness to uphold its test usefulness within the context of alternative assessment (Davison & Leung, 2009).

Washback is considered neutral, as assessments are neither good nor wrongful but only tools to evaluate and support students' learning (Brown & Hudson, 1998). With that being said, certain assessment tasks tend to create more negative washback than the others, for example, timed impromptu essay tests (Weigle, 2007). Since Manson's e-Portfolio program emphasises process writing, self- and peer-assessments, and progress checking, it is likely to exert positive washback on students' learning. For instance, students have adequate online space to learn, correct, and adjust learning with multi-sourced (self, peer, or teacher) and multimodal (audio, textual, or visual) feedback. Albeit instructed by Manson, his students enjoyed lots of opportunities to create, curate, and reflect upon their own drafts in the e-Portfolios, enabling greater levels of learner agency (i.e., involvement in the decision-making process – which drafts should be uploaded for grading). Further, students actively engaged in peer learning and collaborative writing, which made second language writing experience neither daunting nor intimidating. For Manson, the e-Portfolio program had positive washback on his professional practices in the following aspects. First, Manson broadened his instructional approaches (attempts to process writing) and upgraded his computer literacy (trials of Google Classroom and Google Docs). Second, he introduced the 'PASCOLT' elements in the writing instruction, which was not required in his school curriculum. Because of e-Portfolios, Manson could even augment the curriculum contents. Third, other than a language coach, Manson assumed a new teacher identity as *an online language assessor* who provided students with multimodal feedback to consolidate learning. Despite having positive washback, the e-Portfolio program also had negative washback on certain students in the class. As reported by Manson, it appears that some students mainly focused on 'polishing' technological skills more than acquiring language learning skills. A few students reported that they were not proficient in transforming their drafts into scanned copies using mobile phones. The level of students' computer literacy remained a cause for concern when e-Portfolios were implemented. A few students also reported that their data plans did not permit successful uploads and downloads of digital documents due to the large file size. Because of the digital divide, the fairness issue of e-Portfolio assessment, one aspect of washback, was yet to be resolved, especially for those economically disadvantaged students who could not afford costly digital gadgets or data plans (Hockly & Dudeney, 2018).

To judge the practicality of Manson's e-Portfolio program, I evaluate it by referring to Bachman and Palmer's three types of resources: human, material, and time as discussed in the previous section. For human resources, Manson took charge of the entire e-Portfolio program on his own from initial startup to final evaluation as he was the only one to adopt alternative assessment in his school. When asked what administrative support he received, he said none and was solely responsible for all implementation logistics. He recounted that in each form level, colleagues were asked to follow a standardised scheme of work where core contents and essential assessment tasks were strictly adhered to. For material resources, Bachman and Palmer (1996) described them as (i) space, (ii) equipment, and (iii) materials. Space was probably not a concern, since Manson stored and shared all instructional materials on Google Classroom. In fact, Manson mentioned that using free online platforms could ease the issue of storage and largely shorten assignment turnaround time. In any e-Portfolio program, equipment alludes to laptops, tablets, mobile phones, and Wi-Fi network. In Manson's school, each student was provided with an iPad on loan and entitled to use free Wi-Fi on campus. Time resources refer to development time for the entire program, i.e., time for training students' computer skills, managing and scoring e-Portfolios, and time for completing e-Portfolio tasks, e.g., drafting, editing, and revising works-in-progress. Undoubtedly, compared to human and material resources, time resources are likely to mitigate the practicality of Manson's e-Portfolio program, given that he and his students spent massive amount of time to participate in the program throughout the class suspension. Overall speaking, Manson's e-Portfolio program has high to moderate practicality except for time resources. In the next section, I discuss the post-pandemic lessons learnt from the current review.

12.5 Post-Pandemic Lessons Learnt from the Review

E-Portfolios are indeed a viable and laudable alternative in language assessment, but they are less likely to substitute for in-person teaching and assessment after the global pandemic. Teachers and other stakeholders need to evaluate their school-based e-Portfolio programs with test usefulness and its associated test qualities. By so doing, they can strengthen the effectiveness of their newly introduced programs, and ensure that the delivery of these programs is methodically tried and tested. The lessons learnt from the use of e-Portfolios as an alternative assessment approach during the COVID-19 pandemic include: how to increase construct validity, how to create positive washback on teaching and learning, and how to warrant high practicality and dependability.

To improve construct validity, teachers should develop an awareness of the assessment purposes, ensuring what specific language sub-skills and grammar patterns will be summatively evaluated. The mapping of intended learning outcomes and their corresponding assessment activities has to be congruent. During the pandemic, due to disruptions to face-to-face teaching, some teachers merely recycled their discrete-point tests without matching with virtual teaching contents. E-assessment activities are supposed to align with TLU domains (e.g., online task-based learning) in order to facilitate students' development of communicative competence. Thus, they can seamlessly convert into real-life tasks to enhance authenticity and construct validity. Such a constructive alignment between curriculum and assessment requires teachers to plan and develop test specifications of an e-Portfolio task rigorously, so that it measures what it purports to measure. Also, the scores generated by the e-Portfolio task are truthfully indicative of a student's language ability within a specific TLU domain.

To create positive washback on language instruction, teachers need to upgrade assessment literacy by incorporating assessment for learning practices into their e-Portfolio programs, namely mini-research projects, peer-assessment exercises, and collaborative writing assignments. Without having these student-centred elements, e-Portfolios are only reduced to a digital container, in which students serve as a content supplier by uploading PDF files. Teachers should provide students with timely, actionable, and succinct feedback, since most e-Portfolio platforms characterise synchronisation, interactivity, and learner agency which are all conducive to high-quality learning. Concerning washback on learning, students need to be trained to manage their e-Portfolios proactively, namely how to manipulate e-Portfolio interfaces for compilation and curation of artefacts; how to act upon e-feedback to adjust learning; and how to augment online participation in diverse e-Portfolio activities (i.e., break-out room discussion, chatroom posts, and interactive learning apps like Mentimeter). In times of pandemic, teachers and students need to step up their assessment and computer literacy respectively in order to deal with the ever-changing virtual pedagogical environment.

To achieve high practicality and dependability, teachers should take human, material, and time resources into consideration. For human resources, learning how to score students' e-Portfolios summatively requires skills and extra time. Hence, teachers are advised to elicit clerical and technical support from school to expedite such a complex undertaking. For material resources, teachers may get sponsorship from small grants, applied research funds, or professional development subsidies to start up their e-Portfolio programs, since they need to pay subscription fees of commercial e-Portfolio systems, purchase essential digital gadgets, and acquire some e-learning or e-assessment software tools. In terms of time factors, teachers may consider introducing e-Portfolio programs alongside the existing English curriculum. They could try out the program by creating a critical mass, say among four teachers in one grade level to save preparation time and share instructional materials. If time permits, they are encouraged to conduct action research to validate the usefulness of their e-Portfolio programs. Concerning dependability, e-Portfolio assessment promotes students' originality in their works, because every e-Portfolio is unique in terms of language, content, and rhetoric. Students' continuous efforts to compile the portfolio of works are likely to avoid cheating and suspected plagiarism, as teachers are able to check on students' artefacts at various stages of their e-Portfolio construction. In the final section, I conclude the chapter by discussing three implications if e-Portfolios are to be sustained beyond the pandemic.

12.6 Implications and Conclusion

As there is a paradigm shift from a *testing* culture to an *assessment* culture, the advent of alternative assessment, e.g., self- and peer-assessments and e-Portfolios amid the assessment *for/as* learning movements can be said to be inevitable (Hamp-Lyons, 2016). Since the turn of the century, we have witnessed more and more teachers adopt alternatives in assessment to improve instruction and to create positive impacts on language education. Nonetheless, it appears that scholars remain sceptical about the test usefulness of alternative assessment in general and paper-based/digital portfolios in particular, because these alternatives may not essentially fulfil all test qualities as described earlier in this chapter, namely construct validity, reliability, washback, and even practicality. Theoretically, it is imperative to legitimise the status of alternative assessment by (a) reaching conceptual clarity to maintain consistency in the implementations of alternative assessment (Brown & Hudson, 1998); (b) developing new understanding and interpretations of test qualities under the teacher-based assessment paradigm as opposed to the psychometric testing paradigm (cf. Davison & Leung, 2009); and (c) enhancing language assessment literacy of the users of alternative assessment (e.g., teachers, administrators, language testers) since they need to be highly proficient in developing, scoring, and evaluating these alternative assessment tasks diagnostically and summatively (Tsagari, 2021).

Pedagogically, owing to the flexible and diverse nature of alternative assessment, teachers may consider attempting an e-Portfolio approach to contextually accommodate their work contexts. For instance, e-Portfolios can be classified into a strong and a weak version (Lam, 2019b). The former refers to a complete overhaul of paper-based language curriculum by emphasising a paperless instructional approach when in-person classes are conducted, whereas the latter adopts a hybrid mode by utilising e-Portfolios as a supplementary tool for remote teaching whenever face-to-face instruction is disrupted. Undoubtedly, the weak version of e-Portfolios can carry on as an adjunct to the existing curriculum, so that students could fall back on a digital dossier to compile, curate, and monitor their language learning reflectively. Hence, teachers are encouraged to fine-tune their classroom-based e-Portfolio programs in accordance with students' levels of computer literacy, students' willingness for participation, availability of fiscal and logistical support, and teachers' beliefs and readiness. With careful design and development, teachers are likely to trial e-Portfolios as an alternative assessment approach more assertively even beyond the pandemic.

Individually, teachers and students need to change their mindsets to accept alternative assessment, e-assessment, e-feedback, and/or e-Portfolios more bravely and enthusiastically. Since we have encountered unprecedented challenges and lots of uncertainties in educational assessment between 2020 and

2022, we are now transitioning into the post-pandemic era as well as 'an alternative era in language testing and assessment' (Fox, 2008, p. 107). Because of this, teachers should be ready for embracing change in instructional and evaluation approaches when in-person teaching could be unexpectedly suspended as a result of natural disasters, global pandemic, public health issues, and other political-driven factors like warfare. Teachers are advised to learn how to master the applications of e-Portfolios through professional development, and to explore the possibility of using e-Portfolios as an alternative to informing language teaching and learning in virtual environments. By so doing, teachers can broaden their repertoires of online pedagogical and assessment skills, which will make them and their students future-ready to resolve most mishaps.

To conclude, this chapter has duly achieved its aims by discussing the notion of test usefulness as well as evaluating an e-Portfolio program with its four test qualities. It then provides teachers and researchers with most insightful and practical post-pandemic lessons based upon the review of the construct of test usefulness. Considering the above discussion, it appears that utilising e-Portfolios as an alternative to evaluate students' language learning is a viable and essential option, since classes can be suspended but not learning, particularly in times of adversity. Online teaching and e-assessment have become a normalcy during the three-time class suspensions in Hong Kong. Although e-Portfolios, like other alternatives in assessment, are no silver bullet for actual learning improvement, they do have numerous benefits in language education, including increased motivation, improved literacy skills, enhanced autonomy, and better peer learning skills, especially when backed by rigorous qualitative and quantitative research data. Regardless of these advantages, e-Portfolios still have some complex issues awaiting to be unravelled if they are to serve as a mainstream assessment tool in the post-pandemic era, namely scoring consistency, standardisation in test contents, assessment, and technology training. While the test usefulness of e-Portfolios remains agreeable, they are only a means to an end. When teachers use e-Portfolios in physical and/or virtual classroom settings, they need to guard against all potential caveats by maximising their construct validity, reliability, washback, and practicality. Lastly, if used ethically and appropriately, e-Portfolios will become a promising assessment tool soon.

Acknowledgements

This work was funded by the Language Fund under Research and Development Projects 2021–2022 of the Standing Committee on Language Education and Research (SCOLAR), Hong Kong SAR. The project reference number is (EDB(LE)/P&R/EL/203/12).

References

Alderson, J. C., & Wall, D. (1993). Does washback exist? *Applied Linguistics, 14,* 115–129.

Allal, L. (2020). Assessment and the co-regulation of learning in the classroom. *Assessment in Education: Principles, Policy & Practice, 27*(4), 332–349.

Aygün, S., & Aydin, S. (2016). The use of e-portfolio in EFL writing: A review of literature. *ELT Research Journal, 5*(3), 205–217.

Bachman, L. F., & Palmer, A. S. (1996). *Language testing in practice: Designing and developing useful language tests.* Oxford University Press.

Brown, H. D., & Abeywickrama, P. (2018). *Language assessment: Principles and classroom practices* (3rd ed.). Pearson.

Brown, J. D., & Hudson, T. (1998). The alternatives in language assessment. *TESOL Quarterly, 32*(4), 653–675.

Chapelle, C. A. (1999). Validity in language assessment. *Annual Review of Applied Linguistics, 19,* 254–272.

Cheng, L. (2008). Washback, impact and consequences. In E. Shohamy & N.H. Hornberger (Eds.), *Language testing and assessment: Encyclopedia of language and education* (Vol. 7; pp. 349–364). Springer.

Cheung, A. (2021). Language teaching during a pandemic: A case study of Zoom use by a secondary ESL teacher in Hong Kong. *RELC Journal.* https://doi.org/10.1177/0033688220981784

Chiu, T. K. F., Lin, T. J., & Lonka, K. (2021). Motivating online learning: The challenges of COVID-19 and beyond. *The Asia-Pacific Education Researcher, 30*(3), 187–190.

Crusan, D. (2010). *Assessment in the second language writing classroom.* The University of Michigan Press.

Cummins, P. W., & Davesne, C. (2009). Using electronic portfolios for second language assessment. *The Modern Language Journal, 93,* 848–867.

Davison, C., & Leung, C. (2009). Current issues in English language teacher-based assessment. *TESOL Quarterly, 43*(3), 393–415.

Fox, J. (2008). Alternative assessment. In E. Shohamy & N.H. Hornberger (Eds.), *Language testing and assessment: Encyclopedia of language and education* (Vol. 7; pp. 97–109). Springer.

Hamayan, E. V. (1995). Approaches to alternative assessment. *Annual Review of Applied Linguistics, 15,* 212–226.

Hamp-Lyons, L. (1997). Washback, impact and validity: Ethical concerns. *Language Testing, 14*(3), 295–303.

Hamp-Lyons, L. (2016). Purposes of assessment. In D. Tsagari, & J. Banerjee (Eds.), *Handbook of second language assessment* (pp. 13–27). De Gruyter.

Hockly, N., & Dudeney, G. (2018). Current and future digital trends in ELT. *RELC Journal, 49*(2), 164–178.

Hughes, A. (2003). *Testing for language teachers* (2nd ed.). Cambridge University Press.

Hyland, K. (2016). *Teaching and researching writing* (3rd ed.). Routledge.

Lam, R. (2017). Taking stock of portfolio assessment scholarship: From research to practice. *Assessing Writing, 31,* 84–97.

Lam, R. (2019a). Teacher assessment literacy: Surveying knowledge, conceptions and practices of classroom-based writing assessment in Hong Kong. *System, 81,* 78–89.

Lam, R. (2019b). *Using portfolios in language teaching* (New Portfolio Series 4). SEAMEO Regional Language Centre.

Lam, R. (2021a). E-Portfolios: What we know, what we don't, and what we need to know. *RELC Journal*. https://doi.org/10.1177/0033688220974102

Lam, R. (2021b). Using ePortfolios to promote assessment of, for, as learning in EFL writing. *The European Journal of Applied Linguistics and TEFL, 10*(1), 101–120.

Linn, R. L., Baker, E. L., & Dunbar, S. B. (1991). Complex, performance-based assessment: Expectations and validation criteria. *Educational Researcher, 20,* 5–21.

Messick, S. (1996). Validity and washback in language testing. *Language Testing, 13,* 241–256.

Moss, P. A. (1994). Can there be validity without reliability? *Educational Researcher, 23*(2), 5–12.

Newton, P. E., & Baird, J. (2016). The great validity debate. *Assessment in Education: Principles, Policy & Practice, 23*(2), 173–177.

Reich, J. (2021). Ed tech's failure during the pandemic, and what comes after. *Phi Delta Kappan, 102*(6), 20–24.

Shepard, L. A. (2006). Classroom assessment. In R. L. Brennan (Ed.), *Educational measurement* (4th ed., pp. 623–646). Praeger.

Shepard, L. A. (2016). Evaluating test validity: Reprise and progress. *Assessment in Education: Principles, Policy & Practice, 23*(2), 268–280.

Taylor, L. (2005). Washback and impact. *ELT Journal, 59*(2), 154–155.

Tsagari, D. (2021). Language assessment literacy: Concepts, challenges, and prospects. In S. Hidri (Ed.), *Perspectives on language assessment literacy: Challenges for improved student learning* (pp. 13–32). Routledge.

Weigle, S. C. (2007). Teaching writing teachers about assessment. *Journal of Second Language Writing, 16*(3), 194–209.

White, E. (1994). Issues and problems in writing assessment. *Assessing Writing, 1*(1), 11–27.

Yancey, K. B. (1999). Looking back as we look forward: Historicizing writing assessment. *College Composition and Communication, 50*(3), 483–503.

Yancey, K. B. (Ed.). (2019). *ePortfolio as curriculum: Models and practices for developing students' ePortfolio literacy.* Stylus.

13

CAN INTERACTIONS HAPPEN ACROSS THE SCREENS?

The Use of Videoconferencing Technology in Assessing Second Language Pragmatic Competence

Shishi Zhang and Talia Isaacs

UNIVERSITY COLLEGE LONDON, LONDON, UNITED KINGDOM

13.1 Introduction

Technology has changed the language assessment landscape over the past several decades, driving research innovation and revolutionising possibilities and practice for operational assessments. One technology that has experienced a substantial uptick during the COVID-19 pandemic in response to self-isolation, social distancing, and restriction of movement orders is videoconferencing technology. Even predating the pandemic, videoconferencing was explored as an alternative to face-to-face speaking interactions for low- and high-stakes second language (L2) assessments (e.g., Kim & Craig, 2012; Nakatsuhara et al., 2016). However, the shift to videoconferencing during the pandemic, even in the case of human-mediated and live scored high-stakes speaking tests (Clark et al., 2021) is unprecedented, likely cementing its future in speaking assessment as a viable alternative to face-to-face provision.

This chapter centres on uses of videoconferencing, particularly emphasising implications for assessing L2 pragmatic competence as part of the speaking construct. After providing some baseline definitions, we foreground research and practice before and during the COVID-19 pandemic, synthesising research and evaluating the benefits and trade-offs of using this technology. We then summarise changes to the assessment landscape by considering past problems, current practices, and future possibilities. Given the slant of the chapter on pragmatic competence and our desire to contribute to further work in this underresearched area, seizing on the new global order catalysed by COVID-19, we highlight future directions of using videoconferencing in assessing L2

DOI: 10.4324/9781003221463-16

pragmatics, including the potential uses of videoconferencing to deliver interactive, multimodal assessments.

13.2 Foundational Concepts and Defining Key Constructs

Before delving into the history of the use of videoconferencing, we first provide some foundational concepts and discuss construct definitions. Videoconferencing can be defined as the transmission of audio and video signals to support real-time communication between people at two or more physically separate locations (Al Hasrouty et al., 2017). Thus, assessments that do not involve remote, synchronous communication between two or more human interlocutors using both visual and audio channels are not included in the definition of videoconferencing. It was first used commercially to support interactions of remote groups in the 1960s (Dustdar & Hofstede, 1999). From the late 1990s, technological improvements such as increased and cheaper bandwidth and more advanced video compression enabled the further development and use of videoconferencing. Videoconferencing was introduced into education as a tool for distance learning. However, the use of videoconferencing for assessment purposes was relatively rare and mostly confined to low-stakes research or pedagogical contexts. It was during the 2010s (with rare exceptions) that a few isolated studies examining the feasibility of videoconferencing for high-stakes assessment purposes began to appear. The use of the technology for standardised tests alongside remote proctoring was catapulted due to restrictions on human movement during the pandemic.

The L2 speaking assessment literature has long distinguished between different modes of test delivery. A direct speaking test, which involves face-to-face communication with a human interlocutor (e.g., examiner, interviewer, another test-taker), can be conducive to communicative, authentic assessments. However, the inclusion of a human interlocutor and the variability of the test environment can work against the reliability of the assessment. This option can be also resource-intensive and expensive and in some contexts is impractical. An alternative is the use of semi-direct speaking tests, which refers to a tape/phone/web/computer-mediated test using pre-recorded input, where test-takers' responses are audio-/video-recorded for subsequent scoring. These tests have the benefit of standardising delivery and removing interlocutor effects (Qian, 2009), and, in the case of computer-mediated semi-direct tests, allowing multimodal task types (Galaczi, 2010). However, direct and semi-direct tests cannot be regarded as equivalent, even though the test scores using these different modes often highly correlate (O'Loughlin, 2001). They differ, for example, in the number and types of functions and topics elicited and the communicative strategies and discourse features reflected through test-takers' oral output (Shohamy, 1994). Thus, test users should choose the suitable type of tests considering the specific context and purpose. For example, for situations where test designers aim at a performance assessment for daily in-person communication (e.g., simulated academic discussions), direct testing is still advantageous (Shohamy, 1994). However, the choice was taken away for some during the pandemic, with lockdowns and the closure of test centres resulting in some established direct tests being rapidly adapted and launched for online use and, hence effectively becoming semi-direct.

Since the 1980s, there has been increasing emphasis on communicative language use of L2 speaking ability (e.g., Bachman & Palmer, 1996), including expressing intentions in socially and culturally appropriate ways, and co-constructing and achieving communicative goals with others (Taguchi, 2019). In communicative competence and language ability models, such abilities are subsumed under the labels *pragmatic competence* (Bachman & Palmer, 1996) and *interactional competence* (He & Young, 1998). Drawing on Timpe-Laughlin and Youn's (2020) definition of pragmatic competence and interactional competence and Galaczi and Taylor's (2018) definition of interactional competence, pragmatic competence refers to the ability to use language in socially, culturally, and contextually appropriate ways to achieve specific communicative goals; interactional competence denotes the ability to successfully employ knowledge of participation patterns, topic and turn management, register, and pragmatics when co-constructing meaning and communicative goals with interlocutors. The use and understanding of the pragmatic meanings of communicative acts is, hence, a defining feature of interactional competence. However, interactional competence goes beyond an individual: it is co-constructed by all participants of a discursive and dialogic practice (Young, 2019).

Over the past 30 years, L2 pragmatic competence assessment centred on measuring discrete skills (e.g., requests and apologies; implicatures or implied meanings). It later proceeded to more discursive, performance-based assessments via reciprocal tasks (i.e., tasks that involve interlocutor interaction and feedback; Timpe-Laughlin & Youn, 2020). Most computer- or web-based tests and paper-and-pencil tests of L2 pragmatics assess a fairly limited construct and, consequently, a limited interpretation of test-takers' L2 pragmatic competence. Alongside the development of L2 pragmatics assessment pre-pandemic, some researchers eliciting pragmatic performance for research purposes selected direct tests with more interactive formats (e.g., roleplays) that resemble real-life conversations for a higher level of construct representation of pragmatic competence (e.g., Grabowski, 2013; Youn, 2015).

The decades-long question remains: Is there a consistent and practical way to assess L2 speaking ability that includes pragmatic competence? The use of videoconferencing retains the co-constructed nature of face-to-face interactions from direct speaking tests through the computer-mediated delivery of semi-direct tests. Thus, videoconferencing is a hybrid that could allow for greater accessibility to test-takers (e.g., not needing to travel to test sites) while still facilitating real-time communication between interlocutors. This chapter overviews the use of videoconferencing in assessing L2 speaking, with a specific focus on assessing pragmatic competence and interactional competence where research evidence is available.

13.3 Research on the Viability of Using Videoconferencing to Assess L2 Speaking Pre-COVID-19

From the early 1990s until the onset of the pandemic, research using videoconferencing for assessment purposes mainly focused on the technological viability, validation of speaking tests through videoconference, test-takers' and examiners' behaviours, and comparisons of test scores obtained through videoconferencing versus face-to-face modes. In general, using videoconferencing for speaking tests was not considered viable in instructional settings given the high costs and technological requirements for smooth transmission of audio and video signals. An early study by Clark and Hooshmand (1992) explored the technological viability of using video teleconferencing technologies in oral tests. They compared oral proficiency interview performance of Arabic and Russian learners of English using in-person versus satellite-based video teletraining, which allowed real-time remote 'screen-to-screen' communication through satellite broadcasting. The authors examined test-takers' and examiners' experience of the testing process and the resulting scores, which were not significantly different across modes. Due to the underdeveloped technology at that time, there were serious signal delays, resulting in brief 'drop-out' periods with no sound when the interlocutors spoke simultaneously, or motion discontinuity with video signals when the interlocutors suddenly moved or used gestures. Hence, it is unsurprising that 57% of the Arabic and 74% of the Russian test-takers preferred face-to-face.

Although initially an expensive high-tech fantasy, by the 21st century, videoconferencing had evolved into a cheaper, more accessible tool, making it possible for anyone with a computer or smartphone and adequate bandwidth to have real-time videoconferencing interactions with interlocutors around the world. Kim and Craig's (2012) study on face-to-face versus videoconferencing benefited from technological advances, including high-bandwidth connection and compression technologies for audio and video file transmissions. Oral interviews performed by Korean learners of English a month apart (counterbalanced order) revealed no significant differences across the two modes. Follow-up interviews showed that most test-takers were satisfied with both modes, although five expressed discomfort with videoconferencing. The authors concluded that videoconferencing is 'suitable for replacing or supplementing face-to-face oral interviews' (p. 273), noting the advantage of drawing on an international pool of interviewers and raters that may not be available locally through cheaper remote testing. Although demonstrating benefits and challenges in using videoconferencing, questions about whether interlocutors behave differently across the two modes and differences in L2 performance quality remained unexplored.

In a series of IELTS-funded outputs exploring the use of videoconferencing for IELTS speaking, Nakatsuhara et al. (2016, 2017), Berry et al. (2018), and Lee et al. (2021) conducted a four-phase study, culminating in trialling a videoconferencing platform for the test and operationalising it in parts of India in November 2019. The main findings are synthesised below to provide evidence for and caution regarding the use of videoconferencing as an alternative to direct speaking tests.

An initial study conducted in the UK, and a larger-scale replication study in China (Nakatsuhara et al., 2016, 2017, respectively) triangulated test-takers' and examiners' behaviours across face-to-face and videoconferencing modes. Technical problems (e.g., sound quality, delayed transmission) improved in the replication study, with examiners tending to inflate lower ability test-takers' scores when they deemed the sound quality problematic. As in the earlier studies, results showed that test scores did not differ statistically across the two modes. Test-takers' language functions were similar across modes, although test-takers asked for clarification more frequently during videoconferencing. There were also differences in examiners' behaviour (e.g., speaking louder or more slowly or using more nods and facial expressions when videoconferencing). Training in the replication study helped ease test-takers' nervousness and perceptions of videoconferencing test difficulty, demonstrating its importance. Examiners were split in their preference for face-to-face versus videoconferencing modes in both studies, with around 84% and 72% of test-takers preferring videoconferencing in the 2016 and 2017 studies, respectively.

In a follow-up investigation, Berry et al. (2018) trialled the use of a videoconferencing platform to deliver IELTS speaking to test-takers and examiners in Central or South America. Participants viewed the extended training sessions positively, although about 80% of the sessions reported technical problems (e.g., sound delays, image freezing). Some examiners' comments suggested that the long turn task might need longer time due to the time lags associated with the task prompt appearing on screen and invigilators' protocols. These matters were the focus of investigation in the fourth operational study, which mainly examined the adequacy of timing of the tasks (deemed sufficient) and the slightly modified interlocutor frame (Lee et al., 2021). Recommendations included incorporating warm-up interactions before the test, flexibility in examiners' scripts, the use of additional scripting to explicitly end the test, the use of headsets, allowing test-takers to see themselves on camera, the provision of general guidance on eye contact, and allowing test-takers to adjust headset volume. The authors underscored the need for further research on the role of communication styles during videoconferencing, especially for non-verbal elements.

Ockey et al. (2019) documented the use of videoconferencing with an ETS-developed task-delivery platform for remote speaking test delivery in group discussions. Test-takers in the US and Mainland China participated in 45 to 60 minutes sessions comprised of three test-takers and a moderator. After completing four oral tasks, test-takers completed follow-up questionnaires centring on the task and technology. Results showed that the videoconferencing was susceptible to technical disruptions for varied reasons, such as slides not being visible to test-takers or dropped video or calls in about a third of the sessions with the US test-takers and in every session with the Chinese test-takers. Despite the technical problems, the study showed that test-takers generally felt they had effectively completed the test in an enjoyable way with minimal test anxiety. The researchers concluded that the video-mediated interactive speaking test has the potential to assess a broader L2 speaking construct than that which is assessed by most semi-direct tests, while highlighting technological challenges. They underscored the need for further research on partner/interlocutor effects in videoconferencing tests and cautioned that more research was needed before such assessments could be adopted for high-stakes purposes.

In sum, improvements and efficiencies in online infrastructure, processing power, computer memory, data sharing, video transmission, and so forth (Al Hasrouty et al., 2017) have facilitated greater uptake of videoconferencing in language education and L2 assessment research. The finding that test-takers perform no differently face-to-face versus videoconferencing in the studies discussed above is encouraging. Taken together, pre-COVID-19 research has highlighted the usefulness of videoconferencing as a medium for language learning and interactions, notwithstanding technical challenges (e.g., Gillies, 2008). Although interactional and pragmatic features were rarely a focus in this body of research, findings or recommendations on the oral proficiency construct (Ockey et al., 2019), test-takers' language functions (Nakatsuhara et al., 2017), and scoring criteria (Kim & Craig, 2012) bear some relevance. For example, Ockey et al. (2019) included the ability 'to negotiate and develop topics with appropriate pragmatic use for a given context' (p. 1) in the construct; Nakatsuhara et al. (2017) specified a number of speech acts in the target language functions, such as agreeing and disagreeing, persuading, and suggesting; Kim and Craig's (2012) scoring criteria featured the ability in using appropriate language to realise the functions for specific scenarios.

13.4 Research on the Use of Videoconferencing in L2 Speaking Assessment during the COVID-19 Pandemic

Since the World Health Organization declared COVID-19 a pandemic in March 2020, there was a marked and accelerated uptake of videoconferencing for instructional and assessment purposes. In some settings, schools, university campuses, and testing centres were abruptly closed to conform to government movement or social distancing restrictions designed to contain the spread of the virus. This pushed test providers to rapidly bring to market an option that could allow test-takers to demonstrate their language proficiency in home-based tests (Isbell & Kremmel, 2020). Online webinars and international conferences in language testing and higher education invited discussions on fundamental issues related to the development and delivery of home-based language tests, and the potential and challenges of using videoconferencing for test delivery and online proctoring. For example, at the Association of Language Testers in Europe's (ALTE, 2021) 1st International Digital Symposium, themed 'Safeguarding the future of multilingual assessment in the COVID world' in April 2021, videoconferencing and online proctoring were key discussion points, with events held through videoconferencing. For the symposium, participants were shown as avatars on screen and could video call other avatars (fellow conference attendees) to initiate a conversation. The next section describes evolving assessment practices using videoconferencing technology during the pandemic.

Due to pandemic-related constraints, there was a push to rapidly develop in-house speaking tests with a videoconferencing component to replace tests that could not be administered in person at some universities, two of which cases in the US context are overviewed below. First, Temple University developed a screening and placement test for international teaching assistants using videoconferencing delivered via Zoom (Wagner & Krylova, 2021). Advantages compared to the externally developed semi-direct test that had been used previously (SPEAK Test), which involved test-takers recording responses into a microphone, included more flexible timing of test delivery to facilitate making earlier course placement decisions and better capturing interactional competence through on-screen interactions. Second, the Community English Language Program at Columbia University developed and launched a new general English online placement test for non-credit bearing courses, replacing an asynchronous test administered through an adapted online survey tool in a computer lab with human proctors (Purpura et al., 2021). The authors deemed Honorlock, which offers live online proctoring with artificial intelligence to review any suspicious test-taker behaviours, acceptable for their purposes but noted concerns about privacy. In addition, the complex procedures and instructions could be problematic for test-takers, especially with lower L2 proficiency and/or computer literacy.

The closure of test centres during the pandemic also resulted in testing organisations needing to adapt pre-existing tests. IELTS Indicator, which was launched in April 2020, was one such test. Certain elements of a remotely conducted speaking component for IELTS, including video call, were already being developed pre-pandemic but were rapidly launched due to pandemic-related disruption to operational testing (Clark et al., 2021). With four sections (listening, reading, writing, and speaking) using the same tasks as the traditional IELTS, IELTS Indicator was marketed as unique in providing the speaking test via video call with an examiner. Scoring was the same, except that it was conducted in real-time remotely rather than face-to-face. Roever and Ikeda's (2022) point that interactional competence is not particularly elicited through traditional IELTS tasks nor reflected in the scoring rubrics also still applies to IELTS Indicator. The test was launched before remote proctoring was available. Due, in part, to security concerns, test scores from IELTS Indicator were said to be provisional, and it was advised that a regular IELTS test should be taken when possible (Clark et al., 2021). Largely for reasons of test security, IELTS Indicator was in use for a short period of time till October 2021 (see Chapter 2 in this volume) but the at-home option of the IELTS test remains. Starting from 2022 in limited countries (IELTS, 2022), test-takers of the IELTS Academic test will have the option of IELTS Online, which seems to be the same as IELTS Indicator except that it has remote proctoring to ensure test security and fairness.

The TOEFL iBT Home Edition, which is identical to the regular TOEFL iBT test in content, tasks, and scoring, was launched in March 2020. Unlike with IELTS, rating is conducted using test recordings rather than live. Test-takers need to schedule live proctoring via ProctorU, a real-time, video-based online proctoring tool, which is used together with technology that can monitor activities and settings on the test-taker's computer (Papageorgiou & Manna, 2021). In August 2021, ETS launched a new English proficiency test, the *TOEFL Essentials*, applicable to university and more general settings and designed to be taken at home (Papageorgiou et al., 2021). Speaking skills are measured with three scored task types: *Read Aloud*, *Listen and Repeat*, and *Virtual Interview*, with a pre-recorded interviewer shown in video clips. Test-takers also record an unscored 5-minute personal video statement as part of the test, although it is unclear how these will be used to inform consequential decision-making. For both tests, videoconferencing is incorporated in online proctoring but is not used in test delivery. Speaking tasks are semi-direct with computer-mediated multimodal input but without reciprocal interactions with an interlocutor.

Notably, the TOEFL iBT Home Edition and IELTS Indicator could not be used in some parts of the world during the pandemic in 2020 (Isbell & Kremmel, 2020). Thus, for those test-takers, before more at-home test options became available (e.g., TOEFL Essentials), they needed to choose other tests to demonstrate their language proficiency in order to apply for universities abroad (e.g., Isbell & Kremmel, 2020; Wagner, 2020). There was also a time lag for all test users between the closure of test centres and the launch of home versions of traditional tests, which took time to bring to market, even if done at an expedited pace. Due to its flexibility as a test that can be taken at any location anytime, the Duolingo English Test (DET), which pre-dated the pandemic (originally launched in 2014), filled the vacuum as the ready-to-go option for at-home testing, seizing much of the market share and gaining inroads as a university entrance test for English language proficiency before its competitors had adapted their tests for home use (Isbell & Kremmel, 2020). The fully automated (i.e., machine delivered and scored) DET is an internet-based adaptive test that measures general English language skills in a non-academic genre (Wagner, 2020). The machine-scored speaking tasks elicit predictable test-taker output, mostly at word- or sentential-level and feature an unscored extended speaking task provided to institutions (Cardwell et al., 2021). Thus, scored items do not measure discourse or interactional competence (Wagner, 2020). DET's videoconferencing is solely used for online proctoring (Isbell & Kremmel, 2020).

13.5 Benefits and Trade-offs of Using Videoconferencing in Assessing L2 Pragmatics

To evaluate the use of videoconferencing to assess spoken proficiency that includes interactional and pragmatic competence, we refer to six test qualities from Bachman and Palmer's (1996) Test Usefulness framework. Given the growing attention of language testing researchers and exam boards on accommodations for test-takers with special needs and matters of equitability (Fairbairn & Spiby, 2019), we also comment on accessibility.

13.5.1 Reliability

Reliable test delivery presumes a functional digital device, microphone, speakers, and stable internet connection. Conversely, technical issues such as dropped video-calls or failure in test content delivery may affect test-takers' or interlocutors' performance, potentially leading to inconsistent test scoring (Ockey et al., 2019). Also, as in all dialogic, human-scored direct speaking tests, test-takers may score differently depending on the rater scoring their work and the interlocutor they are paired with (Isaacs, 2016). These effects can be mitigated through rater and interlocutor screening and training but may not be completely avoided (e.g., Berry et al., 2018).

13.5.2 Construct Validity

Videoconferencing can simulate the interactive, co-constructed nature of face-to-face interactions, allowing a relatively broad L2 speaking construct to include interactional and pragmatic components (Wagner & Krylova, 2021). One limitation of using videoconferencing, including when interaction is involved, is that it is more difficult to judge body language and non-verbal behaviour online than in person, restricting construct coverage to non-verbal elements visible through video. Variable sound quality and online delays can introduce sources of construct-irrelevant variance. This is particularly problematic when these features interfere with understanding of speech and smooth communication.

13.5.3 Authenticity

Videoconferencing test tasks with carefully selected topics and situations could reflect natural language use in real-world domains (Kim & Craig, 2012). It is also multimodal in nature and can allow test-takers to demonstrate a wide range of oral language proficiency resembling everyday communication (Ockey et al., 2019). However, it should not be ignored that the non-verbal modes via videoconferencing can be different from face-to-face interactions. The camera frame and positioning restricts mobility, body language and gestures, exaggerates physical-movement effects and denies real eye contact (e.g., Kern, 2014). These factors could limit the overall authenticity and interactiveness of videoconferencing speaking tests. Considering that videoconferencing has become a major means for communication in the current era, besides comparing videoconferencing with the face-to-face test performance, it is also worth comparing it to real-life videoconferencing scenarios (Lee et al., 2021). However, task types are decisive in performance assessments and the extent to which interactional and pragmatic components can be elicited. For examiner-led oral interviews, which have been widely used in speaking tests, even though test-takers can talk with a live interlocutor via videoconferencing, the interactional competence and discursive pragmatic competence elicited are limited. The use of videoconferencing also opens up the possibility of selecting an interlocutor from a language background or speaking a language variety that test-takers are likely to encounter in real-world settings, potentially catering to contextual differences and exposing test-takers to different global Englishes (Isaacs & Rose, 2022).

13.5.4 Interactiveness

Interactiveness refers to the degree and type of test-takers' involvement in carrying out a test task (Bachman & Palmer, 1996). Videoconferencing can facilitate high interactiveness through simulating face-to-face interactions and allowing for meaningful communicative exchanges. When used with test tasks such as roleplays, videoconferencing can enable test-takers to utilise a wide range of speaking skills in demonstrating a broad construct of speaking ability. Besides verbal skills, videoconferencing allows the exchange of certain non-verbal elements such as facial expressions, which are important for conveying meaning and achieving communicative goals. However, similar as for authenticity, the non-verbal elements are limited and could be distorted. Compared with face-to-face communication, contextual cues in interactions are also limited through videoconferencing. These factors could limit the overall interactiveness and authenticity of videoconferencing speaking tests. The chat function is a feature that could potentially be used in a speaking test that would involve a degree of multi-tasking and attention switching on the part of the interlocutors and that is another avenue for exploration, particularly for integrated task types (Plakans & Gebril, 2012).

13.5.5 Impact

Impact denotes the effect of test-taking and test scores on society and educational systems and the individuals within these systems (Bachman & Palmer, 1996). Videoconferencing speaking tests help expose test-takers to a wide range of skills needed in a certain language use domain. The use of the technology may not, in itself, provoke anxiety, at least in some settings for some test-takers (Nakatsuhara et al., 2017; Ockey et al., 2019). It could give test-takers access to interlocutors who are not simply confined to the local area, where L2 proficiency may be limited, and could ultimately help foster intercultural communicators across geographical boundaries. The use of interactional task types to measure a broad L2 speaking construct could have positive washback effects.

Introducing videoconferencing into at-home tests, however, could threaten personal privacy and data protection. This is especially the case when videoconferencing is used for online proctoring, as test-takers could be required to show the environment they take the test in throughout the duration of the test. Videoconferencing platforms are not immune to security vulnerabilities and cyberattacks that could lead to unauthorised parties accessing testing sessions or data. Moreover, promoting the use of videoconferencing could result in unequal access to needed resources such as technologies and comfortable test-taking space, which might exacerbate existing inequalities in educational resources and possibly increase social disparities.

13.5.6 Practicality

Through connecting participants across screens, videoconferencing provides an online option to assess interactional and pragmatic abilities and saves the need of co-locating interlocutors in the same physical space. Setting up the hardware and software for videoconferencing and ensuring smooth testing procedures through multiple trials can be labour- and time-intensive, in tandem with preparing guidelines for test-takers and examiners and providing on-site or remote technical support. Also, it might be more costly to provide the full videoconferencing facilities for tests. However, in line with greater practicality of semi-direct speaking tests for test providers (Galaczi, 2010), after the initial set-up, it should be more efficient and economical than face-to-face alternatives.

13.5.7 Accessibility

The use of videoconferencing greatly enhances accessibility of tests to test-takers, making it possible for anyone with a computer with videoconferencing equipment and a stable internet connection to take the test from any location. This is especially helpful for test-takers and examiners who live in places that cannot support in-person tests (e.g., remote areas), have mobility or access issues, and in times of crisis when in-person tests are restricted (e.g., war, pandemic). The use of captions (although not always accurate) and font modification to make functionalities more accessible to all test-takers, particularly those with specific learning differences are important considerations. There is some anecdotal evidence that the use of videoconferencing platforms can be less stressful for people with autism, who may actually find less access to non-verbal cues facilitative to communication (Lawrence, 2021), although this remains to be systematically examined in relation to tests. There is likely to be further work in this vein if the use of videoconferencing becomes a mainstay post-pandemic as an alternative to direct speaking tests.

13.6 Changes in the Assessment Landscape: COVID-19 and Beyond

Time-sensitive pandemic-related challenges have spearheaded radical changes in the assessment arena, particularly spurring greater reliance on technology to pursue alternative ways of carrying on with business during the crisis. Videoconferencing tools have been prominent in this endeavour, moving away from mostly being a source of exploration for assessment purposes in empirical studies pre-pandemic to being rapidly adopted to facilitate at-home testing that informs consequential decision-making during the pandemic. The research synthesised in this chapter suggests the potential of videoconferencing to support remote test delivery, including online proctoring, and to elicit a broad speaking construct using reciprocal tasks. The use of the technology also makes assessments more accessible to stakeholders and may be more cost-effective and less resource-intensive than face-to-face provision. Despite such benefits, there are trade-offs, including technical issues that could threaten the reliability of the assessment, the introduction of interlocutor and/or rater effects (although this is no different from direct human-scored interactional tests), more limited access to non-verbal cues, privacy and potential invasiveness when dealing with test security, and perpetuating or increasing inequalities due to access disparities to the relevant resources. More research is pressing on how best to accommodate test-takers with special needs for tests that use this technology.

There is a dearth of videoconferencing research for L2 assessments centring on pragmatic and interactional competence specifically. Direct tests would be more amenable to assessing these aspects of L2 speaking due to greater access to verbal and non-verbal cues and no risk of signal delays, which could facilitate turn-taking compared to videoconferencing tests. The decades-old debate about the relative merits of direct and semi-direct tests is not completely settled, even with the use of videoconferencing. There is surely no perfect way to assess L2 speaking but only a comparatively more appropriate way that can be used to maximise the benefits and minimise the trade-offs to suit a particular assessment context and purpose. To assess a representative construct of pragmatic competence for speaking, reciprocal interactions are needed. Practical constraints are a major obstacle to their implementation in operational and particularly large-scale assessment settings (Roever & Ikeda, 2020). We expect that the use of videoconferencing would help operationalise the assessment of L2 pragmatic competence and potentially be a main medium through which to realise interactive, multimodal assessment.

At the time of writing this chapter, COVID-19 is still spreading around the globe. Some L2 assessment practices that experienced a substantial uptake or have become entrenched during the pandemic, including the use of videoconferencing, are likely to continue post-pandemic. The pandemic has changed the landscape of language assessment and has pushed language testers to be pragmatic, innovative, and, in some cases, move forward with available resources as a matter of survival in a rapidly changing reality. It has pushed test providers to harness the use of technology, including videoconferencing, at a speed of adoption that was almost unthinkable for standardised testing pre-pandemic. The COVID-19 pandemic is a seismic event. It is impossible to know what the future holds. Language testers should be prepared for such eventualities (Isbell & Kremmel, 2020) so they can act proactively and not just reactively in the future.

References

Al Hasrouty, C., Olariu, C., Autefage, V., Magoni, D., & Murphy, J. (2017). SVC videoconferencing call adaptation and bandwidth usage in SDN networks. *GLOBECOM 2017 – 2017 IEEE Global Communications Conference* (pp. 1–7). Institute of Electrical and Electronics Engineers. https://doi.org/10.1109/GLOCOM.2017.8254135

ALTE. (2021, April 28–30). *Safeguarding the future of multilingual assessment in the Covid world* [Conference]. ALTE 1st International Digital Symposium, Online.

Bachman, L. F., & Palmer, A. S. (1996). *Language testing in practice: Designing and developing useful language tests.* Oxford University Press.

Berry, V., Nakatsuhara, F., Inoue, C., & Galaczi, E. (2018). *Exploring the use of videoconferencing technology to deliver the IELTS Speaking Test: Phase 3 technical trial.* IELTS Partners. https://www.ielts.org/-/media/research-reports/ielts-research-partner-paper-3.ashx

Cardwell, R., LaFlair, G. T., & Settles, B. (2021). *Duolingo English Test: Technical manual.* (Duolingo research report DRR-21-04). Duolingo. https://duolingo-papers.s3.amazonaws.com/other/det-technical-manual-current.pdf

Clark, J., & Hooshmand, D. (1992). "Screen-to-screen" testing: An exploratory study of oral proficiency interviewing using video conferencing. *System, 20*(3), 293–304. https://doi.org/10.1016/0346-251X(92)90041-Z

Clark, T., Spiby, R., & Tasviri, R. (2021). Crisis, collaboration, recovery: IELTS and COVID-19. *Language Assessment Quarterly, 18*(1), 17–25. https://doi.org/10.1080/15434303.2020.1866575

Dustdar, S., & Hofstede, G. J. (1999). Videoconferencing across cultures—A conceptual framework for floor control issues. *Journal of Information Technology, 14*(2), 161–169. https://doi.org/10.1177/026839629901400205

Fairbairn, J., & Spiby, R. (2019). Towards a framework of inclusion: Developing accessibility in tests at the British Council. *European Journal of Special Needs Education, 34*(2), 236–255. https://doi.org/10.1080/08856257.2019.1581404

Galaczi, E. D. (2010). Face-to-face and computer-based assessment of speaking: Challenges and opportunities. In L. Araújo (Ed.), *Computer-based assessment (CBA) of foreign language speaking skills* (pp. 29–51). European Commission.

Galaczi, E., & Taylor, L. (2018). Interactional competence: Conceptualisations, operationalisations, and outstanding questions. *Language Assessment Quarterly, 15*(3), 219–236. https://doi.org/10.1080/15434303.2018.1453816

Gillies, D. (2008). Student perspectives on videoconferencing in teacher education at a distance. *Distance Education, 29*(1), 107–118. https://doi.org/10.1080/01587910802004878

Grabowski, K. (2013). Investigating the construct validity of a role-play test designed to measure grammatical and pragmatic knowledge at multiple proficiency levels. In S. J. Ross & G. Kasper (Eds.), *Assessing second language pragmatics* (pp. 149–171). Palgrave Macmillan. https://doi.org/10.1057/9781137003522_6

He, A. W., & Young, R. (1998). Language proficiency interviews: A discourse approach. In R. Young & A. W. He (Eds.), *Talking and testing: Discourse approaches to the assessment of oral proficiency* (pp. 1–24). John Benjamins. https://doi.org/10.1075/sibil.14.02he

IELTS. (2022). *IELTS Online*. https://www.ielts.org/for-test-takers/ielts-online

Isaacs, T. (2016). Assessing speaking. In D. Tsagari & J. Banerjee (Eds.), *Handbook of second language assessment* (pp. 131–146). De Gruyter Mouton. https://doi.org/10.1515/9781614513827-011

Isaacs, T., & Rose, H. (2022). Redressing the balance in the native speaker debate: Assessment standards, standard language, and exposing double standards. *TESOL Quarterly, 56*(1), 401–412. https://doi.org/10.1002/tesq.3041

Isbell, D. R., & Kremmel, B. (2020). Test review: Current options in at-home language proficiency tests for making high-stakes decisions. *Language Testing, 37*(4), 600–619. https://doi.org/10.1177/0265532220943483

Kern, R. (2014). Technology as Pharmakon: The promise and perils of the Internet for foreign language education. *The Modern Language Journal, 98*(1), 340–357. https://doi.org/10.1111/j.1540-4781.2014.12065.x

Kim, J., & Craig, D. A. (2012). Validation of a videoconferenced speaking test. *Computer Assisted Language Learning, 25*(3), 257–275. https://doi.org/10.1080/09588221.2011.649482

Lawrence, A. (2021, August 25). How Zoom helped the neurotypical world hear my autistic voice. *Nature*. https://www.nature.com/articles/d41586-021-02325-9

Lee, H., Patel, M., Lynch, J., & Galaczi, E. (2021). *Development of the IELTS video call speaking test: Phase 4 operational research trial and overall summary of a four-phase test development cycle*. IELTS Partners. https://www.ielts.org/-/media/research-reports/lee-patel-lynch-galaczi.ashx

Nakatsuhara, F., Inoue, C., Berry, V., & Galaczi, E. (2016). *Exploring performance across two delivery modes for the same L2 speaking test: Face-to-face and video-conferencing delivery. A preliminary comparison of test-taker and examiner behaviour*. IELTS Partners. https://www.ielts.org/-/media/research-reports/ielts-partnership-research-paper-1.ashx

Nakatsuhara, F., Inoue, C., Berry, V., & Galaczi, E. (2017). *Exploring performance across two delivery modes for the IELTS speaking test: Face-to-face and video-conferencing delivery (Phase 2)*. (IELTS Partnership Research Papers, 3). IELTS Partners. https://www.ielts.org/-/media/research-reports/ielts-research-partner-paper-2.ashx

O'Loughlin, K. J. (2001). *The equivalence of direct and semi-direct speaking tests*. Cambridge University Press.

Ockey, G. J., Timpe-Laughlin, V., Davis, L., & Gu, L. (2019). *Exploring the potential of a video-mediated interactive speaking assessment* (Research Report No. RR-19-05). ETS. https://doi.org/10.1002/ets2.12240

Papageorgiou, S., Davis, L., Norris, J. M., Garcia Gomez, P., Manna, V. F., & Monfils, L. (2021). *Design framework for the TOEFL Essentials test 2021* (Research Memorandum No. RM-21-03). ETS. https://www.ets.org/Media/Research/pdf/RM-21-03.pdf

Papageorgiou, S., & Manna, V. F. (2021). Maintaining access to a large-scale test of academic language proficiency during the pandemic: The launch of TOEFL iBT Home Edition. *Language Assessment Quarterly*, *18*(1), 36–41. https://doi.org/10.1080/15434303.2020.1864376

Plakans, L., & Gebril, A. (2012). A close investigation into source use in integrated second language writing tasks. *Assessing Writing*, *17*(1), 18–34. https://doi.org/10.1016/j.asw.2011.09.002

Purpura, J. E., Davoodifard, M., & Voss, E. (2021). Conversion to remote proctoring of the community English language program online placement exam at Teachers College, Columbia University. *Language Assessment Quarterly*, *18*(1), 42–50. https://doi.org/10.1080/15434303.2020.1867145

Qian, D. (2009). Comparing direct and semi-direct modes for speaking assessment: Affective effects on test takers. *Language Assessment Quarterly*, *6*(2), 113–125. https://doi.org/10.1080/15434300902800059

Roever, C., & Ikeda, N. (2020). Testing pragmatic competence in a second language. In K. P. Schneider & E. Ifantidou (Eds.), *Developmental and clinical pragmatics* (pp. 475–495). De Gruyter Mouton. https://doi.org/10.1515/9783110431056-016

Roever, C., & Ikeda, N. (2022). What scores from monologic speaking tests can(not) tell us about interactional competence. *Language Testing*, *39*(1), 7–29. https://doi.org/10.1177/02655322211003332

Shohamy, E. (1994). The validity of direct versus semi-direct oral tests. *Language Testing*, *11*(2), 99–123. https://doi.org/10.1177/026553229401100202

Taguchi, N. (2019). Second language acquisition and pragmatics: An overview. In N. Taguchi (Ed.), *The Routledge handbook of second language acquisition and pragmatics* (pp. 1–14). Routledge. https://doi.org/10.4324/9781351164085-1

Timpe-Laughlin, V., & Youn, S. J. (2020). Measuring L2 pragmatics. In P. Winke & T. Brunfaut (Eds.), *The Routledge handbook of second language acquisition and language testing* (pp. 254–264). Routledge. https://doi.org/10.4324/9781351034784-28

Wagner, E. (2020). Duolingo English Test, revised version July 2019. *Language Assessment Quarterly*, *17*(3), 300–315. https://doi.org/10.1080/15434303.2020.1771343

Wagner, E., & Krylova, A. (2021). Temple University's ITA placement test in times of COVID-19. *Language Assessment Quarterly, 18*(1), 12–16. https://doi.org/10.1080/15434303.2020.1862849

Youn, S. J. (2015). Validity argument for assessing L2 pragmatics in interaction using mixed methods. *Language Testing, 32*(2), 199–225. https://doi.org/10.1177/0265532214557113

Young, R. (2019). Interactional competence and L2 pragmatics. In N. Taguchi (Ed.), *The Routledge handbook of second language acquisition and pragmatics* (pp. 93–110). Routledge. https://doi.org/10.4324/9781351164085-7

14
THE USE OF TECHNOLOGY FOR REDESIGNING L2 LANGUAGE ASSESSMENTS

Tasks, Rubrics, and Feedback in Emergency Remote Teaching Contexts

Ana Maria Ducasse

RMIT UNIVERSITY, MELBOURNE, VIC, AUSTRALIA

14.1 Introduction

Before the Pandemic online delivery was the professional domain of many institutions. For trained experts, online delivery employing dynamic and interactive tasks and simulations (e.g., Gierl & Haladyna, 2012) is a well-honed skill. However, the sudden transition from traditional testing mode to virtual assessment surprised most educators who struggled with the steep learning curve. Known early on as 'Emergency Remote Teaching' (ERT) (Hodges et al., 2020), in the initial stages of the crisis, university language teachers were thrust into a sudden overhaul of their pedagogical activities while learners searched for stable Wi-Fi and screen access. For the fortunate, the affordances of widespread Wi-Fi and access to technology-enabled education continue in the face of disruption with or without the required skills for remote teaching and learning on the part of teachers and learners. The crisis provoked an unexpected process to convert courses from face-to-face to virtual delivery mode where the teacher/assessor's autonomy and dynamism (Clark et al., 2021) were indispensable when keyboards replaced pens and screens became the whiteboard.

Upskilling was rapid, with little time for training, offering scope for creativity and inventiveness in the virtual environment where the roles of teacher and learners had not yet been fixed (Hampel & Stickler, 2005). Rising to this challenge, there was a need for Language and Culture Educators (LCEs) to adopt an 'interpretive, reflective and reflexive stance' (Scarino, 2022, p. 1) towards language learning. LCE creativity played a significant role (e.g., Zhu

DOI: 10.4324/9781003221463-17

et al., 2013) in maintaining momentum in language education during the Pandemic. LCEs made adaptations and took the decisions required by 'recognising and working with the knowledge, perspectives, expectations, and values that learners br[ought]' (Scarino, 2022, p. 9) to their virtual classroom. In addition, the resilience of the student response (Lee et al., 2021) cannot be denied. The virtual space prompted global reflection on the processes around learning, communication, teacher instruction, and the effectiveness of assessment practices that ensued via changes to course design and delivery through digital platforms. Overall, despite the challenges it brought, it also afforded teachers an opportunity for innovation and learners an educational pathway.

14.2 Literature Review

Language testing has always reacted to and been driven by social and contextual factors (Fan & Jin, 2020), and the response to the Pandemic is a case in point. It had a galvanising effect on the education sector globally. Institutions expected teachers to develop tools to digitally promote and evaluate learning (Pellegrino et al., 2001). Learners were to demonstrate new knowledge and skills within their disciplinary and pedagogical contexts from individual cognitive and emotional profiles (Shute et al., 2016). While the Pandemic sowed fear, learners and teachers managed multiple unknowns and insecurities in a virtual classroom.

An understanding of the notion that teaching and learning are both cognitive and emotional activities for teachers and their learners (Sternberg & Horvath, 1995) remains crucial to individual teacher and learner responses to the situation. In classroom-based contexts, the responsibility and the complexity of designing at-home assessment tasks and appropriate feedback with all its challenges fell on the shoulders of individuals, a context that contrasts with that reported by Clark et al. (2021), who enjoyed social and contextual factors of collaboration between testing partners by working in a high-stakes testing environment.

Although detailed feedback with productive potential (i.e., assessment *for* learning – AfL) is time-consuming, it matches the type of feedback that interests learners, which is 'usable, detailed, considerate of affect and personalised to the student's work' (Dawson et al., 2019, p. 25). Frequently second language (L2) writing assessment is summative (i.e., assessment *of* learning – AoL) (Lee, 2016), possibly because learners are not shown how to take up feedback for learning by their time-poor teachers. A summative assessment style can result in time-poor teachers quickly assessing more assignments but risks learners learning less from teacher time spent correcting and consequently learning more slowly from reduced feedback opportunities overall.

In this research, *ad hoc* teacher feedback, based on observations of learner in-class performance, became difficult or impossible with teaching during the Pandemic, so a more student-centred individualised approach to L2 writing assessment was implemented for assessment to include alternate feedback opportunities. The teacher (T henceforth) invited learners to be actively involved in monitoring their progress and deciding how to address the gaps in their learning. This focus based on learning objectives and assessment criteria, known in higher education research as Assessment *as* Learning (AaL) (Torrance, 2007), placed learners at the centre of classroom assessment when T adapted assessment tasks for remote virtual delivery.

14.3 Rationale

Despite the education sector's challenges, two years since the precipitation to 'online everything', Crawford (2021) argues that there is only partial acknowledgement of the efforts undertaken to maintain resilience and reports on failed interventions are scant. By piecing together, the patchwork of responses from global practitioners, we may be able to construct a path for future iterations beyond the crisis, which is essential. By exposing the experiences of a range of practitioners assessing language proficiency in reaction to ERT, the language testing community might benefit from the process of tests adaptation for virtual online platforms in various local contexts.

There is a growing number of studies specifically on language assessment that make up the Pandemic response narrative (e.g., Isbell & Kremmel, 2020); so, building on these by describing the particulars of adaptation to online in a particular context and disseminating current practices could enable practitioners to prepare for and make decisions about future changes in language assessment (Fan & Jin, 2020) going forward. These might include, for example, more discussions of adapting tasks, rubrics, and feedback mechanisms on the one hand for Classroom-Based Assessment (CBA); and, on the other hand, changes to constructs, timelines, platforms, and remote proctoring during the Pandemic (Clark et al., 2021) in high-stakes testing.

14.4 The Study

The study seeks to understand the processes for adapting assessment tasks, rubrics, and feedback within a higher education context characterised by the challenges and the affordances of the Pandemic. Through a document analysis that compares Spanish language assessment tasks before and after the Pandemic, the study addresses two questions:

> Research Q1 How were assessment practices influenced by the Pandemic?
> Research Q2 What were learners' views of language assessments in a virtual mode during the Pandemic?

14.4.1 Context

The Australian context pertains to working in the Pandemic through the southern hemisphere winter, in an Anglo-phone country of multiple languages and cultures, at a public university where previously it was unusual to teach and assess 100% via a platform and in virtual space. Staff bore the swift decision-making around the immediate, overnight adaptation of assessment to remote teaching in an environment that they were teaching themselves to negotiate and navigate.

The study follows the researcher/lecturer over two semesters and three consecutive levels. Language and Culture Education classes ran remotely and synchronously regardless of the difficulties, i.e., 2× two-hour online synchronous teaching marathons for each class, per week, for two years. We did not offer online asynchronous teaching, as opted for in other disciplines with lectures, readings and possibly face-to-face online tutorials. Most changes were made for ERT in Semester 1 and then applied as required for Semester 2 with less stress. Melbourne remained in lockdown and recommenced face-to-face teaching in Semester 1, 2022. Students and instructors were also more accustomed to ERT from their second to the fourth semester of remote synchronous study.

14.4.2 Methodology

This case study presents the perspective of a LCE (T) who, as a teacher/researcher, is also a teacher/assessor and task/rubric designer. T adapted most assessments, during initial lockdowns and restrictions of movement in Melbourne, Australia. Teaching in the virtual space required a re-alignment of assessments for the new learning environment in which the learners were acquiring knowledge and skills differently. Hence, it was vital to ensure the suitability of the assessment for measuring specific knowledge and skills and consequently improve the validity of inferences made about learner progress (Shute et al., 2016).

The adapted tasks and rubrics presented and discussed consider theoretical issues related to AaL pedagogy. The approach is innovative in CBA. Although educators frequently find themselves in this position globally, there are scant examples of AaL from practitioners reflecting on CBA tasks adaptation for Learners (Ls) during the Pandemic.

14.4.3 Data

The students in the Spanish Program are enrolled in the Bachelor of International Studies, where four consecutive semesters of an additional language are compulsory. Most are young adults studying for their first degree.

The levels comprise approximate Common European Framework of Reference levels. Semester 1, 2020, Spanish 3/A2 comprised 41 students (30% male/70% female). From Semester 1 A2, 50% continued to Semester 2, Spanish 4, which comprised 33 students (30% male/70% female), the remainder of the cohort comprised students who completed Spanish 3 in previous semesters or had tested into the level. Semester 1 B2/Spanish 5 comprised 19 students (40% male/60% female), some of whom had continued from Spanish 4 in 2019, but others were new and had taken a placement test for this level.

In Semester 1 2020, the course had run for only the first two weeks of instruction; then, it was delivered virtually for the remaining ten weeks. At the time of that transition, switching to ERT, only two weeks remained before the first assessed task, scheduled for Week 4. Consequently, these assessments urgently needed to be adapted.

The tasks and adaptations are divided by course level, followed by a more general discussion on the context and processes to address RQ1. To gather a range of learner responses to the challenges and affordances of online assessment tasks from their perspective, RQ2 was answered based on the results of the content analysis of free-text responses documents from university-wide voluntary and anonymous Course Exit Surveys across three sequential Spanish L2 levels, i.e., Semester 1 2020 through Semester 1 2021. Students are encouraged to respond to the end of semester surveys for every class in their course; they decide whether to take up the feedback option. In Semester 1 2020, level 3 received 24 free-text comments, level 5, 12 comments, and in Semester 2, level 4 received 38 comments. The comments match the cohort followed for assessment tasks in RQ1.

14.4.4 RQ1 How Were Assessment Practices Influenced by the Pandemic?

14.4.4.1 Spanish 3

The major challenge addressed in level 3, regardless of the delivery format, is the return to language study after a four-month break. Many have low vocabulary retention from 24 weeks or 96 hours of study in the previous year and cannot remember conjugations. The stimulation of fun interactive activities to help stimulate recall was hard to replicate online because they are typically oral and involve walking around the room. Instead, students wrote in a chat but first translated online, which is undoubtedly a different skill to speaking face-to-face (hands-free from a mobile) to gesticulate your meaning to a partner.

Initially, the early assessment task for level 3 was a reading passage with short answer questions and a video listening comprehension of a monologue with short comprehension questions. It is a passive task in the sense that learners listen or read, write free text responses, and can write verbatim parts of what is understood. Both tasks had been adapted from materials online, considering several key factors.

For example, the online adaptation of the task resulted in a paragraph summary of a daily routine video taking into consideration cheating in unsupervised performance and issues of test validity and reliability. The assessor wrote the summary text, not a video transcript, in ten short consecutive sentences, each with a blank for the learners to complete. It demonstrated comprehension of the listening and the written paragraph with gaps. Any correct option was accepted and added to the assessor's predicted list of accepted responses for automated marking within the CANVAS Learning Management System (LMS).

Cheating and unsupervised performances necessitated changes in the testing format as learners might have phoned or texted for help during the test or looked up words online. Nevertheless, when T increased the task difficulty, learners had to engage with the listening text at a higher cognitive level. Learners listened to the 3-minute video as many times as needed within the time limit. T took this decision to provide learners with a sense of agency and the ability to check their responses repeatedly. Learners may have slowed the video or used transcription technology. Still, filling the gaps was a challenge that made it more difficult to 'find' the answer without comprehension. Course analytics in CANVAS showed that the new task resulted in an even spread of answers. In the top 27%, there were 11 answers; in the middle 46%, there were 21 answers; and in the bottom 27%, there were 8 answers, and one student did not submit a task.

Another adaptation was the need for over-explaining so that learners could make sense of online material when they were not in class. It meant that the task instructions were overly long, as indicated below. At our institution, all discussion of assessment tasks is in English, as are the task instructions. See below the Task 1 extract from the LMS.

> Watch the video and complete the blanks in the paragraph to show you understood what you heard. You may change answers at any time during the test. You will have time to replay the video and check your answers. Do not forget to click SUBMIT once you have finished. If you do not Submit, the last answers count as your final ones. **NOTE**: Do not use any punctuation in the gaps. Use options if you have not installed a Spanish keyboard, for example, è –> e'; à –> a', etc. and ñ> n~. You will receive an automated mark for responses that match the correct answers, but the teacher will check all responses. All single word correct answers are accepted and added to the list of possible correct answers.

Originally in the course guide, before ERT, the pen-and-paper task was to be written and handed in at the end of class before leaving. Then T marked it up for correction following learner requests for correction on their writing to ensure feedback met their expectations. It was returned as a document for learners to add to a digital e-portfolio of written texts and corrections, the entire process of which is explained in Ducasse and Hill (2019). The instructions for the digital adaptation of the written task involved several steps, as explained below in the LMS extract:

> Ten short paragraphs will be set over the semester, and three will be expanded for submission as part of a test. After the first feedback engagement task, the tutor will not offer more feedback until the previous suggestions are attempted and submitted in the email chain. This includes feedback for test drafts.
>
> Write your short paragraph on the weekly topic to practise class material. Try to write with as little help from resources as possible to convey your ideas. Reference words or phrases with (D= dictionary) where you use the dictionary for help.
>
> You will be asked to talk about your ideas on the topic you prepared with a small group in the next class.
>
> Copy and paste your text into an email to the tutor using the LMS inbox. Subject heading 'Engagement Feedback'. Always write in the same chain because you will submit a pdf of your entire semester's engagement for a mark in the LMS at the end of the semester. You can keep track of your edits and compare previous feedback as you write.
>
> You will receive a marked-up version from the tutor with suggestions on where to edit and improve your text. Here is the key your teacher will use. You can ask for clarification X <> Y swap words;/\insert words; (Z) delete words; *ABC edit single word; *(DEF) edit phrase in brackets.
>
> Resubmit your edited written homework texts by email chain showing your edits (corrections) in capital letters within your text.

The last instruction below was to guide students to learn from feedback and apply the feedback from previous tasks to the following one.

> NB Lecturer provides feedback on your next text draft only after you have made the requested edits on the task that was corrected before each new submission.
> Task 2 extract from LMS

It is explained as a learning dialogue: T comments and Ls responds. Ls break the flow if they do not edit after T's suggestions. To continue the dialogue, each learner needs to take up the dialogue where it broke off by reflecting and acting on feedback from previous tasks before requesting more feedback. If they have not edited previous feedback or submitted the edits, the T does not offer feedback for the subsequent assessment draft. That was a built-in catch because every third feedback engagement task matched the submission for a formative assessment where each revision was entered on a template to raise the awareness of corrections and learn from the assessment process (see Appendix for the rubric).

14.4.4.2 Spanish 4

Some of the challenges addressed in level 4, regardless of in-person or online delivery, comprise lexical variety, increasing accuracy, and the ability to write longer coherent texts. The internet was good for developing learner autonomy. In Semester 4, the last in the compulsory language study for the degree, it meant that students had more confidence in their abilities, and we made them feel proud that they would write an essay in their L2 of two years. Feedback online was constructive and more successful than in the past.

The first assessment for level B1, in previous pen-and-paper years, had included tests of listening, reading, and grammar in context with a written production task. B1 has a summative essay as the final assessment on the life and times of an artist. Therefore, feedback and drafting were a focus. In the move towards AaL and adaptation to a virtual classroom, T maintained the listening task but changed from audio to video with a paragraph blank completion task instead of a combination of Multiple-Choice Questions, True/False and short answers used previously. The writing task for the first assessment followed the pattern of Spanish 3 above. Course analytics in CANVAS showed that the adapted first assessment task also resulted in an even spread of answers. There were 9 answers in the top 27%; in the middle, 46%, 15 answers; and in the bottom, 27%, 8 answers, and one student did not submit.

The weekly emailed feedback and editing task continued in Semester 2 with level 4. This course had two tutors, which means that each had 16 short paragraphs to mark up each week.

14.4.4.3 Spanish 5

Regardless of delivery, the challenges addressed in level 5 are the disparate class levels combined at B2.1 level. Students may have travelled, completed internships or language exchanges, be from a Spanish speaking heritage, have taken high school Spanish, be fluent in other Latin languages, and among them all are students who have studied four semesters of L2 continuously from beginners' level over two years at our university. Online allows students to progress at their pace in reading, writing, and grammar study, which is a plus for more proficient students who view their learning as more autonomous (O'Reilly, 2014).

However, after two years of Pandemic online teaching and having taught Spanish 5 to students fresh and receptive to online, when it was weird but novel, and conversely, to students tired and frustrated by the lack of interaction with other students online, post-Pandemic it is refreshing to engage with students in a room, a corridor, or a stairwell. The same students previously online, seemingly unreachable and on the other side of a screen, have become class characters, all with a role to play in their university life experience. At B2 level, where they can speak and write, in the language classroom they come to learn from each other and reinforce each other's progress as they join groups to discuss readings and videos or perform group work. They are motivated to choose their cultural group study topics (Wu, 2003) and the classroom atmosphere enhances their self-direction (e.g., Nicholson, 2013). Leaving the post-Pandemic class after the first assessment reported on here, a student said 'I feel I have learned more in these four weeks than the four semesters online'. It was simply a candid personal perception but a perceptive comment on our classroom environment online compared with face-to face.

Before ERT, this level was given a traditional pen-and-paper test with reading, listening, and grammar questions in context. The student feedback for this first test had frequently been that the listening was too fast and that the reading was too difficult. Using the affordances of technology and taking advantage of learners working remotely, T decided to give the learners more agency and adapted the first 10% assessment to be more authentic for online delivery. T asked the Pandemic year class to select an online article as a pre-assessment task. Students read, then listed vocabulary and noted new expressions for the assessed task a week later. It consisted of writing a summary of their article in Spanish, finishing with a reflection on what they learned from the cultural content. Below is the Task 3 extract from LMS:

Part 1 pre-task activity 5%.

1. Locate a recent online article in Spanish relating to food in the Spanish speaking world that interests you.
2. Read it and make a note of new vocabulary and structures.
3. Use the red SUBMIT button to upload a screenshot or a scanned pdf version of your selected article, the list of vocabulary and structures you identified to learn and use for a written summary and reflection in the next class.
4. In class, use your article notes to write a summary and reflect on the cultural content.

Part 2 summary task 5%:

You have 20 minutes to write a 200–250-word summary of your chosen text, including, as necessary, any unfamiliar words and structures that you have selected.
CONDITIONS For this assignment, the use of other resources is NOT permitted. You had time to prepare beforehand. You must have a pdf of the selected text you will summarise uploaded into the assignment with the vocabulary list.

Use the text, your prepared vocabulary list, and your notes if you have a draft summary or dot points to improve during class time.

Type directly into the box and submit when finished. You can re-read and edit within the time limit

The student focus nature of this assessment aligns with the principles of AaL. Course analytics in CANVAS showed that the new task resulted in an even spread of answers. There were eight answers in the top 27%; in the middle 46%, seven answers; and in the bottom, 27%, three answers and one student did not complete.

In an earlier study, T analysed transcripts of oral personal reflection tasks spoken by the students who completed this summary task with the cohort above (Ducasse, 2022). Students reflected on research skills, e.g., '*I like this task because it forced me to explore Spanish news and internet sources that I do not do enough of. And since then, I have begun to read more Spanish media*'; on self-awareness, e.g., '*I have been bad at this before because before this task I copied too much of the original text*' and their affective response, '*I believe it was a good start to the assessment tasks in the course. In my opinion, it helped me feel at ease the rest of the semester*'. The learners' awareness offers instructors information regarding Multi-Modal Digital Assessments enabling individual learning goals.

14.4.5 Challenges Encountered Adapting Assessments Tasks for ERT

T redesigned the tasks, with little discussion or consultation available. T searched online for help with the Instructure CANVAS platform and struggled. For two weeks, the Spanish 3 task marks disappeared for the entire cohort, and though the learners had seen initial feedback, the final mark was not appearing in the grade report. Technical support was not available remotely since the university outsourced IT support in the Pandemic, and the solution was uncovered through trial and error by T by changing test dates and lists of learners who had taken the test. It was a nerve-wracking baptism of fire. Marks are always recorded separately for safekeeping, but it was the first time working with student digital assessments. For the remainder of the semester, T felt continuously on edge, concerned that the internet would not work and that the record of the learners' work online in the platform might disappear.

T did not use an exam-proctoring system, i.e., a lockdown browser or sound and video monitoring. T redesigned the assessments so that although using a dictionary or asking a friend or family might occur, it was not so much a security breach in terms of the task response. The distribution of marks reported above for the assessments completed online showed that with the adapted tasks, where students engage more with the task process than with an assessment product, the results are still spread across a range of marks. It suggests that encouraging online writing tool usage, with the introduction of a new rubric to include digital editing skills, has not led to higher marks or a reduction in distribution.

The reading, writing, listening, and speaking tests were all converted for delivery as CANVAS tests. The written instructions, the images, and audio files for each test task were included. In the style of previous practice tests with solutions, a sample of tasks for the different skills was developed for learners to practice using the technology for completing tasks and uploading answers before taking the live tests.

In class, T extended the time for the tests to reduce the stress the technology caused. T reassured learners that if the browser closed, the system saved their work, and they could recommence unattempted questions with a second attempt. Some learners had to creatively find ways to submit final written drafts when the platform did not allow them to upload. On the other hand, if Ls used a pdf or image, the work did not appear in the marking screen and required T to download, mark, save, snip, and upload. Providing feedback became very burdensome with such additional steps.

14.4.6 RQ2 What Were Learners' Views of Learning a Language in a Virtual Mode during the Pandemic?

The response rate for the Course Evaluation Surveys for the Pandemic years was much lower than usual, hypothesised to result from student disengagement with studying from home. While most learners found the virtual classroom assessments stressful, some found them convenient and were not negatively affected: especially when they were resilient and went with the flow. T learned from the comments that many were unhappy and lacking in motivation while studying remotely for a course they had enrolled in face-to-face mode, but they appreciated feedback, were understanding and were interested in the cultural content.

In Ducasse (2022), student reflections on assessments in the online course, not free-text course evaluations, were reported. The main content analysis themes were 'learning language and content', 'completing assessments tasks', and 'reflecting on learning and completing assessments from the personal and interpersonal perspective'. In the analysis of the selected free-text comments connected to assessment for this study, learners expressed issues that affected them personally. These ranged from their ability to be motivated to engage with learning and assessment via technology to an awareness of tasks they perceived helped them improve via redrafting and teacher feedback and the enjoyment of learning cultural content via the target language.

14.4.6.1 The Technology

Across three semesters, what stood out was that learners were unhappy with changes involving technology. They had complaints about the platform, e.g.,

'The platform that we do our classes and the online assessment format, particularly in the group presentation are the parts that need the most improvement. Especially for a language, I would love to see all efforts go towards having face to face options for classes' (level 5). At all levels, students encountered technical difficulties during assessments, e.g., 'There were a lot of technical difficulties in assessed tasks and that put a lot of stress on the learners' (level 3). Perhaps the worst issue for students who had never studied online was lack of satisfaction and inability to engage with others, e.g., 'I am not satisfied with the course being online. It is very difficult to engage with others and express confusion' (level 3). These circumstances led to reduced motivation, e.g., 'at least in my case, it was very hard to stay motivated or want to contribute' (level 3) and the result was that course numbers declined from the Pandemic, with its impact on students felt in the following years.

14.4.6.2 Assessments

Students recognised that 'the assessments are mostly fair and reasonable based on learning format (level 4)'. However, the most significant number of unsolicited comments was on feedback, i.e., 'the best aspect of this course was the paragraph writing that we sent and got feedback for. We then used online tools to make our paragraph better' (level 3). Furthermore, in the following semester, a continued sense of personal fulfilment was expressed, e.g., 'the weekly engagement task has been a great way to keep improving my writing' (level 4). Comments recognise the regularity and timeliness, i.e., 'she always makes sure to comment on your work' (level 3) and the perceived quality of the tasks and feedback. For example, 'I think the weekly engagement tasks are great and constant feedback on my Spanish writing has been extremely helpful!' (level 4). Apart from 'the feedback on assignments hav[ing] been good and helpful' (level 3), students' perception of the impact on their learning from submitting redrafts was also made explicit in the comments. For example, 'this helps me refine my writing skills and also to practise my grammar and sentence structures' (level 3) and 'it is great for keeping me on track' (level 3), and it 'provides an opportunity to synthesise what I've learnt while getting valuable feedback' (level 3). This task, amid all the tumultuous change, allowed students to perceive that they had achieved autonomy from redrafting with internet tools and teacher guidance that made them feel they 'had learnt the most out of that task' (level 3) and also that they were 'really challenged [myself] and learnt lots this semester' (level 3).

14.4.6.3 Cultural Assessments

The cultural assessments comprise group oral presentations, and summaries or essays that are longer by proficiency level. Level 3 tasks cover UNESCO sites in the Spanish Speaking world. Students who studied beginner levels appreciate completing research in Spanish: 'I think Spanish is really interesting both as a language and as a culture. This course goes beyond learning grammar and vocab' (level 3). Level 4 tasks cover art and artists in a Spanish speaking socio-historical context and students write their first essay in Spanish. Level 5, covers gastronomy in the Spanish speaking world: mobility, sustainability, and fair trade. Students enjoy the authentic materials: 'The contents and components of the course are interesting and diverse, and I have enjoyed this year's focus on cultural topics immensely' (level 5).

14.5 Discussion: Affordances for Post-Pandemic

Perhaps as practitioners, while we rapidly effect change reactively, we are being swept along by what will become paradigm shifts in hindsight. T, an experienced teacher and researcher, was inspired to reflect on and discuss experiences of 'change under pressure' because, within our contexts as educators, we can be left with no choice but to operate quickly and, even at times, blindly. The Pandemic times were no different because, *inter alia*, it was a global crisis for education. On reflection, T would not like to repeat the same stress; however, the affordances are worth maintaining despite the challenges to keep working in this space. The practical implications suggest that T will continue to implement, adapt, and further improve assessments in the future; the changes made across the three courses proved more authentic, offering learners increased agency over their learning.

The ERT time during the Pandemic was important: on the one hand, for collegiality and pastoral care, but on the other, the sink or swim context resulted in breaking with tradition and changes of mindset borne out resilience. T observed how well learners and lecturers adapted to new modes of teaching, assessment, and feedback delivery. It is perhaps because educators face constant decision-making in situations calling for professional judgement in all aspects of their work, that this energy was also channelled into teachers teaching themselves new skills. Lecturers kept their positions, maintained their students engaged and interested in learning while showing increased empathy for colleagues and learners alike.

Despite that, remote teaching is not for everyone. Some learners appeared uncomfortable from feedback received after the course, though others found it suited their needs. Unfortunately, some frustrated learners could not find what they needed on the platform or could not open the files or submit responses which caused distress. It will be preventable in the future with instructional videos informing and guiding learners about how to use the platform without countless unsuccessful clicks.

Regarding T's 'tools' to promote and evaluate AaL during the Pandemic, T learned new skills required to design, adapt, develop, and evaluate digital classroom-based tests. T used contextual knowledge from within Global

Studies to engage the learners with authentic cultural content in Spanish. Reflecting on the time learners spent alone, perhaps not knowing how to study without classmates to guide them, tasks were broken down into steps.

Gaining fluency and enjoyment of in-class language learning are critical motivators for Spanish learning (Parma & Bustin, 2021). The inherent challenges of teaching L2 synchronously and remotely made it challenging to maintain student motivation through achieving fluency and enjoyment. Nevertheless, students who persisted demonstrated intrinsic motivation by the possibility of using Spanish in its linguistic community and a professional setting. Anecdotal evidence suggests that a higher-than-average number of students from Melbourne applied for paid teaching placements in Spain through the Spanish Ministry of Education's teach English abroad program during the Pandemic years, to escape lockdown and pursue dreams of fluency and enjoyment!

14.6 Conclusion

The key message is that authentic assessments and tools to provide timely feedback for virtual and remote language learning, supported by practical formative assessments, helped learners view AaL tasks, the central tenet of AaL. Although achieving this appears challenging for educators, in the context of this Australian case study, there were reasonable class sizes, online teaching infrastructure, and participative learners willing to engage with the affordances and address the challenges. It bodes well for future classes to benefit from the experience.

The study helps us understand why authentic assessments, streamlined feedback processes, and more interesting cultural artefacts online all resulted from the Pandemic. The question to ponder is what will remain of these assessment tasks and AaL teaching focus adaptations into the future, beyond the Pandemic. In sum, the changes made to the design of tasks and feedback processes, and the learners' views presented, have added to a growing number of studies on the narrative of ERT, in crisis mode during the Pandemic, with an eye to carrying the affordances into the future.

14.7 Ethical Approval

RMIT University Ethics approval #2020-23688-13090

Acknowledgements

This paper is framed within the research project Inter_ECODAL: Interculturality and inter-comprehension assessing plurilingual discourse competence: digital student feedback literacy (grant number PID2020-113796RB-I00), co-funded by the Spanish Ministry of Science and Innovation and the Agencia Estatal de Investigación.

References

Clark, T., Spiby, R., & Taviri, R. (2021). Crisis, collaboration, recovery: IELTS and COVID-19. *Language Assessment Quarterly*, *18*(1), 17–25. https://doi.org/10.1080/15434303.2020.1866575

Crawford, J. (2021). During and beyond a pandemic: Publishing learning and teaching research through COVID-19. *Journal of University Teaching & Learning Practice*, *18*(3), 02. https://doi.org/10.53761/1.18.3.2

Dawson, P., Henderson, M., Mahoney, P., Phillips, M., Ryan, T., Boud, D., & Molloy, E. (2019). What makes for effective feedback: Staff and student perspectives. *Assessment & Evaluation in Higher Education*, *44*(1), 25–36. https://doi.org/10.1080/02602938.2018.1467877

Ducasse, A. M. (2022). Oral reflection tasks: Advanced Spanish L2 learner insights on emergency remote teaching assessment practices in a higher education context. *Languages*, *7*(26). https://doi.org/10.3390/languages7010026

Ducasse, A. M., & Hill, K. (2019). Developing student feedback literacy using educational technology and the reflective feedback conversation. *Practitioner Research in Higher Education*, *12*(1), 24–37. http://insight.cumbria.ac.uk/id/eprint/4574/

Fan, J., & Jin, Y. (2020). Standards for language assessment: Demystifying university-level English placement testing in China. *Asia Pacific Journal of Education*, *40*(3), 386–400. https://doi.org/10.1080/02188791.2019.1706445

Gierl, M. J., & Haladyna, T. M. (2012). Automatic item generation: An introduction. In M. J. Gierl, & T. M. Haladyna (Eds.), *Automatic item generation: Theory and practice* (pp. 3–12). Routledge.

Hampel, R., & Stickler, U. (2005). New skills for new classrooms: Training tutors to teach languages online. *Computer Assisted Language Learning*, *18*(4), 311–326. https://doi.org/10.1080/09588220500335455

Hodges, C. B., Moore, S. L., Lockee, B. B., Aaron Bond, M., & Jewett, A. (2020). An Instructional design process for Emergency Remote Teaching. In Burgos, D., Tlilja, A. & Tabacco, A. (Eds.), *Radical solutions for education in a crisis context*, (pp. 37–51). Springer. https://doi.org/10.1007/978-981-15-7869-4_3

Isbell, D. R., & Kremmel, B. (2020). Test review: Current options in at-home language proficiency tests for making high-stakes decisions. *Language Testing*, *37*(4), 600–619. https://doi.org/10.1177%2F0265532220943483

Lee, I. (2016). Putting students at the centre of classroom L2 writing assessment. *Canadian Modern Language Review*, *72*(2), 258–280. https://doi.org/10.3138/cmlr.2802

Lee, K., Fanguy, M., Lu, X. S., & Bligh, B. (2021). Student learning during COVID-19: It was not as bad as we feared. *Distance Education*, *42*(1), 164–172. https://doi.org/10.1080/01587919.2020.1869529

Nicholson, S. J. (2013). Influencing motivation in the foreign language classroom. *Journal of International Education Research*, *9*(3), 277–286. https://doi.org/10.19030/jier.v9i3.7894

O'Reilly, E. (2014). Correlations among perceived autonomy support, intrinsic motivation, and learning outcomes in an intensive foreign language program. *Theory and Practice in Language Studies*, *4*(7), 1313–1318. https://doi.org/10.4304/tpls.4.7

Parma, A., & Bustin, A. (2021). Uncovering the key motivational factors behind students' enrollment in Spanish classes at institutions of higher education. *Journal of Spanish Language Teaching*, *8*(1), 32–47. https://doi.org/10.1080/23247797.2021.1921949

Pellegrino, J. W., Chudowsky, N., & Glaser, R. (2001). *Knowing what learners know: The science and design of educational assessment*. National Academy Press.

Scarino, A. (2022). Language teacher education in diversity – A consideration of the mediating role of languages and cultures in student learning. *Language and Education*, *36*(2), 152–169. https://doi.org/10.1080/09500782.2021.1991370

Shute, V. J., Leighton, J. P., Jang, E. E., & Chu, M. (2016). Advances in the Science of Assessment, *Educational Assessment*, *21*(1), 34–59. https://doi.org/10.1080/10627197.2015.1127752

Sternberg, R. J., & Horvath, J. A. (1995). A prototype view of expert teaching. *Educational Researcher*, *24*(6), 9–17. https://doi.org/10.3102/0013189X024006009

Torrance, H. (2007). Assessment as Learning? How the use of explicit learning objectives, assessment criteria and feedback in post-secondary education and training can come to dominate learning. *Assessment in Education*, *14*(3), 281–294. https://doi.org/10.1080/09695940701591867

Wu, X. (2003). Intrinsic motivation and young language learners: The impact of the classroom environment. *System*, *31*(4), 501–517. https://doi.org/10.1016/j.system.2003.04.001

Zhu, C., Wang, D., Cai, Y., & Engels, N. (2013). What core competencies are related to teachers' innovative teaching? *Asia-Pacific Journal of Teacher Education*, *41*(1), 9–27. https://doi.org/10.1080/1359866X.2012.753984

Appendix

Feedback rubric Semester 1 Task 1 Spanish 3 A2

	1 under level 1.5 pass	2 at level credit	2.5 distinction	3 high distinction	/15
Text flow use of connectors and connected content					/3
Range and level of vocabulary					/3
Range and level of expression					/3
Edits marked in capitals	50%+ errors edited correctly	60%+ edited	70%+ errors edited	80% + errors edited	/3
Choice of tools to edit final text & reference in edits	Autocorrect (A) Spelling and accents Dictionary online (D)	(CN) Conjugator online Translator online (T)	Class notes (C) Keyboard for accents/ ñ, ü (K)	PPT from class (PPT) Memory (M)	/3

15
RETHINKING THE ONLINE PLACEMENT TEST FOR A COLLEGE-LEVEL JAPANESE LANGUAGE PROGRAM DURING THE COVID-19 PANDEMIC

Akiko Imamura, Catherine Ryu, and Mariko Kawaguchi

MICHIGAN STATE UNIVERSITY, EAST LANSING, MI, UNITED STATES

15.1 Introduction

Placement tests are widely recognised as an essential component of any language program articulation at the post-secondary level (Bernhardt et al., 2004). Placing students in appropriate language courses, however, is not a simple task since it requires balancing the competing demands of stakeholders, (i.e., students, instructors, and administrators, in addition to addressing each program's unique circumstances). Although effective course placements are essential for optimal language learning, the placement test requires efficiency in terms of time and human resources. Prior to the pandemic, the Japanese Language Program (henceforth, JLP) at Michigan State University (MSU) has relied on hard-copy written tests and interviews performed in person, on a single day, at the end of summers. The pandemic, however, made in-person testing no longer tenable. To address this pressing challenge, the program newly implemented an online placement test. This chapter delineates the assessment procedures and reports a preliminary analysis of test results regarding the effectiveness of online testing and its sustainability in the post-COVID-19 era.

Previous studies have shown that achieving a balance between effectiveness and efficiency of placement tests is a common challenge to large-scale university foreign language programs (Bernhardt et al., 2004). The JPL at MSU faced similar challenges, even though the program itself is not as large as other language programs (e.g., the Spanish programs). There are four levels of the Japanese language at MSU, each organized with a sequence of two courses. The first half of each level is offered in Fall and the second half in Spring. Each year approximately 450 students are enrolled in our language courses.[1] Students who have studied Japanese elsewhere and do not wish to start with JPN101, the first semester of Japanese at MSU, must take the placement test before beginning the Fall semester. Similar to other large-scale college-level language programs, time constraints and intense labour needs were the main challenges when we administered an in-person pencil and paper placement test for multiple levels. Thus, the program had been keenly aware of the issues with the test delivery format, not to mention the need to manage the test and course placement data more effectively in relation to the program's curriculum development. The arrival of the pandemic in 2020 left us no choice but to shift the placement test to a 100%-online format. The pandemic thus catapulted the program to take a giant leap and swiftly build and launch an online placement test in the Summer of 2020 in time for the course placements in the Fall of 2020.

15.2 Placement Test and Its Implementation

15.2.1 Overview of Literature on the Placement Test

Placement tests are conducted for two purposes: assessing students' language proficiency and placing individual students based on their proficiency (Brown, 2005). The test utility depends highly on the predictive validity of a placement test since 'unless the test can correctly predict where a student should be placed in a sequence of courses (for optimal learning), the test is less than useful' (Bernhardt et al., 2004, p. 358). To maintain predictive validity, each program's curriculum and course syllabi must be considered for the placement decisions (Kondo-Brown, 2017). From students' viewpoint, placement tests are high-stake assessments as its result could directly impact students' language learning experience and, more broadly, their entire academic plans.

Additionally, many language programs face a number of challenges in administering placement tests. As Kondo-Brown (2017) pointed out, developing or even adopting a test that can yield highly valid and reliable placement results is burdensome. Lack of time and complicated logistics are other typical impediments (Bernhardt et al., 2004). Individual students' course placements often must be completed in a relatively limited time by a small number of instructors or administrators. Given such constraints, administering a comprehensive placement test is quite challenging even for a program with a limited number of students to assess, while it is ideal to assess a wide range of language skills, including grammatical knowledge, listening, reading, writing, and oral proficiency. Adopting a large-scale test developed by a third party may increase efficiency; however, such an adoption necessitates verification of its utility as an appropriate placement tool for the language program. In other words, a pilot testing among the current pool of students and investigating a correlation between student performance in each course before and after its adoption are critically important. Thus, while third-party tests have their benefits, it poses a significant challenge for language programs attempting to choose one for their programs (Kondo-Brown, 2017).

Besides the challenges of identifying a reliable placement test, meeting students' demands is another critical factor when administering a placement test. Not to mention the need for speedy and effective course placements, students desire to enrol in a specific course level based on their self-assessment and academic plans. Placements in a lower-level course than anticipated may cause both emotional and heavier financial burdens for some students. In a nutshell, the course placements involve a multi-layered consideration of the unique circumstances, including a test selection, stakeholders' needs and demands, as well as the chosen test's effectiveness and efficiency.

The COVID-19 pandemic exacerbated the challenging nature of administering a placement test, prohibiting in-person tests and face-to-face interviews. MSU's Japanese program thus had to address an urgent need to implement the placement test entirely online. Yet, transitioning to an online placement system itself was a welcoming shift. The widely recognized merit of the computerized placement test lies in its flexibility, convenience, and efficiency (see Banno et al., 2010; Chapelle & Voss, 2016; Eda et al., 2008; Sakai & Kobayashi, 2012). For instance, students can schedule their testing time regardless of their geographic locations. Moreover, instructors can save time and effort for grading and record-keeping. The flexibility of computerized online placement tests thus opens up an opportunity to secure the time for oral assessments (Bernhardt et al., 2004).

Another critical advantage of computerized tests is the possibility of administering a computer-adaptive test (CAT), which 'control[s] the adaptivity based on test takers' performance on each item on the test' (Chapelle & Voss, 2016, p. 117). CATs often rely on 'a psychometric method called item response theory to control the adaptivity' (Chapelle & Voss, 2016, p. 117); the results of test item analysis based on the theory are applicable to any group of test-takers (Kondo-Brown, 2017). By adjusting to students' proficiency level, a CAT 'can be administered using a relatively small number of question items' (Burston & Neophytou, 2014, p. 20).

15.2.2 Japanese Placement Test

For the Japanese language, a few third-party Japanese tests or testing platforms are currently available as placement tests: Tsukuba Test-Battery of Japanese (TTBJ), Japanese Skills Test (JSKIT), Japanese Computerized Adaptive Test

(J-CAT), and Standard-Based Measurement of Proficiency (STAMP) (Eda et al., 2008; Hatasa & Watanabe, 2017; Hirotani et al., 2017; Kobayashi, 2016; Kondo-Brown, 2017). These systems measure multiple aspects of language abilities, such as grammar knowledge, listening, and reading. Among the tests listed above, STAMP includes speaking tests along with assessments of other skills. In terms of the cost, J-CAT and STAMP requires some fees,[2] while TTBJ and JSKIT are free. For speaking skills, a couple of third-party tests are also available. Kondo-Brown (2017) reported that many JLPs use the American Council on the Teaching of Foreign Languages (ACTFL)'s Oral Proficiency Interview (OPI) as a placement test. Since 2006, there has been an internet-mediated variation known as OPIc.

15.3 Guiding Questions for the JLP's Pilot Project

Given the complex and challenging nature of determining the most appropriate placement test for our JLP, this pilot study was designed to answer two guiding questions:

1. How can we design an online placement test as a single assessment system containing all levels that can be implemented with limited financial and human resources during the pandemic and that can be sustainable in the post-pandemic era as well?
2. To what extent can the new online placement test as a single assessment system accurately differentiate each student's language ability in relation to our Japanese language curriculum?

15.4 Pre-COVID-19 Era System

The JLP at MSU offers four levels of language courses, JPN 101, 102, 201, 202, 301, 302, 401, and 402 as a sequence. The first half of each level, JPN 101, 201, 301, and 401, are only offered every Fall, and the second half, JPN 102, 202, 302, and 402, every Spring. The majority of JLP's placements occur before the fall semesters start; thus, most test-takers are placed into JPN 201, 301, or 401. Students may start from the second half of each level with a break from Japanese for a fall semester, although it is not necessarily recommended.

Before Summer 2020, the JLP at MSU administered in-person pencil and paper placement tests, which took about two hours to complete. It usually took place a few days prior to the beginning of the Fall semester. On average, the program placed 20–30 students every year. The pre-pandemic placement system used three individual tests for second, third, and fourth-year language courses. Each test was based on the final written exam of its corresponding level and included only grammar, reading, and writing portions. Since the placement test was administered in a single classroom in which all students took their respective tests of different levels, and due to the time constraint and lack of human resources, neither a listening test nor an oral interview was included. However, the test administrators (i.e., the language instructors) did engage with the students in Japanese, for instance, when checking their IDs before the test. This was an informal way of observing their proficiency levels based on their responses.

This in-person placement test required intense labour of the instructor(s) in charge, even though the number of learners who took the test did not exceed over 50 each year. Handling 20–30 students over two hours was not only challenging but also chaotic, resulting in a lot of confusion and sometimes errors. Even though the tests had multiple-choice questions, the instructors had to check the answers manually. It took time, and errors were found in the answer key in some cases. While the multiple-choice questions were being graded, the students worked on a written essay, and when they finished their essays early, students had to wait for the instructors to grade their written tests. Moreover, the test materials were not updated regularly due to a relative lack of sustained program-wide discussion on placement-related issues.

15.5 New Japanese Placement Test at MSU

15.5.1 New Placement Procedure and Logistics

Between the onset of emergency remote instruction in March and the beginning of the Fall semester in 2020, it was impossible for our program to conduct a pilot study to determine the utility of any third-party tests. This was due not only to time constraints but also to a lack of human resources. That is why we designed a single assessment system with some adaptive nature to differentiate, to the extent feasible, the proficiency levels of our students.

With the necessity of implementing a fully online placement test, we developed a system comprised of three parts: (1) an online student information survey, (2) an online placement test, and (3) a virtual oral interview. To implement this multi-layered system in a streamlined interactive manner, we adopted a web-based survey tool, Qualtrics. In addition to its built-in notification systems for sending out reminders, other tracking functions, and data importing and exporting capacity, Qualtrics also has the real-time auto-scoring ability except for essays. All placement test-related information was published on the program website, including the anonymous link to the student information survey and a tentative schedule for oral interviews to inform potential test-takers about the testing process and procedure.

With this system, a student first accessed the student information survey, which collected learners' language backgrounds, and which functioned as the registration for the online test. The survey requires students to register with their MSU email addresses, opening a communication channel with individuals using MSU credentials. In this way, the test administers were able to identify all test-takers' answers, along with their demographics and learning background information. The student information survey and online test were linked in the Qualtrics workflow platform so that the completion of the survey automatically triggered the transmission of a personalized link to the online placement test. A reminder email was pre-scheduled for the online test if a registered learner did not take the test. This automated system remained accessible throughout Summer 2020.

In mid-August, the test administrator in charge screened the online test results and used them to make tentative placement recommendations based on the online test. The tentative placement recommendations enabled the program to sort out the students who could proceed to the oral interview tests. Before the Fall semesters, all qualified students were interviewed on the same day by the Japanese language instructors via Zoom for about five minutes each.[3] Based on the instructors' recommendations, the final course placements were determined, and the students were notified of their placements within a day or two after the interviews.

The new online assessment system allowed the JLP to manage time and human resources effectively, while ensuring that students be placed in a timely fashion before the beginning of the new academic year. Simultaneously, the system greatly increased the scheduling flexibility of the text without adding to the administrator's workload.

15.5.2 Structure of the Placement Test and Its Adaptive Nature

The online test built on Qualtrics contains four sections: grammar, reading, listening, and writing, which must be completed within an hour. Qualtrics automatically tracks the progression of test-taking. Each level of the test includes 20–30 questions selected from the final exams used in previous academic years in each language course. The questions are chosen to assess students' linguistic and socio-linguistic competences that are necessary to reach the proficiency goals of individual levels. To automate grading, a combination of multiple-choice and matching formats is used for all grammar, reading, and listening sections. In the writing section, students typed short essays in Japanese, which were manually graded.

The key feature of our online placement is its dual-level structure. To operationalize this design concept, we utilized Qualtrics' branch logic capacity. The test is structured with five blocks, JPN102, 201, 301, 401, and 402. To reiterate, each block includes questions selected from the final exams of MSU Japanese courses. The questions were collected from the exams one-level lower than the level being tested. For example, the JPN 201 block contains questions selected from the final exam of the JPN 102. Students initially select

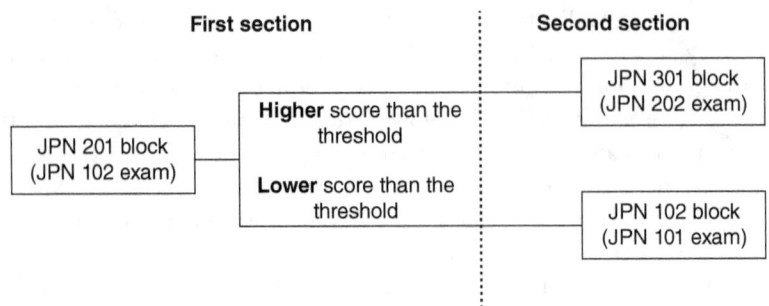

FIGURE 15.1 Dual-level placement flow chart.

their desired level out of JPN 201, 301, or 401, for the first section of the test. This is because only the first half of each level, JPN 101, 201, 301, and 401, are offered in the Fall semester. Depending on the resulting score, they are then automatically assigned to another block of questions that is either higher or lower than the initial level. In other words, the dual-level structure of our placement test requires all registered students to complete two blocks out of the five. A JPN 102 block was added (a spring course), in case students need the second block lower than JPN 201. We also included JPN402 (a spring course) to identify students who might not need any language courses. With this system, for instance, a student who wants to enrol in JPN 201 will begin with the JPN 201 block. Based on the scores they earned (See the next section for the criteria), the student would be assigned to the block for JPN 301, which corresponds to JPN 202 level exam, or the block for JPN 102, corresponding to JPN 101 (see Figure 15.1).

While this test design does not use item-based adaptivity relying on an algorithm (Chapelle & Voss, 2016), it is still adaptive in nature because Qualtrics' branch logic automatically determines the combination of test blocks based on the test-taker's performance on the first block of questions. This system is thus capable of generating more performance data points than the previous placement test, which in turn helps the JLP to identify more accurately than before the proficiency levels of test-takers. Furthermore, this structure was expressly designed to determine each learner's optimal course placement more precisely and efficiently than the previous single-level placement.

As for designing oral interviews, we created interview prompts collaboratively involving all language instructors in charge of the individual language courses. Each interview included questions relevant to the respective levels' proficiency goals (e.g., talking about preference in hobby for JPN 201; memorable events with friends for JPN 301; and pros and cons of online education for JPN 401). All questions were shared with all interviewers in advance to enable the interviewers to adjust the questions based on the interviewee's responses. By the time of oral interviews, the instructors had access to all student's test scores and their tentative placement recommendations.

15.5.3 Placement Criteria

As mentioned briefly above, the placement decision involved two steps: asynchronous online tests and oral interviews. The asynchronous online test provides the two test scores along with the essay. The essay was holistically evaluated by the administrator based on the organization and cohesion, structural variation, accuracy, spelling, and adherence to Japanese writing conventions. When students earned above 85% on the first test block for their desired level on Qualtrics, they were tentatively placed into the desired levels, regardless of the second test block result for the next higher level, and assigned to the interview for the desired level. The threshold of 85% was chosen as the benchmark for a practical reason.

When a student earned below 85% but above 60% on the first block, the scores of the second block, targeting the next lower level, had a significant impact on the tentative decision. In such a case, the placement decision would require a holistic judgment by comparing the two scores of the online test along with the quality of the essay and the oral interview performance. In some cases, we postponed narrowing down the tentative recommendation to one. For instance, a student might be tested for both JPN 301 and 201 in an interview if a student selected JPN 301 as the desired level but earned only 70% for the first block test and a similar score for JPN201 for the second block test.

When students earned less than 60% for the first test block, their tentative placement would be lower than their initially desired levels. Although the interview was conducted to validate the initial recommendation, some students were not invited to an oral interview if their desired level was 201, but the scores for both test blocks were under 60%. While an oral interview was a vital aspect of the placement procedure, it was also time-consuming. By identifying only the students whose course placements required oral interviews in this way, we were able to assess their speaking abilities efficiently.

After the online test, the administrator made a tentative recommendation for each student, and the recommendations were shared with the language instructors before the oral interviews. Students' oral interview performance was evaluated holistically in terms of contents, cohesiveness, linguistic complexity, accuracy, and socio-linguistic/pragmatic appropriateness. The instructors' final decisions were made based on whether each student is proficient enough to keep up with one's desired level in an integrated fashion. This was done by comparing the tentative recommendation made by the administrator and the student's oral performance. The oral interviews served as an opportunity to verify the viability and reliability of the tentative recommendation made prior to the oral interviews.

TABLE 15.1 Placement Results for Fall 2020 and Fall 2021

	FS2020				FS2021			
	Survey	Online	Oral	Final	Survey	Online	Oral	Final
101		N/A	N/A	10		N/A	N/A	9
102		N/A	N/A	9		N/A	N/A	8
201		29	21	12		19	15	6
301		4	3	4		7	3	2
401		3	2	1		3	3	4
Total	44	36 (81.8%)	26 (59%) (72%)	36	42	29 (69%)	21 (50%) (72.4%)	29

15.6 Online Test Results and Placement Decision

The JLP at MSU developed the online assessment system in Summer 2020 and placed approximately 70 students over the last two academic years. This section presents the placement test results collected from Fall 2020 and Fall 2021, together with the preliminary analysis. The number of learners who completed the student information survey was 44 for Fall 2020 and 42 for Fall 2021. Among these test-takers, 36 students in 2020 and 29 in 2021 finished taking the online placement test and received their final course placements. These numbers amount to 81.8% and 69% of those who completed the survey in their respective years. The final results of the placement decision are shown in Table 15.1. Among students who had initially completed the student information survey, 59% and 50% of students proceeded to oral interviews in their respective years. This corresponds to 72% and 72.4% of students who took the online test. For the most part, the course placement decisions made over the past two years were not contested by students, indicating the relatively high accuracy level of the assessments thus made. In 2020, for example, only a single case of course change occurred after the onset of the semester. In 2021, no course changes were reported.

15.6.1 Oral Interviews and Placement Decision Change

In the past two iterations of the new assessment system, oral interviews have served as an effective verification tool to calibrate accurate placement decisions for individual students. In Fall 2020, four among 26 students who took an oral interview were placed in a lower-level course than their tentative placement decisions. This amounts to 15.4% of the total number of interviews. In Fall 2021, we observed many more decision changes after oral interviews. Nine students' placement decisions (42.9% of all interviews) were adjusted based on their oral interview performances. Six students, or 19%, of interviewees, were placed in a lower course after their interviews. Significantly, in Fall 2021,

TABLE 15.2 Differences in Students' Desired Level and Placement for JPN201 and 301

FS2020

Desired level	Final recommendation			
	101	102	201	301
201 (29)	41.3% (12)	20.7% (6)	37.9% (11)	
301 (4)		25% (1)	25% (1)	50% (2)

FS2021

Desired level	Final recommendation			
	101	102	201	301
201 (19)	47.4% (8)	31.6% (6)	26.3% (5)	
301 (7)	14% (1)	28.6% (2)	14% (1)	43.4% (3)

three students' final placement (14.3% of all interviews) was determined to be higher based on their oral interview performance. While the number of changes made is different in terms of percentage, the results demonstrate that oral interviews enhanced tailoring the placement decisions according to the characteristics of individual test-takers.

15.6.2 The Discrepancy between Students' Desired Level and Final Decision

Table 15.1 is notable for illuminating the disparities between students' desired levels chosen at the beginning of the online test and their final course placements in the past two test operations. In the past two years, only one student was placed into a higher-level course than the student's desired level. Meanwhile, it was common that a student's placement performance did not exceed the expectation of their desired levels (see Table 15.2). This tendency was prominent among the students who wished to enrol in JPN 201 and 301. For example, in 2020, 11 out of 29 students (37.9%) were placed in JPN 201 as they wished. In 2021, only five among 19 students (26.3%) were placed at their desired level. That is to say, in both years, much more than 50% of students were placed in lower-level courses than their originally desired course. Moreover, even among students who chose JPN 301 as their desired course, two out of four students (50%) were placed in JPN 102 or 201 in 2020.[4] In 2021, four out of seven students (57.1%) were recommended to start at the lower level than their desired level.

15.7 Discussion

The online assessment system shed new light on the discrepancy between students' self-assessment of their language skills and their actual course placements. In fact, this outcome supports the previous studies on language learners' self-assessment, reporting that learners' self-assessed proficiency often does not coincide with the assessments based on other means (Tigchelaar et al., 2017). In other words, learners cannot necessarily evaluate their current proficiency level accurately. To address such a disparity, it is certainly possible to emphasize to the students the intensive nature of college-level Japanese courses. However, another critical issue pertaining to this disparity is the question of potentially negative emotional or psychological effects on the students. A lower-level course placement might be understood as the denial of their previous training and efforts, which might have a tremendously negative impact on the students' future motivation to pursue Japanese studies. In addition, the placement results suggest that there might be more students whose speaking skills are relatively lower than their other language skills. This finding is valuable to the JLP as we continually develop the current language program articulation.

The study corroborated that one of the marked benefits of the online assessment system is efficiency and flexibility for both test-takers and administrators. The online system enables the program to launch the placement process much earlier than the previous in-person pencil and paper placement tests by distributing various phases of the placement assessment during the summer. Students were notified of their tentative and final placement decision before the Fall term started. It allowed students to adjust their expectations in the program before their arrival and use the summertime efficiently to review Japanese. The new online assessment system thus provided a conduit through which new and transfer students could interact with the program before they joined MSU. From the administrator's viewpoint, the flexible nature of the system allowed the program to reduce the intensity of work for the instructors and academic advisors. Instructors' burden to grade all tests within a couple of hours was significantly reduced. By determining tentative recommendations much earlier than before, academic advisors no longer needed to override 20–30 students' enrolment at once.

With the online single assessment system in place, we can now collect more data points with less work and a less intense schedule. Compared to the previous system, the current online system allows a collection of a few more additional data points: background information survey, listening, and oral interviews. Thus, it facilitates making complete placement decisions while striving toward a greater degree of efficiency and accuracy. For example, no students, with the exception of one in 2020, have changed their course enrolment since the implementation of the online assessment system. The rarity of course enrolment change so far thus demonstrates the relatively high accuracy of the current assessment system. In fact, placement accuracy is one of the essential factors when evaluating the utility of the placement test in terms of predictive validity (Hatasa & Watanabe, 2017). Given the purpose of this particular test, the ultimate goal is to find the optimal course for the registered learners so that they would benefit the most in the specific sequence of MSU's Japanese language courses.

Furthermore, changing the delivery format of the placement test also opened up an opportunity for the JLP to rethink this method of assessment critical piece of the Japanese Studies curriculum and its articulation. By using Qualtrics, we could collect and store both students' background information (e.g., the length of previous learning experience and previously used materials) and their online placement test performance. A more comprehensive analysis of these data will provide a greater understanding of how to better support our incoming students and better prepare them for our program. In other words, the technology-mediated integration of student performance information resulting from the online assessment system can potentially foster further pedagogical improvements.

The additional programmatic advantage of implementing the new placement system is that it provides an opportunity for all our instructors to collaborate as a team. During regular semesters, individual instructors do not have opportunities to discuss their opinions on cross-level assessments. The administration of the single assessment system for all levels facilitates many collaborative opportunities (e.g., sharing their final exam questions, taking a pilot version of the test, and running oral interviews). This enabled, and will continue to enable, faculty members, to gain a holistic perspective of the JLP beyond the individual courses they teach.

15.8 Post-Pandemic Lessons

Redesigning the placement test had many benefits beyond determining appropriate course placements for students in an efficient, accurate, and timely manner. Despite its advantages, challenges still remain with the current assessment system. One issue is the adequacy of using Qualtrics as the authoring tool (cf. Chapelle & Voss, 2016). A survey tool, Qualtrics, is not designed to create language tests. While it contains a variety of question types, the design of Qualtrics constrains the display of test questions and formats for answering the questions. For instance, test-takers sometimes would need to scroll the screen back and forth repeatedly when previewing the tests. Although this may not be an issue limited to Qualtrics, the current test has room for practical improvements. Additionally, Qualtrics does not have an item banking system. Lack of such features could present some inconvenience if the program were to continue using Qualtrics. Administering the assessment system with Qualtrics is still time and labour-intensive, and it sometimes requires extensive research and consultation with the technical support staff.

Furthermore, when running the second iteration of the placement test system, the program updated some portions of online tests in May 2021.

However, the updates needed to be rushed to prepare all the tests before the language faculty's contract expiration. Given the disadvantages, one issue to address for the post-pandemic era is whether this new placement system is the most optimal choice for the program in the long term. Shifting to a third-party online test, such as TTBJ, is an option in the future, even if we need to investigate how our students' performance in TTBJ corresponds to the level of each language course. Once we have these data, we may no longer need to update the online tests. Adopting a third-party test will help ease the language faculty's workload, and there would be no significant disadvantage for incoming students as long as there is no fee involved.

Meanwhile, we as the program need to carefully deliberate on how much technology use is most advantageous for all stakeholders. Despite technology's significant impact and improvement on various aspects of the placement test, its implementation entirely relies on computer and internet access. Issues of students' lacking adequate devices and internet access have been pointed out in the development of a proliferation of computer-assisted language learning (Winke & Goertler, 2008). The pandemic has amplified the question of technology access and remains a continuing issue of equity, especially for learning communities, including college students, even in the 21st century (Moser et al., 2021; Reich et al., 2020). The equity issue needs to be always taken seriously so that the lack of access does not affect the students' placement experience or its result.

15.9 Conclusion

This chapter has presented the development of a new online placement test procedure conducted by the JLP at MSU during the COVID-19 pandemic. The urgency of implementing fully remote instruction led us to develop an online single assessment system in a relatively short time, over two months in Summer 2020. The dramatic changes in the testing modality brought about many logistical and practical improvements, not to mention our newly gained administrative ability to offer a single assessment system for all levels. In the post-pandemic era, further adjustments to the testing procedures should be considered to maintain a sensitive balance between efficiency and placement accuracy, which will lead to an effectively streamlined articulation of the Japanese language curriculum at MSU.

Notes

1 The number is the approximate of the total enrolments for both Fall and Spring. A student might be counted twice when they registered for both Fall and Spring courses.
2 To the authors' best knowledge, J-CAT costs approximately $10–40 depending on the version (Japanese Language Education Support Association, n.d.). STAMP

also requires a test fee but their website does not include the specific price (Avant Assessment, LLC, n.d.)
3   A couple of students did not show up for the interview. The final placement decisions for these students were made solely based on the online test results.
4   As mentioned before, JPN 102 is not offered for Fall semesters. This means that the students may not take a Japanese course for the fall, if they are recommended to take JPN 102.

References

Avant Assessment, LLC. (n.d.). *STAMP Guides for testing coordinators: Frequently asked questions.* https://avantassessment.com/stamp-frequently-asked-questions

Banno, E., Watanabe, T., & Okubo, R. (2010). Development of an online Japanese placement test. *Bulletin of Higher Education, Okayama University, 6*, 107–117.

Bernhardt, E. B., Rivera, R. J., & Kamil, M. L. (2004). The practicality and efficiency of web-based placement testing for college-level language programs. *Foreign Language Annals, 37*(3), 356–366.

Brown, J. D. (2005). *Testing in Language Program: A comprehensive guide to English language assessment* (Revised ed.). McGraw-Hill.

Burston, J., & Neophytou, M. (2014). Lessons learned in designing and implementing a computer-adaptive test for English. *The EUROCALL Review, 22*(2), 19–25.

Chapelle, C. A., & Voss, E. (2016). 20 years of technology and language assessment in Language Learning & Technology. *Language Learning & Technology, 20*(2), 116–128.

Eda, S., Itomitsu, M., & Noda, M. (2008). The Japanese Skills Test as an on-demand placement test: Validity comparisons and reliability. *Foreign Language Annuals, 41*(2), 218–236.

Hatasa, Y., & Watanabe, T. (2017). Japanese as a second language assessment in Japan: Current issues and future directions. *Language Assessment Quarterly, 14*(3), 192–212.

Hirotani, M., Matsumoto, K., & Fukada, A. (2017). The validity of general L2 proficiency tests as oral proficiency measures: A Japanese learner corpus based study. *Japanese Language and Literature, 51*(2), 243–270.

Japanese Language Education Support Association. (n.d.). *Nihongo tesuto shisutemu J-CAT* [Japanese test system J-CAT]. https://j-cat.jalesa.org/?page_id=176

Kobayashi, N. (2016). Japanese language proficiency assessment with the Simple Performance-Oriented Test (SPOT) as a primary focus. In M. Minami (Ed.), *Handbook of Japanese Applied Linguistics* (pp. 175–198). De Gruyter Mouton.

Kondo-Brown, K. (2017). *Introduction to assessment for Japanese language teachers.* Kuroshio.

Moser, K. M., Wei, T., & Brenner, D. (2021). Remote teaching during COVID-19: Implications from a national survey of language educators. *System, 97*, 1–15.

Reich, J., Buttimer, C. J., Fang, A., Hillaire, G., Hirsch, K., Larke, L. R., Littenberg-Tobias, J., Moussapour, R., Napier, A., Thompson, M., & Slama, R. (2020, April 2). *Remote learning guidance from state education agencies during the COVID-19 Pandemic: A first look.* https://doi.org/10.35542/osf.io/437e2

Sakai, T., & Kobayashi, N. (2012). *Tsukuba Nihongo Testoshu (TTBJ) no kaihatsu to shiyo (1)* [Development and use of the Tsukuba Test Battery of Japanese (1)]. *Conference*

Proceedings of the 5th International Conference on Computer Assisted Systems For Teaching & Learning Japanese. 1–4.

Tigchelaar, M., Bowles, R. P., Winke, P., & Gass, S. (2017). Assessing the validity of ACTFL can-do statements for spoken proficiency: A Rasch analysis. *Foreign Language Annals, 50*(3), 584–600.

Winke, P., & Goertler, S. (2008). Did we forget someone? Students' computer access and literacy for CALL. *CALICO Journal, 25*(3), 482–509.

16
CONCLUSION

Lessons Learned and Lessons Not Learned

Karim Sadeghi

URMIA UNIVERSITY, URMIA, IRAN

16.1 Introduction

In their introduction to a special issue they edited for *System* on the challenges of teaching and learning languages online during the COVID-19 pandemic and the responses by language teachers, learners as well as other stakeholders, Tao and Gao (2022, p. 1), quoting Albert Einstein that 'in the middle of difficulty lies opportunity', rightly acknowledge that despite all hardships associated with the crisis, it 'did generate ample opportunities for language educators to experiment with online learning technologies and gain valuable experience for their future integration in language education'. The emergency situation which was viewed as a curse or disaster in many respects (health-wise and economy-wise, for example) has eventually been found to be a blessing in disguise when it comes to education, including language education (Cheung, 2021). Although the special issue in *System* (with its 26 articles) has no study related to language assessment, few people will dispute a similar role technology has played in the field of language assessment in the wake of the COVID-19 pandemic. For sure, initially the global crisis disrupted language assessment more severely and for longer periods than any teaching- and learning-related activity such that in contexts with no access to technology and the Internet, assessment either fully stopped or was postponed for a later date. Apart from large-scale language tests such as internet-based Test of English as a Foreign Language (TOEFL iBT) that already relied on technology for delivery and which could continue in very limited forms depending on availability of human supervision, most other practices of classroom-based language assessment became only second to teaching. These assessments could resume only when teachers gradually started learning about remote assessment processes and practices and only when schools, administrators, teachers, and students had access to basic technological resources such as computing facilities, the needed software, and stable internet connections.

Although at the time of writing this chapter (June 2022) the pandemic has eased in many ways, reliance on technology for language assessment seems to be a mainstay for the foreseeable future. Viewed from this angle, the COVID-19 pandemic can be seen as a blessing in disguise for the field of second language assessment as it has helped renovate the whole field, forcing students, teachers, and assessment experts to upgrade their technological skills and knowledge. Despite this advantage, there still are numerous teachers and students worldwide who do not have access to the proper technology required for online or remote test delivery for a variety of reasons including wars, economic conditions, digital literacy issues, and so on. Despite the initial hardships scholars of language assessment experienced during the first few months of the pandemic, as this volume documents, researchers and practitioners in the field started looking for solutions as early as they understood the pandemic was there to stay with us for a long time. This book is one of the first to document some early attempts to tackle the problem of remote language assessment, although a special issue of *Language Assessment Quarterly* (edited by Ockey, 2021) focuses on challenges of placement testing at some US universities during the COVID-19 pandemic. With a view to learning from the challenges experienced to inform technology-mediated language tests in the future, this conclusion chapter briefly reviews some of the major lessons learned from the emergency integration of technology in language assessment for post-pandemic times, as seen through the eyes of the contributors to the volume. The chapter ends with the lessons that have not been learned yet, inviting all human beings including scholars in the field of language assessment to ponder before another more disastrous pandemic hits.

16.2 Lessons Learned

The contributors to this volume reflect in some detail on the post-pandemic lessons learned in their specific testing contexts, some of which could well extend beyond their immediate contexts. The resulting emergency remote teaching, for example, led to higher degrees of collegiality and pastoral care among teachers, students and testers as well as making them more resilient; in Ducasse's (this volume) words, 'the sink or swim context result[ed] in breaking with tradition and changes of mindset borne out resilience' and in Balteiro's terms, the pandemic did 'contribut[e] to teachers' trust of and sympathy with students'. For Clark et al. (this volume), the major benefit of the pandemic was related to the convenience that at-home online testing afforded taker-takers within the context of International English Language Testing System (IELTS) Indicator. Although technology-mediated language assessment can be very inconvenient if the right infrastructures are not in place (e.g., test-takers do not have access to the required technological equipment, relevant software, high speed internet, and even an appropriate physical environment), the fact is that as soon as these resources are made available, language tests delivered from a distance will save candidates the time and money needed to travel to test-centres (as Neiriz et al., this volume, document). Similar convenience can be envisaged for test administrators who relinquish almost all their responsibilities on the shoulders of technology. There are obvious parallel benefits for other stakeholders as Zhang and Isaacs (this volume) observe: 'The use of the technology also makes assessments more accessible to stakeholders and may be more cost-effective and less resource-intensive than face-to-face provision'. The highest burden seems to be placed on test-makers themselves who need to make sure that online delivery happens securely enough and that the online test is as valid, as reliable, and as fair as its parallel paper-based (or computerised) version which is administered at the presence of a human proctor.

One of the most serious issues, or inconveniences, with unsupervised online assessments remains to be cheating (or what Farhady, this volume, calls academic dishonesty). Although some technological tools are already in place to contribute to test security and minimise academic disintegrity (Neiriz et al., this volume, for example, talk about live proctoring as a means to reducing cheating; and Voss, 2023, explain different proctoring options in remote testing), Farhady (this volume) believes that as far as such dishonesty occurs within the context of classroom assessment where the purpose is further learning, the behaviour should be tolerated: 'Of course, it may be possible for a few students to get help from others that is acceptable if the assistance leads to learning'. The same argument is echoed by East et al. (this volume) who propose that 'from an assessment *for* learning perspective, cheating and academic integrity no longer define the central concerns of assessment events'.

One lesson East et al. (this volume) report having learned as a result of the COVID-19 pandemic is that, as far as validity is concerned, there is no one-size-fits-all in assessment, and that a 'mix and match' approach is the best when it comes to integrating technology with assessment, the success of which depends on how creative and inventive teachers and testers are. Indeed one major lesson that the world of education including language assessment has learned from the pandemic is the need for being prepared to make adjustments and modifications to current practices on an emergency basis as many contributors to this volume like Balteiro, East et al., and Hardacre recognise. Such quick adjustments at a global scale would have been next to impossible without the involvement of digital technology, which has also meant an increased focus on continuous, formative, diverse, and 'multimodal' assessment (Carrió-Pastor, this volume) rather than end-of-the-semester examinations.

Apart from existing concerns with issues such as comparability, security, fairness, and other fundamental assessment-related concepts (see, for example,

Sadeghi & Douglas, 2023), and despite the initial challenges such tests introduced to test-makers, test-takers, and educational authorities when everyone had to quickly adapt to new modes of delivery, technology-mediated language assessment is expected to dominate the field, especially due to the convenience it now affords all stakeholders. In Clark et al.'s (this volume) terms, 'online testing has now established itself as a permanent feature of the assessment landscape', and in Mahmoud and Cabrera-Puche's (this volume) terms, 'the pandemic made it incumbent upon stakeholders to think about *assessment without borders*'. Convenience however comes at a cost; and such has been the case with most of the studies reported in this book where frontliners (such as Bruce and Stakounis, this volume) have had to cope with test design, validation, administration, and adaptation on a daily basis, without a proper plan or empirical data, as the pandemic unfolded and as new needs of language testers and test-takers emerged constantly. Some of the reports in this volume document the turmoil in those early days; but as we enter a new phase of (hopefully) post-pandemic period when language assessment has almost returned to normal, the integration of technology into language assessment (especially within the context of classroom testing) as well as remote delivery of small-scale and large-scale language tests is a precious gain. The message to take home is that the language assessment territory may face another shock should a new worldwide disaster hit, with the lesson being that assessment experts should be on their toes and ready for adopting further innovative contingency measures. To survive another unforeseen disaster, accordingly, 'training and upskilling, particularly in the area of digital assessment literacy, are certainly required', in Bruce and Stakounis's (this volume) words. Voss (this volume), similarly highlights the role of teachers', administrators', assessment providers' and test-takers' technological literacy (with test-takers requiring both construct-related and construct-unrelated digital literacy). For him, instructors and test-makers should be able to identify the right technological tool for the language assessment problem at hand: 'the best solution is by identifying technology that supports the planned language assessment for its intended purpose' which can be very difficult for teachers and testers strange with such technological affordances. Advocating e-portfolios, Lam (this volume) likewise underlines the importance of stepping up computer and assessment literacy for teachers and digital literacy for students to enable e-portfolios to lead to positive backwash and to prevent them from remaining as 'digital containers' only.

The two keywords that became buzz word in education during the COVID-19 pandemic were adaptability and flexibility. Mahmoud and Cabrera-Puche (this volume) highlight this stating, 'The COVID-19 pandemic clearly forced thinking about adaptability, and social responsibility. … exams ought to be adaptable to a variety of language learners, including heritage language learners, and other learners in diverse contexts using available resources'. Apart from their technical flavour, these key terms among others such as fairness, equity, and social justice were meant to be lessons to be learned not only by all those involved in education including experts in language assessment but also by all other human beings. Whether these lessons have been learned properly will be discussed in the next section. Indeed one lesson we have learned while integrating technology in language assessment, as Imamura et al. (this volume) identify, is an awareness of the range of challenges ahead such as access to computer and the Internet: 'The pandemic has amplified the question of technology access and remains a continuing issue of equity, especially for learning communities', an issue we will take up below. The following quote from Zhang and Isaacs (this volume) seems to best capture the gist of lessons we have learned as a result of resorting to technology to survive, alerting us to remain vigil lest similar scenarios happen in the future:

> The pandemic has changed the landscape of language assessment and has pushed language testers to be pragmatic, innovative, and, in some cases, move forward with available resources as a matter of survival in a rapidly changing reality. It has pushed test providers to harness the use of technology, including videoconferencing, at a speed of adoption that was almost unthinkable for standardised testing pre-pandemic. The COVID-19 pandemic is a seismic event. It is impossible to know what the future holds. Language testers should be prepared for such eventualities … so they can act proactively and not just reactively in the future.

16.3 Lessons not Learned

As most of the contributors to this volume underline in their chapters, language teachers, test-takers, testing experts, educational authorities, and other stakeholders have learned many lessons from the COVID-19 pandemic, technology-wise and education-wise. Despite its health-related catastrophes, the pandemic was a timely trigger to renovate educational polices and practices, including those of language education and assessment. The educational community seem to have learned the lesson to be more flexible, not to take things for granted, and be prepared for on-the-spot decisions and unplanned scenarios. The success of educational measures taken has depended on the availability of the relevant technology on the one hand, and its affordability for and ease of access by those who needed it as well as their computer literacy on the other. Although technological divide was already there (and was very significant), the pandemic one more depicted the existing unfair conditions more sharply. One big lesson was for stakeholders, authorities and political leaders to act upon such discriminations and make technological resources available to all those who could not afford it. Although an awareness of and a call for promoting fairness and social equity are the outcome one finds whenever and wherever these key issues are debated, very little progress is observed in practice indicating equal access by and parallel advantage of technological affordances on offer to the poor and people living in war-torn contexts.

To me, the COVID-19 pandemic was a divine signal to invite human beings to unity and coherence. This did seem to be effectively working during the early days of the pandemic when members of the same community showed more care towards each other, or even different nations and states tried to join forces to combat the disease together by, for example, producing different medications and vaccines, or wars were temporarily suspended in different parts of the world. These important lessons for humanity unfortunately did not last long and soon there were unhealthy competitions between the more and the less powerful (politically and economically) on access to treatments, medications and vaccines, costing the lives of those who lived in poorer countries or were sanctioned for political reasons. Rather than being meant to save the lives of those who needed such treatments, the relevant industry became a political-economic enterprise.

World leaders who initially seemed to be worried about their people's health have once more, and much worse this time, ignited the flames of different kinds of wars. What happened to the divine signal that was meant to awaken human beings? Where is the world heading for? What has happened to humanity and ethics? Whatever lessons we may have learned at the wake of the pandemic, one big lesson the world has missed is losing its essence: the most precious thing that seems to have been lost post-pandemic is the humanity. The lesson to learn for now before another more disastrous catastrophe hits the world, is for each and every one of us, and more importantly for the world leaders, to stop their greed for more power and exploiting economic resources of those who do not have the resources to defend themselves. Those who oppress the others and commit injustice will never prosper, neither in this world, nor in the Hereafter (The Quran, 6: 135). Hopefully the language assessment world has already learned the lesson by accommodating assessments that allow for fairness and justice, in all their senses.

References

Cheung, A. (2021). Synchronous online teaching, a blessing or a curse? Insights from EFL primary students; Interaction during online English lessons. *System*, *100*, 1–13. https://doi.org/10.1016/j.system.2021.102566

Ockey, G. J. (2021). An overview of COVID-19's impact on English language university admissions and placement tests. *Language Assessment Quarterly*, *18*(1), 1–5. https://doi.org/10.1080/15434303.2020.1866576

Sadeghi, K., & Douglas, D. (Eds.). (2023). *Fundamental considerations in technology mediated language assessment*. Routledge.

Tao, J., & Gao, X. (2022). Teaching and learning languages online: Challenges and responses. *System*, *107*, 1–9. https://doi.org/10.1016/j.system.2022.102819

The Quran. Sura Al-An'am (6), 125.

Voss, E. (2023). Proctoring remote language assessments. In K. Sadeghi and D. Douglas (Eds.). *Fundamental considerations in technology mediated language assessment*. Routledge.

INDEX

academic integrity 39, 41, 50, 115, 118–120, 127, 133, 245
accommodations xv, 12, 17, 155, 204
alternative assessment 13, 182–183, 188–192
Arabic 93–94, 199
argument xv, 12, 17, 20, 35, 37–38, 50, 69–72, 82, 168, 171
articulation 228, 238–240
assessment *as* learning 115, 214
assessment *for* learning 106, 114–115, 182, 191, 213, 245
assessment grid 169–75
assessment *of* learning 9, 105, 112, 114–115, 168, 172, 213
assessment literacy xiv, 37, 39, 42–43, 46, 50, 182, 191–192, 246
assessment strategy 107
attitude 13, 21, 30, 54, 63–65, 119–121, 125, 175
authenticity 10–12, 25, 36, 50, 106, 128, 131, 134, 152, 161, 183, 186, 188, 190, 205–206

canvas 104, 107–108, 110, 112, 132, 136, 138–140, 150–151, 154, 217, 219, 221–222
claim 70–80, 168
collaborative 10, 35, 62, 136, 144, 163, 167–168, 170, 172, 175–176, 184, 187–189, 191, 234, 239

construct irrelevant variance 18, 47, 152, 157, 205
construct 11, 18, 22, 37–38, 40–41, 47, 54–55, 57, 70–71, 75–77, 80–82, 91–92, 105–106, 131, 149, 152–153, 155–160, 170, 183–188, 190, 192–193, 196–198, 201, 204–208, 214, 246
construct representation 149, 152, 157–158, 160, 198
computer adaptive test/testing (CAT) 5–6, 11, 19, 80, 89, 230
computer assisted language assessment (CALA) 5, 12
computer-based testing/assessment 5–6, 20–21, 75, 87–88, 132, 201
corpus 9, 79–80, 163–165, 167, 169–171, 175
COVID-19 xiii–xvi, 3–5, 10, 12–13, 16, 18, 35, 37–38, 45, 54–55, 61–64, 69, 84, 86, 89–90, 92–93, 96, 103–104, 111, 117–122, 126, 132, 134, 137, 144, 148–149, 151–152, 155–156, 160, 163, 166–169, 172, 175, 181, 187, 190, 196, 199, 201, 207–208, 228, 230–131, 240, 243–248

data-driven learning 163
digital assessment 37, 42–43, 46, 50, 246
digital learning object 163, 167–171, 174–176

digital literacy 21, 36, 40–41, 44–45, 48–49, 92, 244, 246
digital technology 3, 5, 145, 245
discrete-point testing 56, 182, 190
dishonesty 64–65, 112, 117, 121–124, 126–127, 132, 134, 145, 245

e-assessment 12, 126, 190–193
e-feedback 191–192
emergency remote education/assessment (ERE/ERA) xv, 4, 34, 39, 212, 232, 244
English for Academic Purposes (EAP) 12, 34–51, 70
English Placement Test (EPT) 148–160
e-Portfolio 181–193, 246
examiner 18, 21–24, 29, 106–110, 15–57, 160, 197, 201

face-to-face 10, 22, 24, 38, 46, 49, 55, 77, 90, 104–105, 107–109, 111–112, 122–123, 127–127, 133, 138, 145, 149, 156, 158–161, 169, 181, 190, 192, 196, 198–201, 203–205, 207, 212, 215, 220, 222–223, 230, 245
fairness xiii, 4, 10–13, 17, 41, 47, 70, 103, 105–107, 135–136, 149–161, 185, 189, 203, 245–248
feedback loop 60–61, 63–64
feeling 121–123, 125, 127
formative assessment 4, 13, 44, 56–59, 85, 107, 115, 119, 123, 126–127, 133, 174, 188, 218, 225, 245

grading 64–65, 137–138, 144, 184, 189, 230, 233
guidelines 5, 38, 90, 94, 134, 137–138, 144, 163, 171, 173–175, 206

heritage language learner 85, 91–92, 96–97, 246
higher education 13, 35–36, 41, 117–119, 126–127, 132, 202, 214
high-stakes xiv, 4, 11, 17–18, 30, 54, 82, 85, 87, 98, 94, 97, 112, 132, 182–183, 196–197, 201, 213–214

IELTS 6, 26, 30, 200, 202–203
IELTS indicator 11–12, 16–23, 26, 30, 70, 202–203
inference 70–82
instructions 6, 8, 11, 26, 60, 62–63, 112, 126, 133, 137–138, 150, 175, 202, 217–218, 222

instructor feedback 137, 145
integrative testing 57
interactional competence 106, 155, 198–199, 202–205, 207
interactiveness 11–12, 131, 183, 205–206
interpretation xiii, 9, 12, 35, 37, 56–57, 69–71, 81–82, 120, 149, 152, 157–158, 182, 184–186, 188, 192, 198

Japanese 13, 93, 228–233, 235, 238–240

learning-oriented assessment (LOA) 46, 59, 182
listening 6, 9–10, 17, 20–21, 27, 36, 39–42, 45, 47–48, 62, 85, 89, 94, 107–108, 111, 122–123, 125, 127, 174, 202, 216–217, 219–220, 222, 229, 231–233, 238
LockDown Browser 41, 150–154, 221

Method era 56–57
Mobile language assessment 87
Multimodal assessment 163, 166–176, 208, 245
Multimodality 164, 166, 168, 171, 173

online assessment 5, 17, 22, 42, 46, 64, 69, 112, 216, 223, 233, 236–239
online delivery 7, 17, 30, 38, 48–49, 106, 108, 212, 219–220, 245
online resources 80, 117
oral interview 59, 232–233, 235–237

peer assessment 63–65, 182, 187–188
peer feedback 45, 49, 132, 134, 137, 144–145
perception 22, 26, 62, 104, 117, 119–123, 127–128, 134, 155, 200
performance 8, 12, 20, 30, 38, 42, 44, 47–48, 50, 54, 57–59, 61–64, 71, 74–75, 77–80, 85, 105, 108, 112, 131, 133–134, 136–137, 139, 141–145, 153, 155, 157, 159, 170–171, 198–200, 204–205, 213, 217, 230, 234–235, 237, 239–240
performance assessment 58–59, 139, 182, 198
placement test/exam 11, 13, 56, 70, 84–97, 119, 148, 150, 153–154, 202, 216, 228–240, 244
practicality 7, 9, 12–13, 19, 38–82, 131, 153, 182–184, 186, 189–193, 206
pragmatic competence 13, 70, 196, 198–199, 204–205, 208

process-oriented testing/assessment 48, 56, 183, 187
proctoring 7, 18–20, 41, 43, 45, 78, 88, 96, 120, 127, 151, 153, 155, 160, 197, 202–204, 206–207, 214, 221, 245
product-oriented testing/assessment 36, 44, 56–57
productive 6–8, 103, 107, 168

Qualtrics 140, 232–235, 239

reliability 4, 10, 12, 30, 35, 39, 48, 64, 77, 79, 85, 103, 105–107, 119–120, 123–124, 128, 131, 133, 135, 149, 152, 157, 182–188, 192–193, 197, 204, 207, 217, 235
remote assessment 4, 10, 69, 72–74, 76–82, 96, 118–121, 128, 243
remote instruction 118, 147, 132–135, 142–144, 232, 240
repository 163, 170–171, 174–176
Respondus Monitor 151–154
rubrics 11, 13, 60, 62–63, 78, 132, 134, 138–139, 144, 203, 212, 214–215

self-assessment 8, 44, 62, 64, 116, 139–141, 176, 230, 237–238
socio-cognitive framework 16–17, 30, 35, 37, 70
Spanish 9, 13, 85, 89, 91, 93–94, 163–165, 167, 214–217, 219–221, 223–226, 229
speaking 6–10, 17, 19, 21–22, 24, 28–30, 36, 39, 45, 49, 61, 76, 85, 88, 94, 103, 105–108, 111, 122–123, 127, 148, 160, 174, 186, 190, 196–208, 216, 219–224, 231, 235, 238
summative assessment 44, 47, 56–59, 85, 109, 112–113, 115, 119, 133, 181, 183, 213, 219
system check 151–152, 154–155

technology mediated language assessment (TALA) 5, 7, 10, 12–13, 107, 114, 244, 246
test impact 17
test method 10–11
test usefulness 70, 181–183, 186, 188, 190, 192–193, 204
test security xv, 4, 7, 12, 18–19, 42, 70, 78, 149, 151, 153–154, 158, 160, 203, 207, 245

University entrance 17, 204

validation xv, 12, 16–17, 20–23, 30, 35, 37–39, 42, 46, 49–51, 69–72, 82, 94, 199, 246
validity 4, 10–13, 17–18, 20–22, 31, 34–35, 37–39, 42–43, 46–50, 64, 69–71, 82, 92, 103, 105–107, 119–121, 128, 131, 149, 157, 173, 182–193, 204, 215, 217, 229, 238, 245
videoconferencing 13, 70, 124, 132, 196–208, 247
virtual classroom 169, 193, 213, 219, 238

warrant 72–80
washback 12–13, 45, 47–48, 57, 131, 159, 182–193, 206
web-based language testing/assessment 5–6, 8, 85–86, 88, 198
WebEx 157, 159
writing 6–9, 13, 17, 19–21, 36, 39, 42, 44–45, 48, 59, 61–62, 75, 76, 80, 89, 94, 103, 105–109, 111, 113, 123, 131–145, 146, 150, 152–155, 174, 181, 184–189, 191, 202, 208, 213–214, 217, 219–220, 222–223, 229, 231, 233, 235, 244

Zoom 10, 104, 108–110, 112, 127, 132, 136–138, 145, 187, 202, 233

For Product Safety Concerns and Information please contact our EU representative GPSR@taylorandfrancis.com
Taylor & Francis Verlag GmbH, Kaufingerstraße 24, 80331 München, Germany

www.ingramcontent.com/pod-product-compliance
Lightning Source LLC
Chambersburg PA
CBHW051353290426
44108CB00015B/1991